72

Introduction to Computers and Application Software

Apple® II Edition

Introduction to Computers and Application Software

Apple® II Edition

Robert H. Blissmer
Systems Consultant

Roland H. Alden
Data General Corporation

Houghton Mifflin Company *Boston*
Dallas Geneva, Illinois Lawrenceville, New Jersey Palo Alto

Printed in the U.S.A.

Library of Congress Catalog Card Number: 86-82664

ISBN: 0-395-41085-1

ABCDEFGHIJ-SM-89876

Contents

Preface

The integration of computers into nearly every facet of modern life has called into being the idea of "computer literacy." This term means different things to different people. In essence, it may be said to signify a fundamental understanding of the way computers operate and how people may interact productively with them. But, in practice, this term has undergone a change in meaning as it is applied to the first course in computing at many colleges and universities.

Not too long ago, in a world dominated by mainframes, the computer literate person was expected to know how computer hardware and software systems worked, and to have mastered at least one programming language. However, with the recent emergence of the personal computer, the idea of "computer literacy" has evolved to mean an understanding of how software programs are used. As with an automobile, instead of learning about the computer's parts or how it works, students are learning how to drive it.

Introduction to Computers and Application Software is intended for a one-term course for which no prior experience with computers is required. The book and its accompanying TriPac™ integrated software teach students basic computer concepts through hands-on training in the three major personal computer applications—word processing, electronic spreadsheets, and data management. The book also outlines a step-by-step methodology for using the computer to solve problems, provides an overview of computer systems ranging from microcomputers to minis and mainframes, offers criteria for selecting and buying a computer, and surveys trends in computing such as robotics and artificial intelligence.

Students using this book learn how to operate a computer, how to run application software, and how to read program documentation and user's manuals, thus preparing them to make the transition to commercial software packages or more advanced computer courses.

TriPac Software

The TriPac application software accompanying the text is especially designed to teach students how to become competent computer users. The program is easy to use, in that all three applications reside on one disk and share a common command structure. Because there is a consistent user interface, learning how to use one application teaches you how to use the others. The TriPac program also emulates features found in the most advanced integrated commercial software. For example, information selected in the spreadsheet and data management applications can be "cut and pasted" into the word processor.

The TriPac program requires an Apple® IIe or Apple IIc with a minimum of 64K of memory and two disk drives. A printer is recommended.

Organization of the Book

The first chapter covers computer background, fundamentals, and the needs that personal computers fill. Chapters 2 through 4 continue the orientation and introduce the major application areas—word processing, databases, and spreadsheets. Each of these three chapters provides an overview of how to use the program and a problem to solve.

Chapters 5 through 10 cover how to use the TriPac application software in detail. The student learns the concepts and principles of each of the three application programs step-by-step. The student applies the programs to problems. As the chapters progress, new aspects of the total software package unfold: the concepts of integration—passing data between applications; the fundamentals of file management; how to develop applications; and advanced software features.

Chapter 11 recognizes the need for a systematic approach to acquiring software and hardware. It builds on the problem-solving method used throughout the text and applies it to the problem of buying a personal computer system.

Chapter 12 provides a comprehensive summary of the potentials and limitations of future personal computer systems that will be of concern to every computer user in the next decade.

Problems and exercises are found throughout the text. A comprehensive glossary explains computer terms and application software concepts.

In short, *Introduction to Computers and Application Software* is the perfect introduction to computers and application software for any student.

Acknowledgments

We are grateful to Mark Esserlieu, whose programming helped make TriPac possible. Thanks to Elizabeth J. Neidich who read the manuscript and made many helpful suggestions. The authors especially wish to thank Harvey Blessing and his students at Essex Community College for class testing an earlier version of the book and making many helpful suggestions.

We would also like to gratefully extend acknowledgment to the reviewers whose comments and feedback helped shape the contents and direction of the book and the software:

Justine C. Baker
Don Berliner, Logical Systems Inc.
Harvey Blessing, Essex Community College
Philip L. Brach, University of the District of Columbia
William E. Burkhardt, Carl Sandburg College
Lawrence Campo, Macomb Community College
James A. Davis, Oregon Institute of Technology
Richard M. Dean, California State Polytechnic University, Pomona
Larry A. Dold, San Joaquin Delta College
Edward Eill, Delaware County Community College
George Fowler, Texas A & M University
George Gintowt, William Rainey Harper College
James Gips, Boston College
Nancy C. Goodwin, MITRE Corp.
Wallace J. Growney, Susquehanna University
Herman Heacker
Rod Heisterberg, Austin Community College
Seth A. Hock, Columbus Technical Institute
Laurence Krieg, Washtenaw Community College
C. Gardner Mallonee, Essex Community College
David John Marotta, Lane Community College
Paul J. McNeil, McNeil Associates
Mona Milbrath, Lakeshore Technical Institute
John L. Moseng, District One Technical Institute
Julius Nadas, Wilbur Wright College
Alex W. Nichols, Cleveland State Community College
Robert C. Panian, Northern Michigan University
Howard L. Perry, Black Hills State College
Ronald Peterson, Weber State College
Therese Phares, Des Moines Area Community College
Ellie E. Rosen, Santa Monica College
Marcy Berman Rosenberg, MBR Software Consulting Services
Judith Scheeren, Westmoreland County Community College
Robert Schuerman, California Polytechnic State University
David R. Sullivan, Oregon State University
Sharon Szabo, Schoolcraft College
Robert Taylor, Berkshire Community College
Erwin C. Vernon, Sinclair Community College
Louis A. Wolff, Moorpark College

A final note of thanks to all those people who suffered through the early versions of the software and uncovered our mistakes and bugs.

R.H.B.
R.H.A.

Introduction to Computers and Application Software

Apple® II Edition

1

Introducing the Personal Computer

PREVIEW

Today, the personal computer is a tool that almost everyone can use. Using a personal computer is a matter of (1) knowing what can be done with a personal computer, (2) understanding the basic concepts and terminology of computers, and (3) acquiring the hands-on skills of operating a personal computer.

This chapter will give you the necessary background to begin using a personal computer yourself. You'll hear about how other people are using their personal computers. You'll learn what a computer system is and what hardware is. You'll learn to recognize the hardware components of a computer system. You'll begin to understand what software is, and you'll become acquainted with the different types of personal-computer software. Finally, you'll learn what an operating system is and does.

Along the way, you'll encounter some concepts basic to all computer systems, and some computer terminology. With this background, you'll be ready for hands-on experience with a personal computer.

In this chapter, you'll discover:

- *Some uses for personal computers*
- *The personal computer as a system of interrelated components*
- *The hardware components of a personal computer*
- *Types of software for personal computers*
- *The functions of application software*
- *The role of operating-system software*
- *How to use your operating system*

An Overview of Personal Computers

Today, it is possible to have at your fingertips more computing power than was available to any computer scientist only thirty years ago. How is this possible? There are two explanations. First, computers have evolved at a dizzying pace over the last thirty years. Remarkable technological advances have made computers steadily smaller, less expensive, and easier to use. The result is the **personal computer**—a computer small enough to fit on a desk top, affordable enough to be owned by a single person, yet powerful enough to perform many different

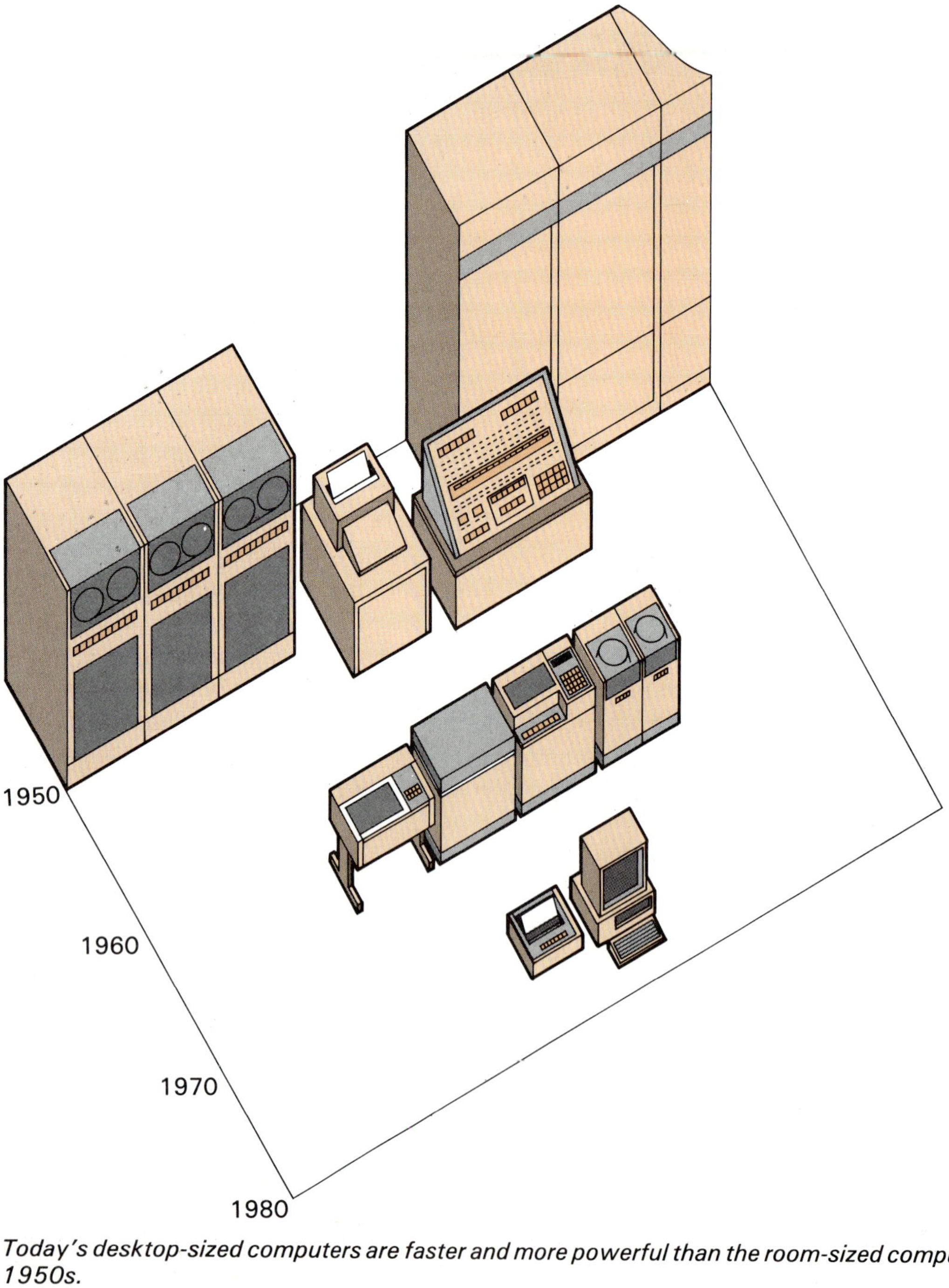

Today's desktop-sized computers are faster and more powerful than the room-sized computers of the 1950s.

tasks. The computer you will use in this class is a personal computer. It is a highly capable assistant, and it greatly simplifies the task of learning basic computer skills.

Meanwhile, an equally remarkable evolution has occurred in **software**—the computer programs or sets of instructions that control the operation of a computer. The first computer users were a handful of scientists and technicians who regarded the computer and its software as a highly specialized tool. But the explosive rate of growth in computers has changed the nature of the tool. Today, most computer users rely on the software industry to simplify the use of the hardware and to equip computers for a wide range of uses.

It is software that makes a computer such a powerful tool. Changing the software in a computer has the effect of transforming the computer into a completely different tool. This is how the same computer can assist you in writing a term paper, alphabetizing a list of names, or preparing a budget. You will be using the software that accompanies this text to put these concepts into practice.

What You Can Do With a Personal Computer

What can you accomplish with the computing power of a personal computer? Because you can change its function by changing the software, the personal computer is a **general-purpose tool.** It can help you write, calculate, analyze, organize, draw, and communicate. The following scenario may help you envision how you might use a personal computer.

Chris Wilson is attending freshman orientation at Altair Community College. This morning's meeting will explain how freshmen are going to use the personal computers they are required to buy. This is the third year that Altair has required all incoming students to own a personal computer. By a special arrangement with a computer manufacturer, Altair offers personal computers to its students at about half the retail price. Altair has also built a state-of-the-art campus communications network, to which students can link their personal computers.

At the meeting, each student is given a "software toolkit," a set of computer programs to use for research, homework, and term papers. One of the programs in the toolkit is a word processor, which students are to use to write papers for all their classes. Chris's English composition instructor is going to assign the class one written paper per week. She will also expect the papers to be revised and handed back in, since the word processor makes the mechanics of revision almost effortless.

Chris's economics classes will be using another program in the toolkit, called a spreadsheet program. In studying the effects of inflation, the class will use the spreadsheet program to project future inflation rates and analyze the impacts of alternative rates.

Another program in the toolkit, the database program, will help index and retrieve lists of references for research papers. The toolkit also includes a drawing program, for use in art classes, and a music synthesizer for music classes. At Altair, every personal computer also comes equipped with a set of communication tools, including a communications program. Students can use these tools to "tap into" the library's computerized card catalog and indexes. They can also use them to communicate with each other and with their professors by sending and receiving "electronic messages" over the communications network.

Altair is confident that its students will be able to do more and better work because the personal computer and software toolkit will free them from the tedious aspects of schoolwork to concentrate more fully on learning.

This scenario is very close to being realized. A number of schools already require their students to buy personal computers; several have campus-wide communication networks. And all of the software tools we have described are in use in colleges and universities.

Acquiring Computer Skills

The most important step in learning what a computer can do for you is to begin to use one. There really is no substitute for hands-on experience. When you sit down at a personal computer and begin to use it, you'll find that learning by doing can be fun. You'll gain the practical skills you need to benefit most fully from using a computer. And you'll begin to get a feeling for the personal computer's potential and functioning, and how it can be used.

If you are unfamiliar with personal computers, you will first need to understand some of the basic features of all computer systems. It really doesn't require a lot of technical knowledge to use a computer. But you do need to understand the answers to a few basic questions: What is a computer system? What is hardware? What is software? How does a computer work? How do you use one? Armed with common sense and the answers to these questions, you will be ready to begin to use a personal computer.

What Is a Computer System?

A system is a set of parts, each with a specific purpose, which work together to accomplish a desired goal. A **computer system** consists of the computer itself, often called hardware; the programs that control the computer, called software; the problem-solving procedures for accomplishing a given task with a computer; and the people who use the computer system to do productive work.

All of the work that a computer system performs is **information processing** of one kind or another. Information processing differs from other work in that the value of its product—information—is determined by its relevance to the problem being solved. Information processing does not need to be done by computer. Typing is information processing; so is adding a list of numbers with paper and pencil. Thinking is also information processing. It makes sense to use a computer for information processing when the information produced with its aid is more timely, more convenient, more accurate, or more effective than could be produced by other means.

When all the parts of a computer system are working together effectively, the result is information that is highly valuable in a particular problem-solving context. Let us examine in more detail each of the parts that make a computer system work.

What Is Hardware?

Hardware—the electronic and mechanical components of the computer—is the tangible part of a computer system. It consists of a collection of parts or subsystems, each of which performs unique functions. Take a look at Figure 1.1, which identifies the parts of a computer. Broadly speaking, the physical parts of a computer system are: a **processor,** which performs the actual information processing and supervises and controls the entire operation of the system; a **memory,** which stores information used by the processor; **input devices,** which convert data into a form that the processor and memory can use; **output devices,** which convert the results of processing into information that people can use;

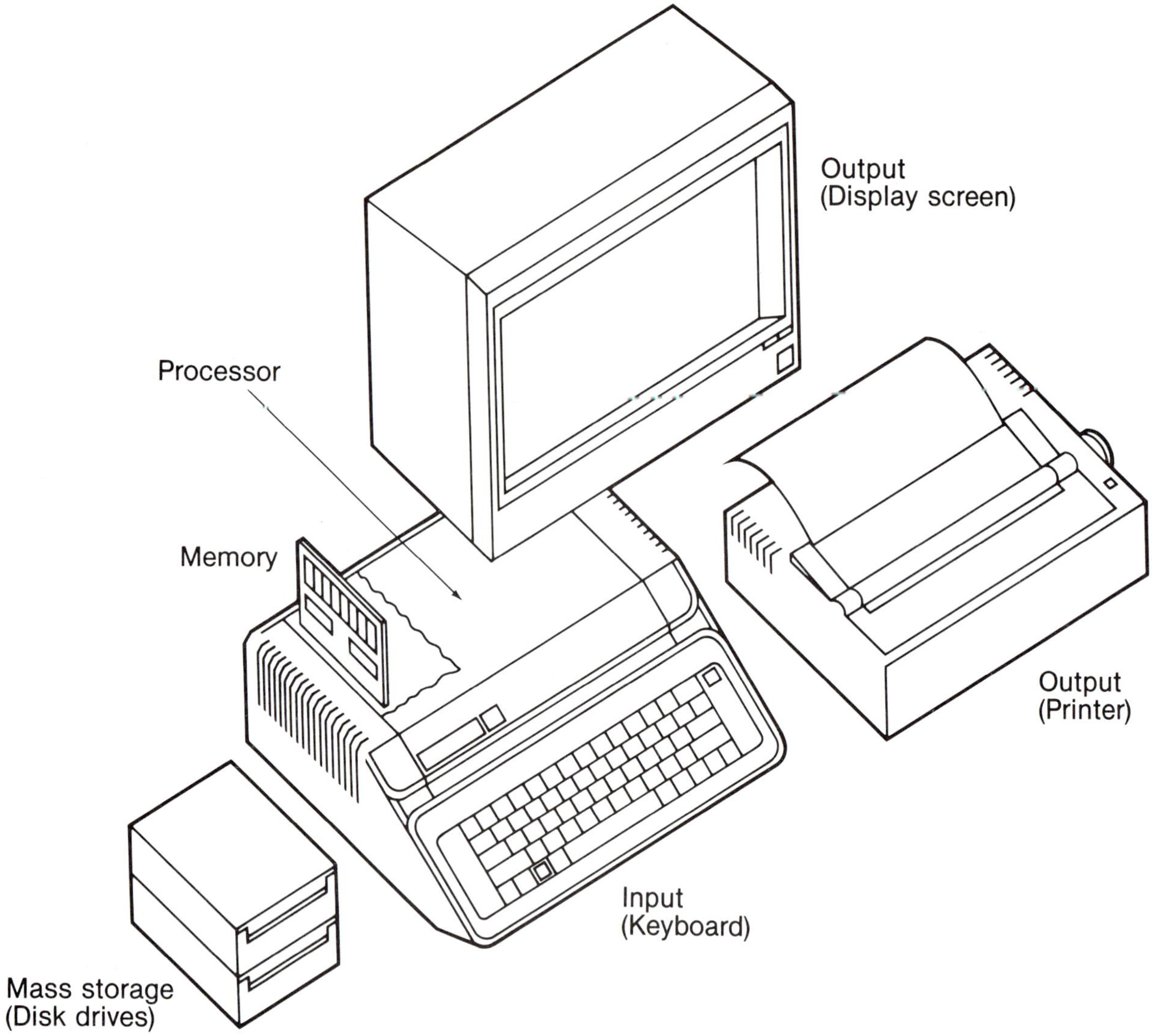

FIGURE 1.1 *Parts of a personal computer system.*

mass storage devices, which store information before and after processing. Let us look at these hardware parts in more detail, to see how each performs its functions.

Input Devices

Input devices have a twofold purpose. First, they accept the commands, from the user, that tell the computer system what to do. Second, they accept data that have been assembled for processing. **Data** are raw facts that are used to create information. An input device converts data and commands into a form the computer can use.

The most widely used input device for a personal computer is a **keyboard**—a device resembling a typewriter keyboard, which converts finger pressure on the keys into electronic codes the computer can recognize. You will use a keyboard to input data and commands to the personal computer you use in this class. In later chapters, we will describe some other kinds of input devices.

The Processor

The processor is the part of the computer that controls its operation and does the actual processing. It is the "brain" of the computer system. Though the comparison between a brain and a processor should not be overstretched, it is a useful analogy to describe what the processor does. Data and programs enter the computer via an input device, and are temporarily stored in the computer's memory, to await their turn for processing.

The processor operates in a cyclical manner. It begins with the first instruction in a program, interprets it, carries out the task specified by the instruction, and goes on to the next instruction. The processor repeats this step-by-step operation until processing is complete. In doing so, it controls all the other functions performed by the system. The processor performs the tasks of information processing and control by means of simple arithmetic and logical operations, such as comparing two numbers and making a decision based on the comparison. All of this happens at incredible speed. The length of time it takes a processor to execute an instruction is measured in millionths of a second.

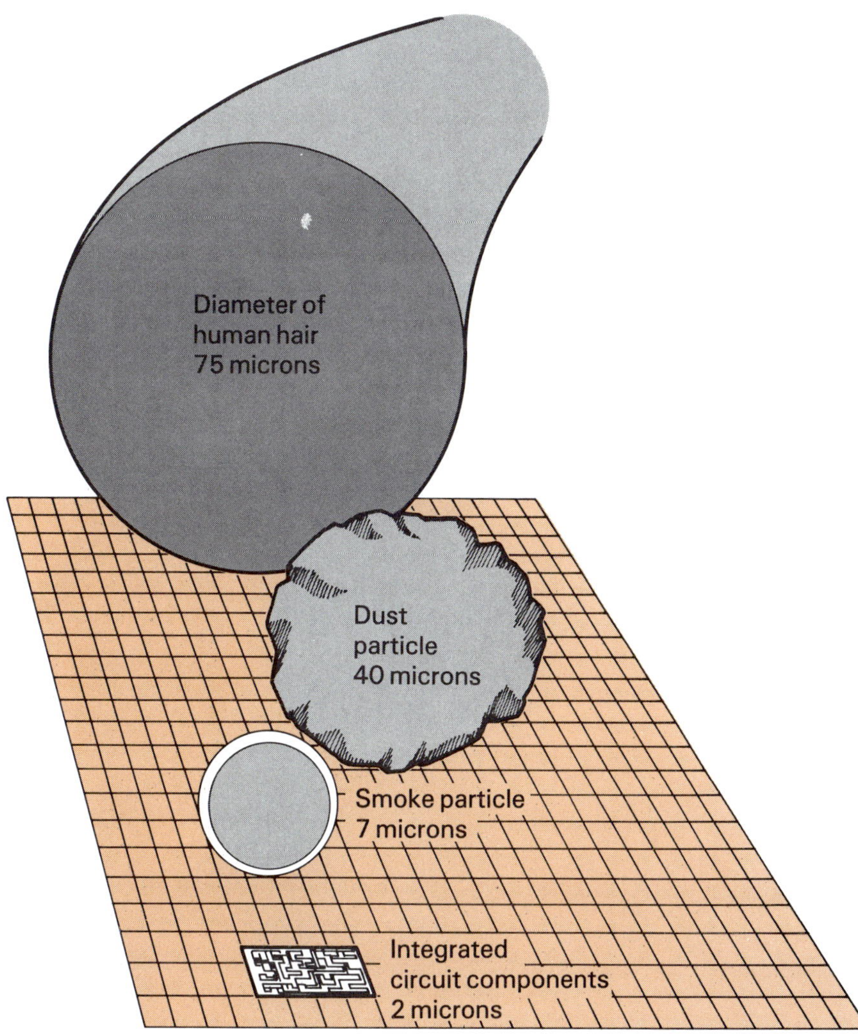

FIGURE 1.2 *In an area the size of the diameter of a human hair, a chip can contain a grid of 200 circuits, each made of lines 2 microns wide.*

Today, processing and control take place in a miniature package called a **microprocessor**—a tiny silicon chip that contains all the circuitry necessary to carry out the instructions it receives. Advances in technology have transformed yesterday's bulky refrigerator-sized components into microscopic versions etched on quarter-inch flakes of silicon. And each new generation of chips manages to cram in more components. As Figure 1.2 shows, the components on today's chips measure in at two microns. (A micron equals 39 millionths of an inch.)

Memory

Memory is a storage area inside the computer. The processor needs a place to store data and programs while it executes individual instructions one at a time. In a personal computer, memory consists of a collection of silicon chips. These memory chips are of two types: random-access memory (RAM) and read-only memory (ROM).

Random-access memory, or **RAM**, is the processor's temporary working area. It is empty until the processor needs to use it—that is, until data and programs are sent to it from an input device. It is also temporary memory, because it is **volatile**. In other words, it loses its contents when the power is turned off. RAM is often called read/write memory, meaning that the processor can both read its contents and write new instructions or data into it.

Read-only memory, or **ROM**, is a permanent memory, containing data and instructions loaded into it at the time the computer was built. Its name signifies that its contents cannot be changed; the processor can read from ROM, but cannot write new information into it. In contrast to RAM, ROM is nonvolatile. It does not lose its contents when the power is shut off.

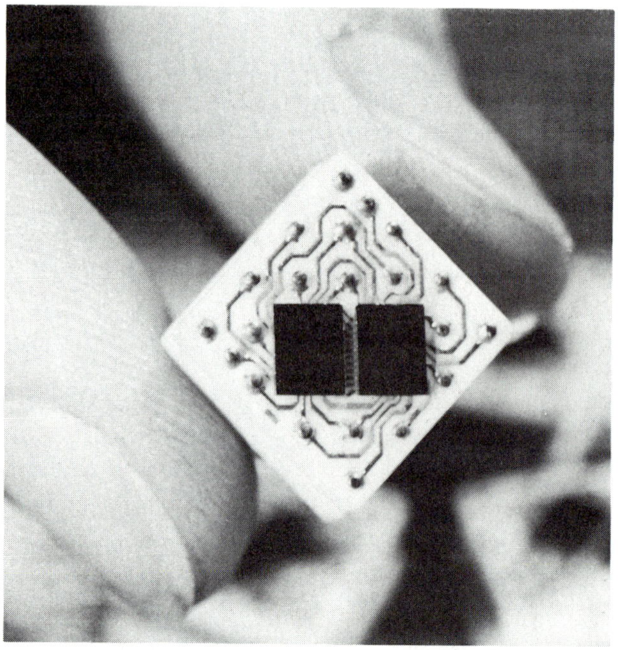

Today's quarter-inch square memory chips can store 1 million bits of information.

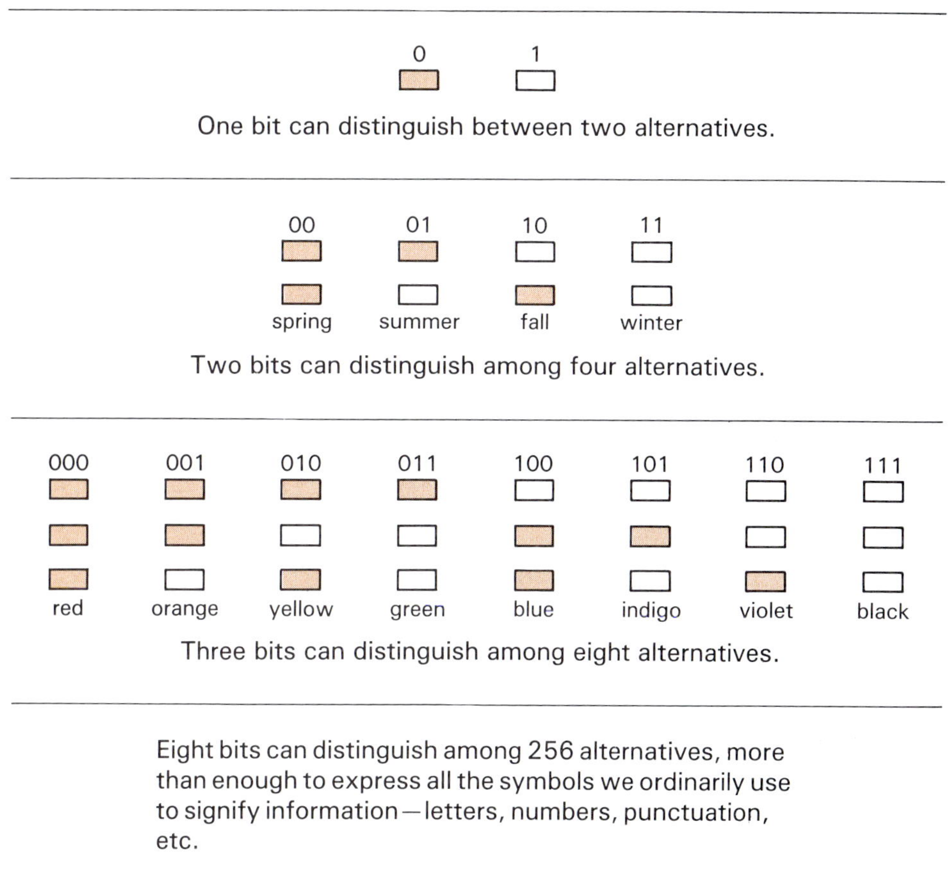

FIGURE 1.3 *How a computer represents information electronically.*

Why does a computer system need two different kinds of memories? Remember that a computer is a general-purpose tool; it can be given many different sets of instructions. Each time you give it a new program, the program is stored in RAM. Thus it is RAM that gives the computer much of its flexibility. Meanwhile, however, certain tasks are being repeated over and over again, always in the same way. One example is starting up the computer, often called **booting.** A set of instructions known as a bootstrap program is permanently in ROM. When the computer is turned on, the bootstrap program is activated, and takes care of loading other programs into memory.

Computer memories are rated in terms of their capacity to store information. The smallest unit of information in a computer system is called a **bit** (short for binary digit). A bit is represented inside the computer by a tiny electronic component, which can be either on or off. Thus one bit can express either of two alternatives: on and off, 0 and 1, yes and no, and the like. Two bits can represent four alternatives, and so on. Figure 1.3 illustrates how a computer represents information with electronic currents.

But while the processor deals with bits, people communicate by means of characters (letters, numbers, punctuation marks, and other symbols). Eight bits (which can represent 256 alternatives) are more than enough to represent all the

TABLE 1.1 *Commonly used abbreviations for memory size*

	Number of bytes	Usage
KB (kilobyte)	1,024	Common memory sizes for personal computers (64KB, 128KB, 256KB, 512KB)
MB (megabyte)	1,048,576	Memory size for minicomputers and mainframes (1MB to 64MB)
GB (gigabyte)	1,073,741,824	Mass storage systems for very large scale computers (1GB to 16GB)
TB (terabyte)	1,094,511,627,776	Experimental mass storage systems such as laser disks (up to 1TB)

commonly used characters. A group of eight bits, treated as a unit and used to represent one character, is called a **byte.** In other words, a byte is a unit of storage that can hold one character of information.

Computer memories are measured in terms of the number of bytes of information they can hold. Table 1.1 shows some commonly used abbreviations for memory capacity. Typical memory sizes for personal computers are 64K, 128K, 256K, and 512K. K stands for kilo, which means 1000. Because computers count in powers of two, not powers of ten like people, 1K is actually 1024 bytes, and 64K is actually 65,536 bytes. But for simplicity's sake, people speak of K as 1000. The same technological advances that have made microprocessors small and inexpensive are also driving down the size and cost of memory. So it is no longer unusual to find personal computers with very large memories.

Mass Storage

Because RAM is temporary memory—it loses its contents when the power of the computer system is shut off—devices are needed to store data and programs outside the computer before and after processing. The most common mass storage medium is a disk.

A **disk** is a circular platter coated with a magnetic material. It stores information in the form of tiny magnetic spots on its surface. A disk is like a miniature electronic filing cabinet, in that it organizes information by grouping it into **files**—sets of logically related information. The TriPac™ disk contains several data files for storing information, and several program files containing the programs that process that information.

A **disk drive** is a device that can read the information on the disk, and write new information on it. It does so by mounting the disk on a spindle and spinning it around much as a record player plays a record. But while a phonograph record stores its contents in a sequential spiral groove, a disk is sectioned off into concentric tracks, each of which is divided into sectors. The disk drive moves different sectors into contact with the read-write head. When you insert a disk and activate the drive, the computer copies information either from the disk into memory or from memory to the disk.

TriPac is a trademark of Houghton Mifflin Company.

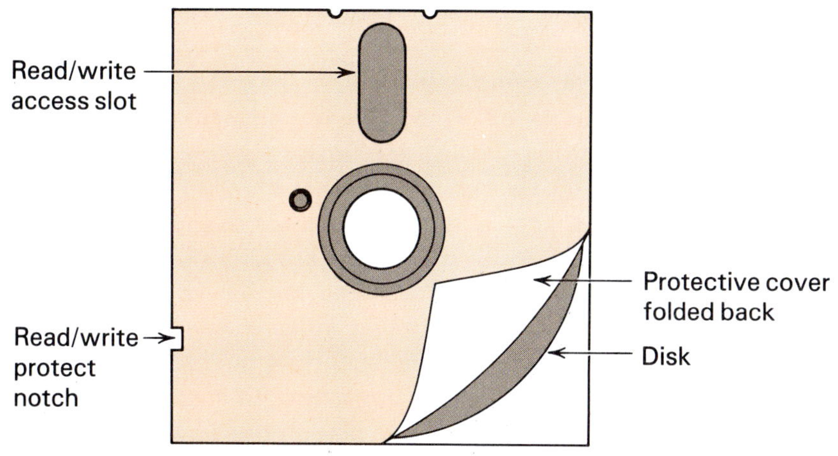

FIGURE 1.4 *A floppy disk in its protective cover.*

There are two broad categories of disks: floppy disks, which are flexible, and hard disks, which are rigid. Figure 1.4 is a diagram of a floppy disk. Floppy disks are either single-sided or double-sided. Single-sided disks can store information on only one side, but double-sided disks can store information on both sides. Disks too are rated according to their capacities. The TriPac floppy disk has a capacity of 143,360 bytes. Hard disks have a speed and capacity advantage over floppy disks. A typical hard disk for a personal computer might store 10 million bytes—10 megabytes—of information. Hard disks combine large storage capacities with fast access to information, but they cost far more than an equivalent number of floppy disks. As a personal computer user's needs grow, he or she often accumulates a large number of data and program files. A single hard disk can store many different programs, along with larger files. The hard disk's capacity and speed offer the user a more convenient way to organize, manage, and access a larger number of files.

Output Devices

Output devices convert the results of processing into a form that people can use. A **display screen**, often called a monitor, is the most common output device. Most use the same cathode-ray tube (CRT) technology as a television screen, slightly modified for computer use. The display screen is how the computer communicates with you, the user. It provides you immediate feedback by displaying the characters you type on the keyboard, or showing you the results of your instructions to the computer. Display screens can be monochrome (one-color) or full-color.

A printer is an output device that provides permanent paper output. When you turn off a computer, the image on the monitor disappears. Paper output means you can retain your output, or, in the case of this class, hand it in to your instructor.

What Is Software?

Software, you will recall, is the collective name for the programs that control the hardware. Hardware is the tangible part of a computer system; software is the intangible part. It is the instructions that determine what tasks the computer system performs.

At first, software may not strike you as a particularly ingenious or unique idea. After all, you are used to controlling appliances and stereo equipment by turning dials and pressing buttons. But there is a difference between these devices and a computer. When you put a new tape into a tape deck, you are merely changing the music, not the function of the tape deck; its function cannot change. But putting a new program into a computer can completely transform the function of the computer. New software gives the computer new capabilities.

Computer hardware is more like a musical instrument than a simple playback device. This is because the combination of hardware and software, like the combination of instruments and music, is a medium of expression. In this class, you will use the TriPac software to write, calculate, analyze, organize, and express solutions to problems.

Though software is intangible, it does have a physical form. A **software package** consists of one or more floppy disks on which the programs reside. It is

A software package consists of the program disks and documentation—a quick reference manual, technical reference manual, and tutorials.

accompanied by a set of books or manuals called **documentation.** The documentation usually includes a User's Guide, a Technical Reference Manual, and a Quick Reference Card that summarizes the functions of the program and how to use them. Along with the program itself, there may be another disk containing a **tutorial**—an interactive program that helps you learn how to use the software.

There are four kinds of packaged software: (1) general-purpose application software, (2) special-purpose application software, (3) programming languages, and (4) operating-system software.

The first category, **general-purpose application software,** is software designed to handle a wide variety of tasks that employ the same general capabilities. For example, word processing is a general-purpose application; you can use a word processor to write a term paper, a business letter, a love letter, or a poem. Today, there are six categories of general-purpose software: word processing, spreadsheets, databases, communications, graphics, and integrated programs that combine several of these applications into a single multifunction program.

Special-purpose application software is tailored to the specific needs of particular kinds of businesses or professions. For example, a lawyer who is contemplating buying a word processor might prefer a program specifically designed to prepare legal documents and contracts. A doctor might find a medical-billing, accounting, and patient-tracking system more useful than a general-purpose database program. A scientist is likely to want a special-purpose statistical-analysis package instead of a general-purpose spreadsheet program.

The third category, **programming languages,** are programs that are used to write other programs. A programming language is a set of precise rules for formulating statements so that a computer can be programmed to understand them. You may be familiar with the names of some programming languages, such as BASIC or Pascal. Thanks to the development of ready-to-use software, you no longer need to know how to program in order to use a computer. Computer systems are designed to serve two types of users. Most users now use existing programs; the small minority of users known as programmers spend their time writing and developing new programs. We will assume that you are in the first category.

The fourth category is **operating-system software**—the programs that control the operation and manage the resources of a computer system. In the case of personal computers that use disk drives, the operating system is usually called a **disk operating system** or, more casually, DOS (rhymes with boss). Some makes of personal computers have their own specific operating systems.

Using a Personal Computer System

Using a computer system involves giving it commands or procedures to carry out. The goal of a computer user is to get the computer to do some useful work. With this in mind, it may be useful to view a computer system as a hierarchy of resources, with the user at the highest level, the application software at the next highest level, the operating system at the middle level, and the hardware at the lowest level of the hierarchy.

At the highest level, the user has an **application** in mind. He or she wants to apply the computer to a particular problem, such as writing a term paper, analyzing a set of numbers, or organizing a list of names. The rest of the computer system is simply a means to this end.

In general, application software performs the high-level work, while the operating system performs the low-level work. By low-level work, we really mean routine work—work that is common to almost all applications. Take, for example, storing information in files. Whether you write with a word processor, analyze problems with a spreadsheet program, or organize information with a database program, you will need to put your information in files.

As we noted earlier, a blank disk is analogous to a filing cabinet without drawers, indexes, dividers, or folders. It is simply "raw" storage space. To be useful as storage, it has to be labeled, indexed, and organized so that users can access the information that is stored there.

This level of organizing and managing the storage space on a disk is accomplished by the operating system. Figure 1.5 illustrates how a disk is organized. The operating system sections the disk into concentric circles called tracks. Each track is then divided into sectors. The operating system also creates a directory, to keep account of which tracks and sectors are in use by which files. A directory is necessary because files are typically in a constant state of change. New files are created, and old files are deleted. Information is added to and deleted from existing files. Unless the disk space is managed efficiently, the information stored on it could become as chaotic as an unorganized filing cabinet.

Guided by the user, the operating system keeps the disk's filing system in order. It can be told to name or rename a file, copy files from one disk to another, read information from a file, and write information to a file. The operating

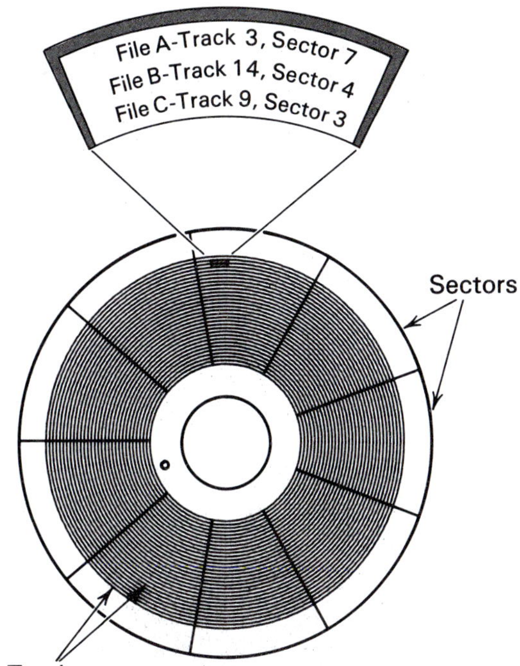

FIGURE 1.5 *How a disk is organized. The operating system divides the disk into tracks and then divides the tracks into sectors. It also creates a directory that lists the location of files on the disk.*

system can also inform the user how much space is left on a disk and how big the files are.

The application software is not concerned with such details. An application program simply "asks" the operating system to do such tasks. The net effect of this hierarchical organization is to insulate the user from all of the "housekeeping" details except those that are necessary to accomplish the tasks at hand. Of course, the user could be responsible for all these details, but that would defeat the goal of using a computer. Hierarchical organization makes it far easier for a user to get the computer to do useful work.

Why doesn't the application program take care of these tasks directly instead of using the operating system? First, tasks such as storing and retrieving data from a disk are routine operations. It makes sense to develop these programs once, and then just let different application programs use them over and over again. Second, and just as important, it would not be feasible for two or more application programs to share a resource, such as a disk, without a "third party"—the operating system—to insure that they do not interfere with each other.

In addition to managing the disks, the operating system also handles such other standard procedures as displaying characters on the screen, accepting input from the keyboard, and sending information to the printer.

Using the Operating System

It might sound as if the user never comes in direct contact with the operating system. In fact, the user does interact directly with the part of the operating system called the command processor—a program that interprets and responds to the commands you type in on the keyboard.

You will often interact with the operating system to run application programs and to communicate with the disk drives and the printer. When the operating system is copied into memory, it takes control of the computer. To run an application program, you then specify its name to the operating system.

The more you use a computer system, the more you will tend to accumulate files and disks. As your "library" of files and disks grows, you will want to learn how to use the file-managing operations of the operating system. These include such commands as: look at a directory, check a disk, copy, save, erase, and rename a file or a disk. These commands are useful for rearranging information on your disks, and for making room for new files.

You are about to begin using a personal computer by applying the concepts you have just learned to a few simple operating-system tasks. You will learn how to format your disks, load and run programs, examine your disks, and make copies of disks and files.

Before you begin, be sure you have the following hardware components:

- An Apple® IIe or IIc computer, equipped with two disk drives and a display device
- A program disk containing the TriPac software and a data disk containing the TriPac data files
- A disk labeled *ProDOS User's Disk* or *DOS 3.3 System Master*
- Two blank disks

Using the Keyboard

To get you started, we will show you one way of interacting with the operating system.

For most tasks, you will use the keyboard to enter the commands that tell the computer what to do. The display screen will give you feedback as you instruct the computer. Typing skill is not necessary at this stage, since operating-system commands are simple and short. But take the time to familiarize yourself with the layout of the keyboard. In this exercise, you will be typing in letters and commands. You will use the Return key to enter a command once you have finished typing it. Figure 1.6 is a diagram of the keyboard. Look at it now to locate the Control key, key, the Return key, the left arrow key, and the Reset key. In Chapter 2, we will look at the entire keyboard in detail.

Handling Disks

Floppy disks are vulnerable to dirt, dust, magnetic fields, mishandling, and human error. Proper handling of disks is essential to prevent damage. Never touch the exposed surfaces of the disk. Handle the disk only by its protective

Apple is a registered trademark of Apple Computer, Inc.

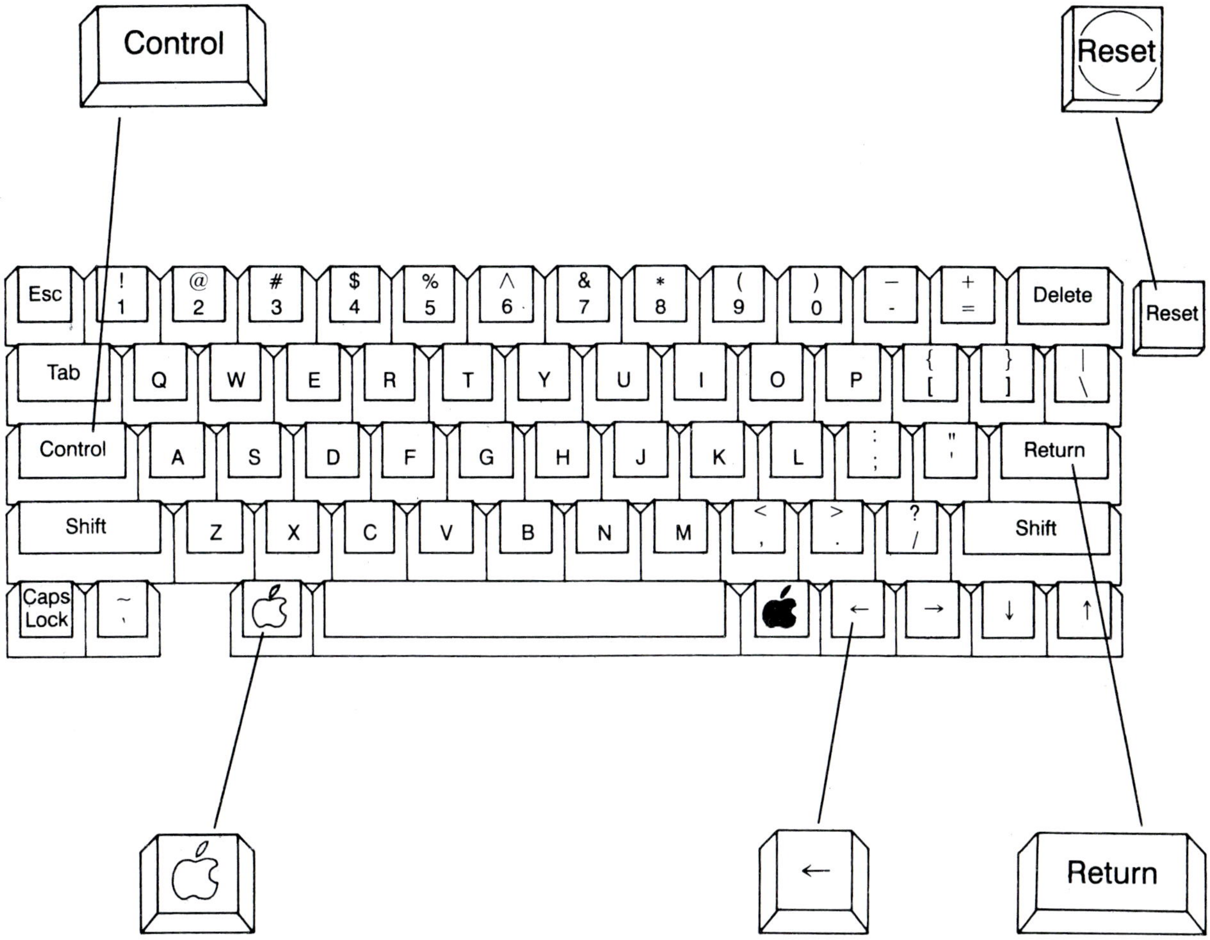

FIGURE 1.6 *Location of the Control, , Return, left arrow, and Reset keys.*

jacket. When not in use, always keep disks in their storage envelopes. Never place a disk on top of the display device. Never place a disk where you might inadvertently spill a soft drink or a cup of coffee on it. And don't place them in a flexible notebook or backpack where they might easily bend.

Operating Instructions

Recall that starting up the computer is often called booting. There are two ways to boot an Apple computer. The computer you are using has two floppy disk drives. The left disk drive is called drive 1. The right disk drive is called drive 2.

Booting the Computer with the Power Off

1. Insert any program disk into drive 1, handling it by the label. Never touch the exposed magnetic surface of the disk.
2. The Apple computer has an on/off switch on the back of the computer. The display device also has an on/off switch. First turn on the display device; then turn on the computer.

Booting the Computer with the Power On

1. Insert a program disk into drive 1, handling it by the label.
2. Hold down the and Control keys while you press the Reset key.

Before you begin using your TriPac software, you will need to place copies of the TriPac program and data files on your blank disks. Your instructor has the master copies. The copy procedure varies depending on whether your computer uses the ProDOS or the DOS 3.3 operating system. Use one of the following procedures to copy TriPac. If your operating system is called DOS 3.3, skip this section and go on to the next section, "Copying TriPac with DOS 3.3" on page 19.

Copying TriPac with ProDOS

The ProDOS User's Disk contains a program for copying disks.

1. Insert the ProDOS User's Disk in drive 1 and boot the computer using one of the procedures described in the previous section.
2. A menu will appear listing your options. Press F to activate the ProDOS filer.
3. Another menu will appear. Press V to activate the Volume commands.
4. A list of volume commands will appear. Press C to copy a volume. (*Volume* is just another name for disk.)
5. The copy program presents you with a number of default (that is, preset) responses. For example, the first default response is

   ```
   --COPY--
     THE VOLUME IN SLOT: (6)
   ```

   Press the Return key four times to use the default responses. Check with your instructor to determine whether the default responses need to be changed.
6. At the bottom of the screen the message

   ```
   --INSERT DISKS AND PRESS <RET>--
   ```

   will appear.
7. Remove the ProDOS User's Disk from drive 1 and replace with the TriPac program disk.
8. Place a blank disk in drive 2. Press the Return key. You'll hear a whirring and clacking noise. The words FORMATTING, READING, and WRITING will alternate on the screen while the program disk is being copied, and the disk drives' lights will flash on and off. When the program is finished, you'll see:

   ```
   COPY COMPLETE
   --PRESS <RET> TO ACCEPT: <ESC> TO EXIT--
   ```

   Remove your new TriPac program disk from drive 2 and label it as the TriPac program disk with today's date and your name.
   Remove the TriPac program disk from drive 1 and insert the TriPac data

disk in its place. Then insert your second blank disk into drive 2. Press the Return key five times. The copy program will be repeated, but this time you'll copy the data files onto your second disk. When the program is finished, you'll see:

```
COPY COMPLETE
--PRESS <RET> TO ACCEPT: <ESC> TO EXIT--
```

Remove your TriPac data disk from drive 2 and label it as the TriPac data disk with today's date and your name. Press the Esc key.

Skip the next section, and go on to the section called "Ending the Session."

Copying TriPac with DOS 3.3

The DOS 3.3 System Master disk contains a program for copying disks.

1. Insert the DOS 3.3 System Master disk in drive 1 and boot the computer using one of the procedures described earlier.
2. A series of messages will appear on the screen. Make sure the Caps Lock key is pressed, type *RUN COPYA*, and press the Return key.
3. The Apple Disk Duplication program will appear. The copy program presents you with a default (that is, preset) response. Press the Return key four times to activate the default responses. Check with your instructor to determine whether the default responses need to be changed.
4. At the bottom of the screen the message

   ```
   --PRESS 'RETURN' KEY TO BEGIN COPY--
   ```

   will appear.
5. Remove the DOS 3.3 System Master disk from drive 1 and replace it with the TriPac program disk.
6. Place a blank disk in drive 2. Press the Return key. You'll hear a whirring and clacking noise. The words READING, INITIALIZING, and WRITING will alternate on the screen while the program disk is being copied. When the program is finished, you'll see:

   ```
   DO YOU WISH TO MAKE ANOTHER COPY?
   ```

   Press the Y key for yes, then press the Return key. The message

   ```
   --PRESS 'RETURN' KEY TO BEGIN COPY--
   ```

   will appear.
   Remove your new TriPac program disk from drive 2 and label it as the TriPac program disk with today's date and your name.

   Remove the TriPac program disk from drive 1 and insert the TriPac data disk in its place. Then insert your other blank disk into drive 2 and press the Return key. When the program is finished, you'll see:

   ```
   DO YOU WISH TO MAKE ANOTHER COPY?
   ```

   Press the N key for no, then press the Return key. Remove your TriPac data disk from drive 2 and label it as the TriPac data disk with today's date and your name. Remove the master TriPac data disk from drive 1.

Ending the Session

At the end of your session with the computer, remove the disks you have been using from the drives and place them in their storage envelopes. Ask your instructor or lab supervisor whether the computer should be turned off or left on for use by the next class.

In Chapter 2, you will begin to learn how to use the TriPac software.

REVIEW AND SELF-TESTING

Key Terms

Personal computer
Software
General-purpose tool
System
Computer system
Information processing
Hardware
Processor
Memory
Input device
Output device
Mass storage device
Data
Keyboard
Microprocessor
Random-access memory (RAM)
Volatile
Read-only memory (ROM)
Special-purpose application software
Programming language
Operating-system software
Disk operating system
Application
Booting
Bit
Byte
Disk
File
Disk drive
Display screen
Printer
Software package
Documentation
Tutorial
General-purpose application software

Questions for Review and Discussion

1. How is it possible for you to have more computing power at your fingertips than was available to any computer scientist thirty years ago?
2. What makes a personal computer a general-purpose tool?
3. Briefly outline the components of a computer system.
4. What is RAM? What is ROM?
5. Why does a computer system have two different memories?
6. Approximately how many characters of information is 1K bytes?
7. How is it possible for personal computers to have large memories?

8. In the broadest terms, what do you have to know to use a personal computer?
9. What is an application? Name some examples of applications.
10. Name one technique that an operating system uses to organize the storage space on a disk.
11. What purpose does the hierarchical organization of a computer system's resources serve?
12. Give two reasons why it is desirable for the operating system to handle details of storing and retrieving information on a disk.

2

Learning to Use Personal Computers

PREVIEW

The TriPac software consists of the Application Manager and three integrated application programs—a word processor, a spreadsheet program, and a database program. The Application Manager provides a consistent, easy-to-use environment for the three application programs.

The Application Manager and the application programs all use similar commands. This means that, once you have learned to use the Application Manager, you can put that learning to use in the application programs.

This chapter will lead you through the TriPac environment, explaining the concepts and commands of the Application Manager. In the process, you will begin to get a sense of how software and users communicate with each other. Then you will be introduced to one of the application programs—the word processor—to see how the Application Manager and an application program work together.

In this chapter, you'll discover:

- *The purpose and function of a user interface*
- *Techniques for communicating with computers*
- *Techniques computers use to communicate with people*
- *The TriPac environment*
- *Other operating environments*
- *The use of the keyboard and display screen*
- *How to use the Application Manager program*
- *The word-processing environment*

Car/driver interface

Computer/user interface

Interacting With a Personal Computer

Learning to operate a personal computer is, in many ways, like learning to drive a car. In learning to drive, you place yourself in an environment—the driver's seat—that equips you with the means to control the operation of the car. You give the car instructions by turning the wheel and stepping on the gas and the brake. The windows, rearview mirrors, and instrument panel give you feedback and enable you to view your progress as you drive. The car/driver interface, in other words, enables the driver to control the car and communicates information to the driver.

You do not have to understand how a car works to learn to drive. You do, however, need to be familiar with the car/driver interface. Though it is complex, most learners take it for granted because they are already familiar with cars. By contrast, the computer is a new technology, and few first-time users are already familiar with it.

Computers differ from cars and other industrial products in one important way. As we saw in Chapter 1, the hardware is simply a vehicle for the software, which is very abstract and intangible. The programs and data files that computers process consist of intangible information, stored in magnetic form on disks.

Learning how to use a personal computer is primarily a matter of learning to use software. To enable the user to manipulate the software, the computer system has to provide an environment in which objects such as files and programs, and actions such as commands and feedback, are made concrete to the user.

The User Interface

Two-way communication with the software occurs through the **user interface**—software that acts as an intermediary between an application program and the person using it. The user interface permits you to communicate with the computer, and to interpret what the computer system communicates to you.

There are several techniques of two-way communication. In Chapter 1, you learned how to give commands to the operating system by typing them in at the keyboard. You also saw the computer's feedback on the display screen. This type of two-way communication works well if you already know the commands, or if you have a reference guide that lists the available commands.

As an alternative, many programs display a **menu** of the commands available to the user. Instead of typing in the command, the user can simply **select** the command he or she wants to use. Many programs will also display a list of files, so the user can select a file instead of typing in the file name.

If the user makes a mistake, the user interface should point it out and give instructions to correct it. These and other instructions often take the form of a **dialog**, consisting of one or more questions from the system and the user's responses to them. A dialog resembles a conversation between you and the user interface.

The Display Screen

The display screen is the primary vehicle by which the user interface communicates to you, the user. It provides you with information and feedback. In effect, the display screen becomes a window through which you receive feedback from the software.

The software uses several techniques to make your interaction with it more concrete. For example, after you select a menu item, it is highlighted in **reverse video** to indicate that it has been selected. Figure 2.1 shows a menu, with the selected command highlighted in reverse video. The cursors and pointers that indicate your position on the screen are also part of the user interface.

Often there is not enough room on the display screen to see the entire contents of a file all at once. For example, many documents you write on the word processor will be too long to display all at once on the screen. To view other parts of the document, you will use a technique called **scrolling.**

The user interface also makes important and frequently used commands highly accessible, and infrequently used ones accessible only when they are needed. The command to open a file is highly accessible because it is frequently used. It can be accessed, for example, by holding down the Control key while pressing the O key instead of going through a menu. The command to rename a file is not used as often, and it is made accessible only when needed.

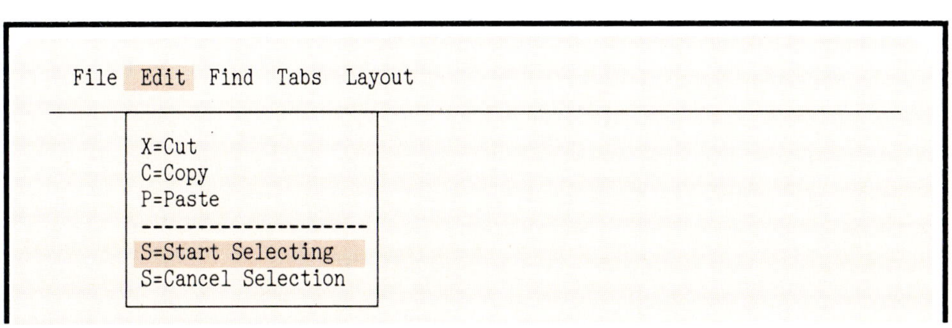

FIGURE 2.1 *Menu with reverse video.*

The Keyboard

The other side of two-way communication—the actions you initiate to control the operation of the computer system—uses the keyboard. As you have already seen, a personal computer's keyboard has several more keys than a traditional typewriter keyboard. These additional keys are used to give the computer instructions and commands. Figure 2.2 shows the keyboard of the Apple IIe personal computer:

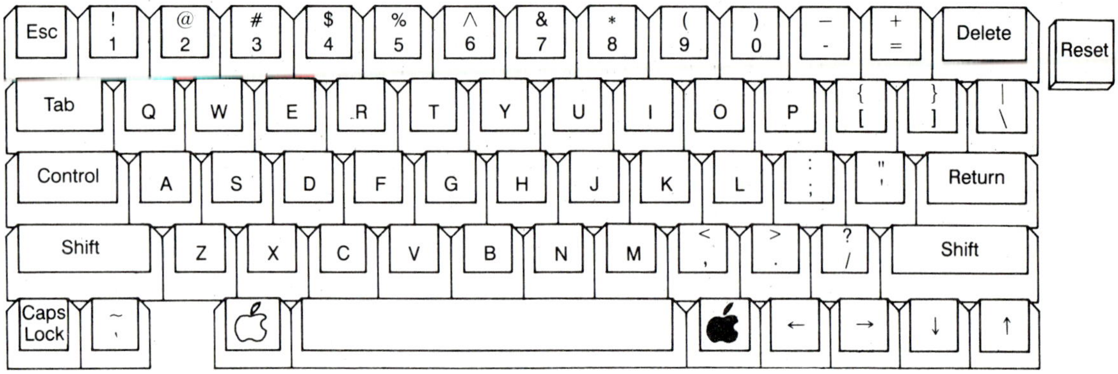

FIGURE 2.2 *The Apple IIe keyboard.*

- Occupying the middle of the keyboard are the traditional typewriter keys, used primarily to enter text and numbers. These keys consist of the letters of the alphabet, numbers, a space bar, and punctuation marks. There are also two shift keys and a Caps Lock key. Letters typed while the shift key is held down appear as capitals. The Caps Lock key holds the shift down until it is released.

Immediately to the left of the traditional typewriter keys is a column of keys that are used to give commands to a program. The TriPac software uses the first three of these keys. Take a look at Figure 2.3.

- The **Esc (escape) key** is used to **toggle** from one mode of operation to another. For example, when you are using the word processor, you are in a mode of manipulating words. If you then want to save a file, you will first use the Esc key to "escape" from that mode into a mode that permits manipulating files. As we will see shortly, toggling between modes is depicted on the display screen as shifting between the upper and lower parts of the screen.
- The **Tab key** is used to move the cursor to a prespecified location left, right, up, or down from its current position. In the TriPac software, you will frequently use the Tab key to respond to questions in dialog boxes. In the word processor the Tab key is used to indent paragraphs, in conjunction with visual markers on the display screen called tab stops. If you wanted to indent five spaces to the right, you would set a tab stop five spaces in from the left margin. Pressing the Tab key would then cause the cursor

FIGURE 2.3 *Escape, Tab, and Control keys.*

cursor to jump five spaces to the tab stop. In the spreadsheet program, the Tab key moves the cursor to the right or left of its current position. In the database program, the Tab key moves the cursor down, up, left, or right when entering and editing data.

- The **Control key** is used as a shorthand way of entering instructions or commands. It is always used in conjunction with another key; pressing it by itself causes nothing to happen. For example, in the TriPac software, holding down the Control key while pressing the O key signifies the command "Open a file for processing." Different programs use the Control key in different ways. The documentation for those programs will explain their use of the Control key.

To the right of the traditional keyboard are two important keys, shown in Figures 2.4 and 2.5:

- The **Delete key** is used to erase the character to the left of the cursor. If you hit the wrong key while typing, simply press the Delete key. This moves the cursor one position to the left, and simultaneously erases the character.

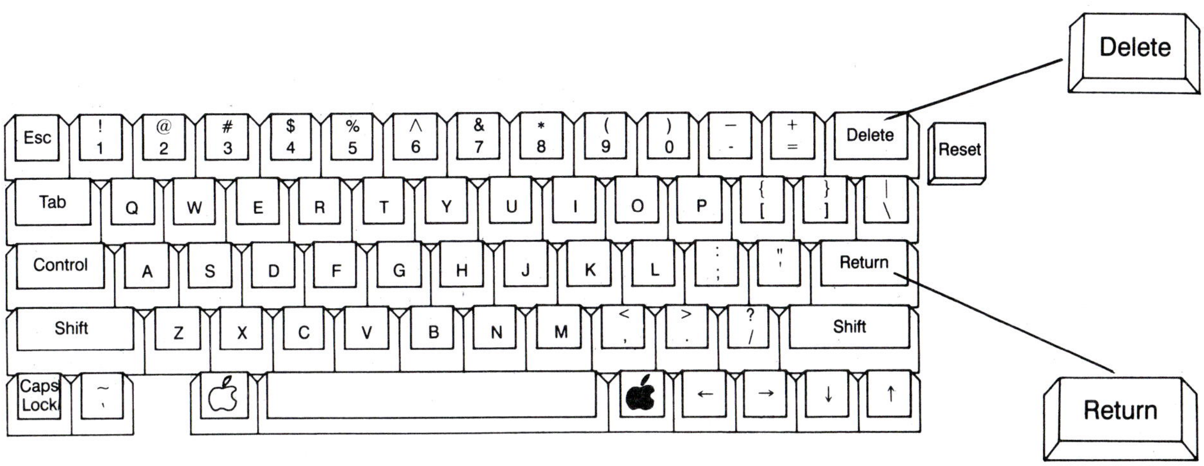

FIGURE 2.4 *Delete and Return keys.*

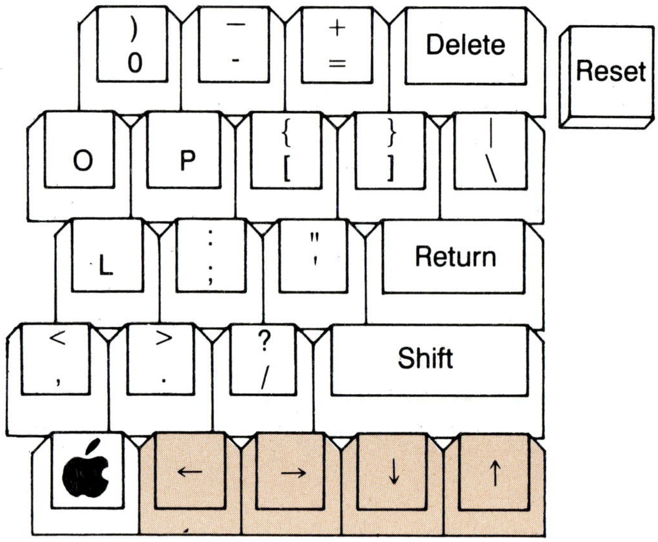

FIGURE 2.5 *Cursor-movement keys.*

Holding the Delete key down will repeatedly erase characters as the cursor moves to the left. This method can be used to erase entire words or sentences.

- The **Return key** is used to enter commands, respond to prompts, and begin new paragraphs.
- To the right of the space bar are the four **cursor-movement keys.** They are inscribed with arrows indicating the direction in which the cursor will move when the key is pressed.

To the immediate left and right of the space bar are the [open apple] and [solid apple] keys, shown in Figure 2.6. They are like the Control key in that they are used in conjunction with other keys to enter instructions or commands. For example, holding down the [open apple] and Control keys while pressing the Reset key will reboot the computer.

The TriPac software uses the [open apple] key in conjunction with the Up and Down arrow keys to scroll the contents of the screen up and down a page at a time. The TriPac software does not use the [solid apple] key.

Different programs use the keyboard in different ways. In other words, the function of certain keys changes depending on which program you are using. For example, the Delete key normally erases characters as it moves from right to left. This occurs when using the operating system and when using the TriPac software. But other programs may employ it differently. Redefinable keys can make software simpler and more efficient, but users have to remember different sets of rules for different programs. The documentation that accompanies a program explains its uses of the keys.

FIGURE 2.6 *The and keys.*

The TriPac Environment

The TriPac environment consists of three general-purpose application programs and an Application Manager program. The **word processor** applies the computer to the work of writing. The **spreadsheet** program dedicates the computer to the work of calculating and analyzing information. The **database** program harnesses the computer to the work of storing, organizing, and retrieving information.

The Application Manager program integrates the three application programs into a common environment. This means that all three share similar menus and commands, which makes them easier to learn and use. It also means that you can pass information from the spreadsheet or database program into the word processor. For example, you can locate a name and address in a database, and then pass that information to the word processor for use in composing a document.

The Application Manager

The **Application Manager** is the part of the TriPac software that manages the three application programs and the files used by those programs. Figure 2.7 shows the relationship between the Application Manager and the three application programs.

The user does not need to be concerned with the technical details of how and where data are stored on a disk. Even so, files are an important concept, and much of what you will "see" the Application Manager doing involves managing files.

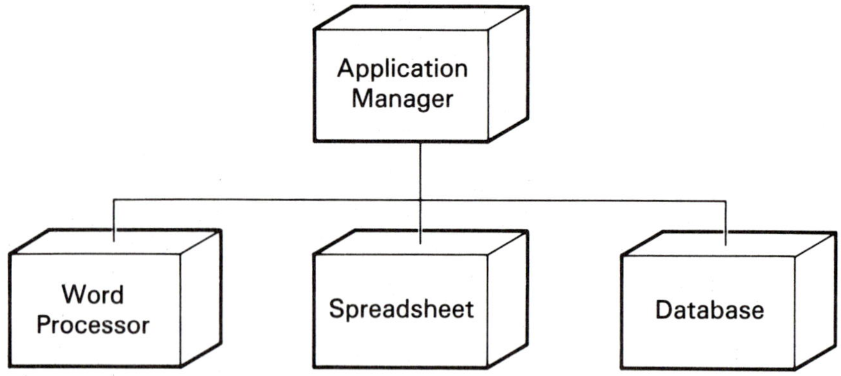

FIGURE 2.7 *Organization of the TriPac software.*

The Application Manager's user interface insulates you from some of the lower-level details of the operating system. Instead of communicating directly with the operating system to run a program or open, copy, rename, or delete a file, you communicate with the Application Manager. It relays your instructions to the operating system.

So far, we have introduced several concepts basic to controlling and communicating with personal computers. We have shown you some commands that you will use to control the operation of the computer. You have also seen some examples of two-way communication between the user and the computer. Now, let us apply these concepts.

Getting Started

Here's how to start using the TriPac software:

1. Remove the TriPac program disk from its storage jacket, handling it by its label, and insert the disk into disk drive 1 (the left-hand drive).
2. Remove the TriPac data disk from its storage jacket and insert the disk into disk drive 2 (the right-hand drive).
3. If the computer is already turned on, hold down the Control and keys while you press the Reset key. If the computer is turned off, use the on/off switches to turn on the display device and the computer.

The red light on disk drive 1 will go on, and the computer will copy the software from the program disk into memory. A title screen will appear. It describes how to use the keyboard and lists a few important features of TriPac. Press the Return key. A dialog box will appear asking you to make sure you have a data disk in drive 2. Press the Return key. The computer will copy the contents of the data disk into memory. Then you'll have your first look at the TriPac software. Figure 2.8 shows what you'll see.

You are now ready to begin using the TriPac software. At first, you are just going to explore the TriPac environment. By the time you finish this chapter, however, you'll have completed your first assignment using the TriPac word processor.

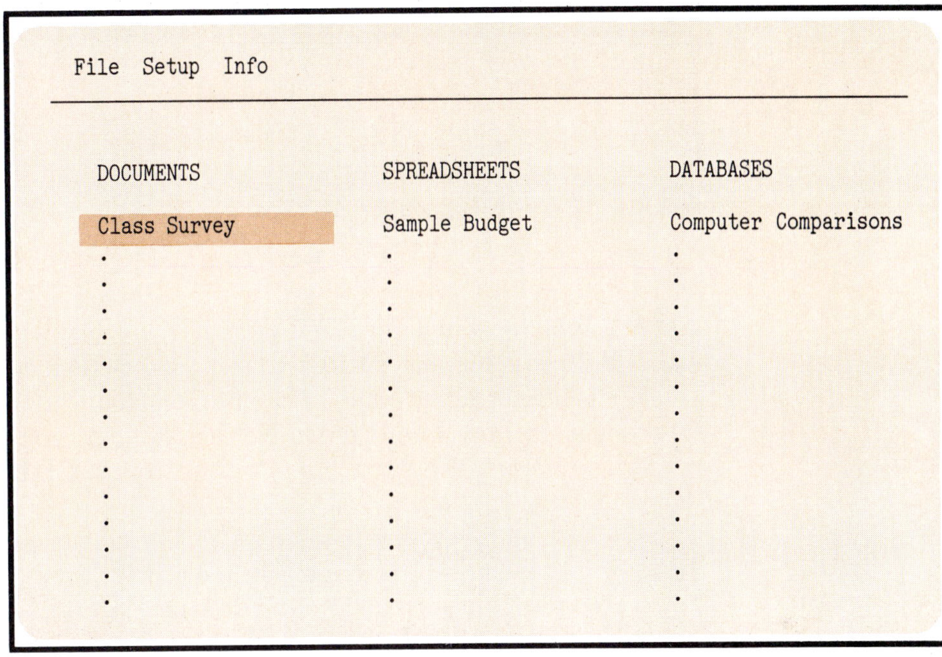

FIGURE 2.8 *The TriPac Application Manager.*

What You'll See

A horizontal line across the top of the screen divides the display into two parts. The larger part below the horizontal line is called the workspace. The workspace currently contains a **directory**—a listing of all the data files on the disk that the application programs can use. In this case, it is a directory of the data files on the disk inserted in drive 2. The directory is subdivided into three categories, DOCUMENTS, SPREADSHEETS, and DATABASES.

Note that the first entry under the column head DOCUMENTS is highlighted in reverse video. Reverse video is a means of highlighting a particular part of the screen. Eventually, you will want to select one of the files in the directory. To select a file, you have to point to it. In this context, the reverse-video highlighting functions as a **pointer** or selection cursor.

The pointer is always movable. Try it, using the Right and Left arrow keys, and then the Down and Up arrow keys. You will notice that holding down an arrow key causes the pointer to keep moving until you release the key. Also note that there are many untitled files in the directory; these are empty unnamed files. Later, when you use the application programs, you will create documents, spreadsheets, and databases and give them names.

As you will see, moving the pointer does not initiate any action, other than highlighting the selection of your choice. The purpose of the pointer is simply to show you where you are on the display.

The display above the horizontal line is called the **menu bar.** Figure 2.9 shows the menu bar for the Application Manager. A menu bar is a list of all the available menus. As we saw earlier, a menu is a list of the commands that you can tell the computer to perform. Each program in the TriPac software has its own menu bar. To access the Application Manager's menu bar, press the Esc

FIGURE 2.9 *The Application Manager's menu bar.*

key. (You will recall that the Esc key acts like a toggle switch; that is, pressing it causes the movable pointer to switch from one mode to another, and from one area of the display to the other.) The File menu in the upper left-hand corner of the display is now highlighted. Note that your original selection in the workspace is also highlighted, but now the arrow keys will move the pointer on the menu bar.

You can see the menu bar, but where are the menus? To view the File menu, press the Down arrow key. The menu will "drop down" from the menu bar. This type of menu is called a **pull-down menu.** Most of the time it is hidden from view; you see it only when you need to consult it. Later, we will explain what the commands in each menu mean. Press the Up arrow key repeatedly and the menu will retract. (Try it.)

You can select other menus listed on the menu bar by using the Left and Right arrow keys. Press the Right arrow key to select the next entry on the menu bar; the selection cursor will shift to the next menu. Practice pulling down and retracting the menus. Also try pressing a Left or Right arrow key while a menu is "pulled down." This is a shortcut method for exploring all the menus on the TriPac Application Manager without causing any other action to occur. Now press the Esc key again. The pointer will disappear from the menu bar.

One of the functions of the Application Manager program is to enable you to open, save, copy, rename, and delete the files used by the three application programs.

For example, in the next section you are going to use the word processor to process an existing document. To activate the word processor, you must tell the system the name of the document you want the program to use. The Application Manager program locates and accesses the files by giving each one a name.

When you position the pointer over the name of a document and then open it, the Application Manager automatically locates and accesses the application program that was used to create the file. It copies the program and the data file from disk into memory, and prepares the file for processing by the application program.

Important: You access the program by accessing one of the files it uses. You do not have to call up or type in the name of the application program separately. This technique is often used when programs are integrated, as in the case of TriPac.

Other file-management operations include creating a new file and deleting an old file. The following exercise will show you how to create and delete files. Be sure to follow the directions exactly, since it is possible to delete any file in the Application Manager's directory.

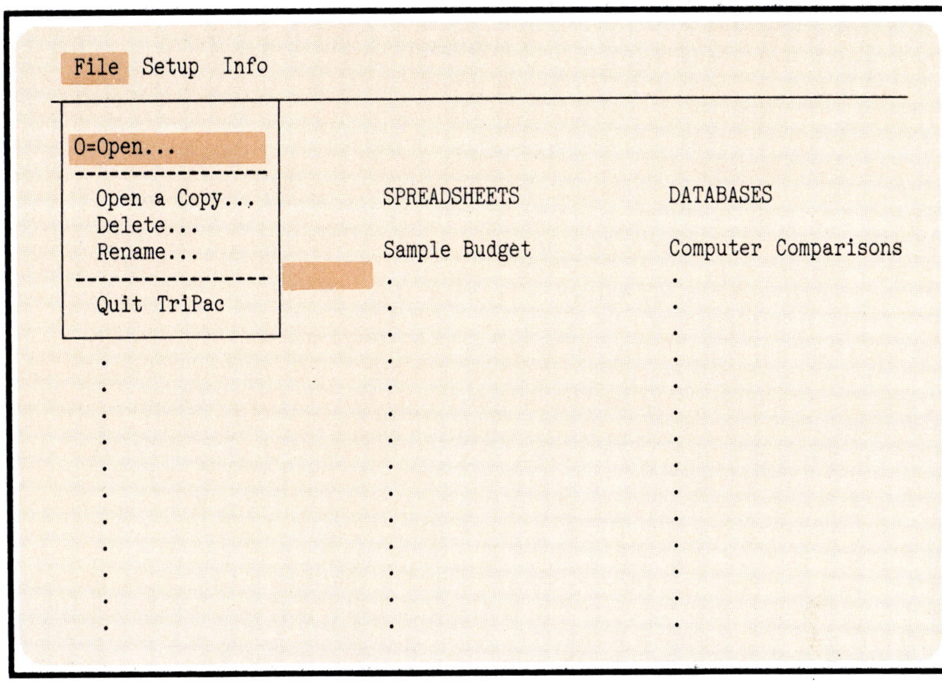

FIGURE 2.10 *Opening a file.*

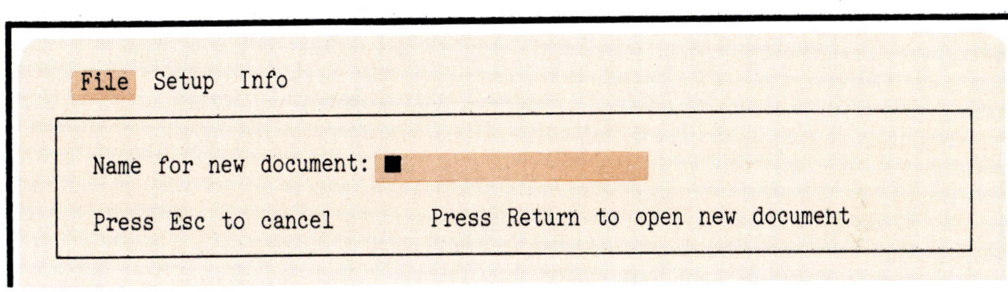

FIGURE 2.11 *A dialog box.*

1. Move the pointer to the first untitled entry in the DOCUMENTS directory. Then press the Esc key.
2. The pointer will highlight the File menu on the menu bar. Press the Down arrow key until the *O = Open* command is highlighted. The screen will look like Figure 2.10. Then press the Return key to select the *O = Open* command.
3. A dialog box will appear. Figure 2.11 shows what it will look like. Because the file you are about to open is untitled, the Application Manager will ask you to name the file. Type in the name *Test Document.* If you make a typing error, use the Delete key to erase the mistake and reposition the cursor.
4. When you press the Return key, the Application Manager will activate the word processor, so you will now see the word processor's workspace. Using the Esc key, toggle to the menu bar. Make sure the pointer is highlighting

the File menu. Then press the Down arrow key until the *Quit Word Processor* command is highlighted. Then press the Return key. After a moment, the Application Manager's workspace will reappear. There you will see that *Test Document* has replaced *untitled* in the DOCUMENTS column.

5. To delete the file you just created, make sure the pointer is highlighting the name *Test Document*. Press the Esc key to toggle to the menu bar. With the pointer highlighting the File menu, press the Down arrow key until the *Delete*. . . command is highlighted. Then press the Return key.
6. A dialog box will appear, asking if you want to "Delete the document named 'Test Document'?" You have a choice. Pressing the Esc key will return you to the Application Manager without deleting the file. Pressing the Return key deletes the file. Press the Return key.

To access the word processor, spreadsheet, or database programs with an existing file, simply point to the file's name in the directory and select the *O=Open* command in the File menu. After the data and program files have been copied into memory, you can begin to work with the data already in the file. You will do this in an upcoming section.

The second menu on the menu bar, the Setup menu, has to do with transmitting data from the computer to the printer. The third menu, the Info menu, is simply a title page for the TriPac software. Note that when these menus are pulled down, each command is followed by an ellipsis (. . .). This is a visual signal that additional information will be supplied in a dialog box when you select a command. To view that additional information in the Info menu, press the Down arrow key and then press the Return key. The dialog box that appears will contain the title information.

Other Operating Environments

Some operating environments are very ingenious in how they visually represent the software and the functions of control. Some use graphic images called **icons** to represent the options in a menu. Figure 2.12 shows an example of a menu that uses icons. Some also divide the display screen into **windows**, variable-sized rectangles capable of displaying different parts of a file or different application programs simultaneously.

Some user interfaces augment the keyboard with a pointing device called a **mouse**, shown in Figure 2.13. The mouse controls the cursor. You point to menu items and options by moving the mouse around on a flat surface next to your computer. The mouse's movements are replicated by the movement of the cursor on the screen. To select the item at which the cursor is pointing, you simply press a button on the mouse. Apple's Macintosh is one example of a computer whose user interface is designed around a mouse pointing device. The system also uses icons and other graphic symbols to communicate with the user.

The Hewlett-Packard Touchscreen computer, shown in Figure 2.14, has a user interface based on a **touch-sensitive screen.** Instead of a mouse, the user uses one finger to input commands and actions.

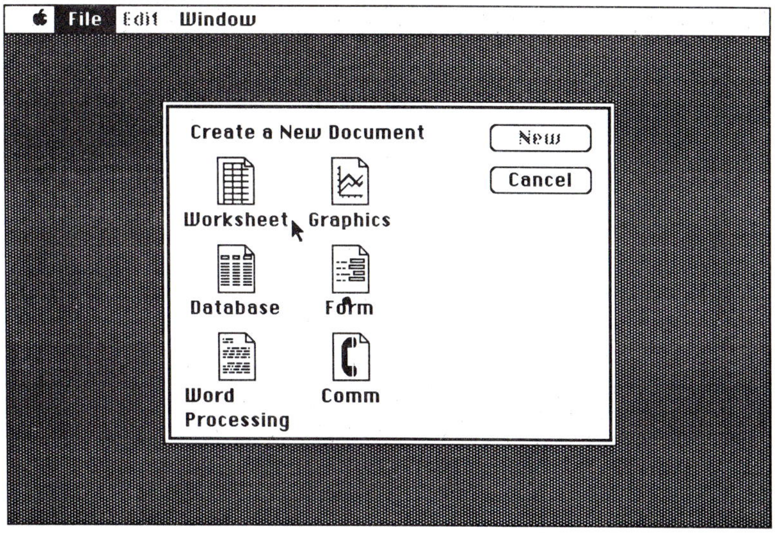

FIGURE 2.12 *Icons in a menu.*

FIGURE 2.13 *As the user rolls the mouse next to the computer, the movement of a ball on the underside of the mouse translates into cursor movement on the screen. Buttons on the mouse allow the user to select what the cursor is pointing to.*

FIGURE 2.14 *A touch-sensitive screen.*

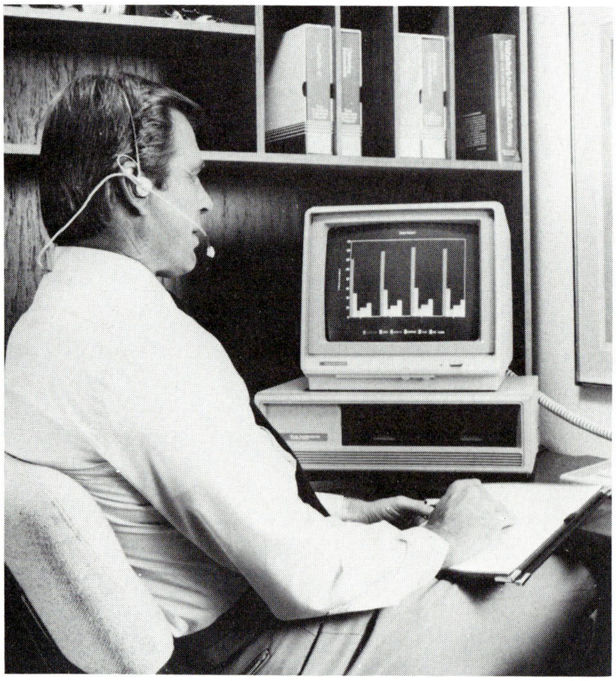

FIGURE 2.15 *A voice-activated personal computer.*

The Texas Instruments personal computer has an optional **voice interface.** Special hardware and software allows the user to "train" the system to recognize simple spoken commands and phrases.

Some application programs have incorporated a **natural-language interface** into their software. Using an application program ordinarily involves typing complex or cryptic requests or commands. A natural-language interface allows the request to be typed in ordinary English. The user interface then translates the English phrase into the necessary commands.

Among the most interesting challenges for designers of user interfaces has been to develop hardware and software for blind, deaf, and physically handicapped users. There are several systems that can translate text into speech, and several ingenious devices for translating movements of the head, toe, finger, or eye into computer commands.

Creating user interfaces for the handicapped forces designers to question their assumptions and think about how people would interact with computers if keyboards and display screens were not the standard conventions of computer use. Their research and experimentation are leading to new ways of interacting with computers that may ultimately benefit all computer users. Figure 2.15 shows a user interface that uses voice input instead of a keyboard.

The Word-Processing Environment

The word-processing environment is very similar to the Application Manager environment. Commands are listed on pull-down menus on the menu bar. The information being processed—the document—appears in the workspace. Let us look at an example of the word-processing environment.

A Word-Processing Example

Your instructor wants to survey your class to find out something about each student's prior experience with computers, and attitudes toward them. You are going to use the word processor to fill out the survey form. In the process, you will be exposed to the basic word-processing operations of cursor movement, scrolling, and entering text.

You are going to use the TriPac word processor to:

1. Select and open the document named *Class Survey.*
2. Answer the survey questions.
3. Save the document on your disk in the file titled *Class Survey.*
4. Print the completed survey to hand in to your instructor.

By the time you have completed this assignment, you will have learned the basic skills of using a word processor. The following instructions will lead you through the process step by step.

1. First, select the document called *Class Survey*. To do so, position the pointer on the name of that document. If the pointer is currently pointing at the menu bar, press the Esc key to toggle into the workspace. Then use the arrow keys to position the pointer on the *Class Survey* document as in Figure 2.16.
2. Press the Esc key to return to the menu bar. Make sure the pointer is highlighting the File menu. Then press the Down arrow key and the pull-down menu will appear. Use the Down arrow key to highlight the *O = Open* command, and press the Return key.
   You have just instructed the computer to (1) copy the *Class Survey* document from disk into the computer's memory, and (2) copy the word processor from disk into the computer's memory.
3. The Application Manager display will disappear from the workspace, and the display shown in Figure 2.17 will appear.

The word processor uses some familiar symbols in unfamiliar ways. A paragraph sign (¶) is visible on the screen. Word processors conserve file space by using a paragraph sign to indicate the end of a paragraph, instead of storing many blank characters. You can point to, select, and manipulate paragraph symbols as you can any other character.

The ^ in the upper left corner indicates the beginning of a page. Again, instead of storing many blank characters, most word processors use a symbol to indicate page breaks in a document. It cannot be selected like other characters.

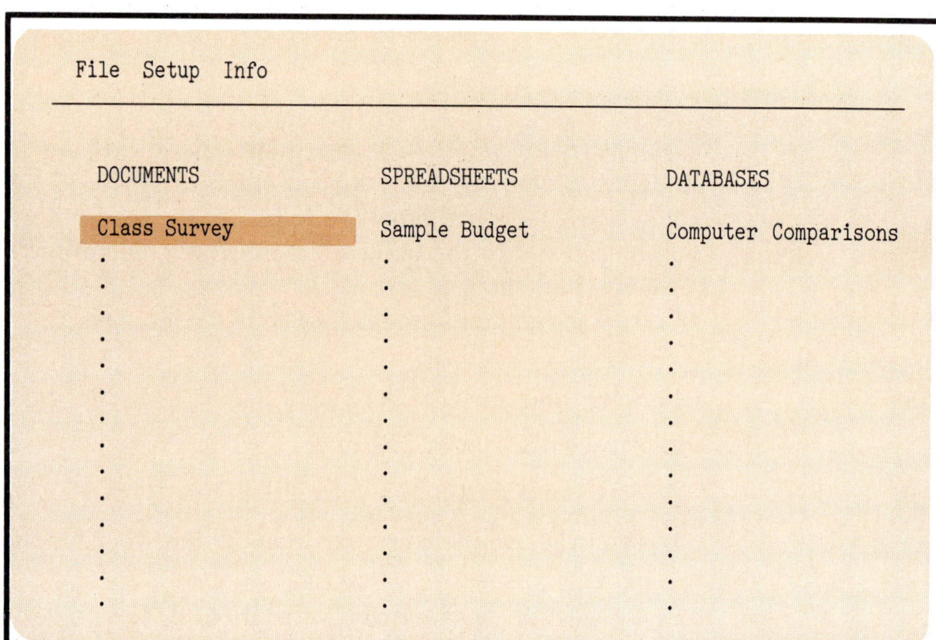

FIGURE 2.16 *Selecting the Class Survey document.*

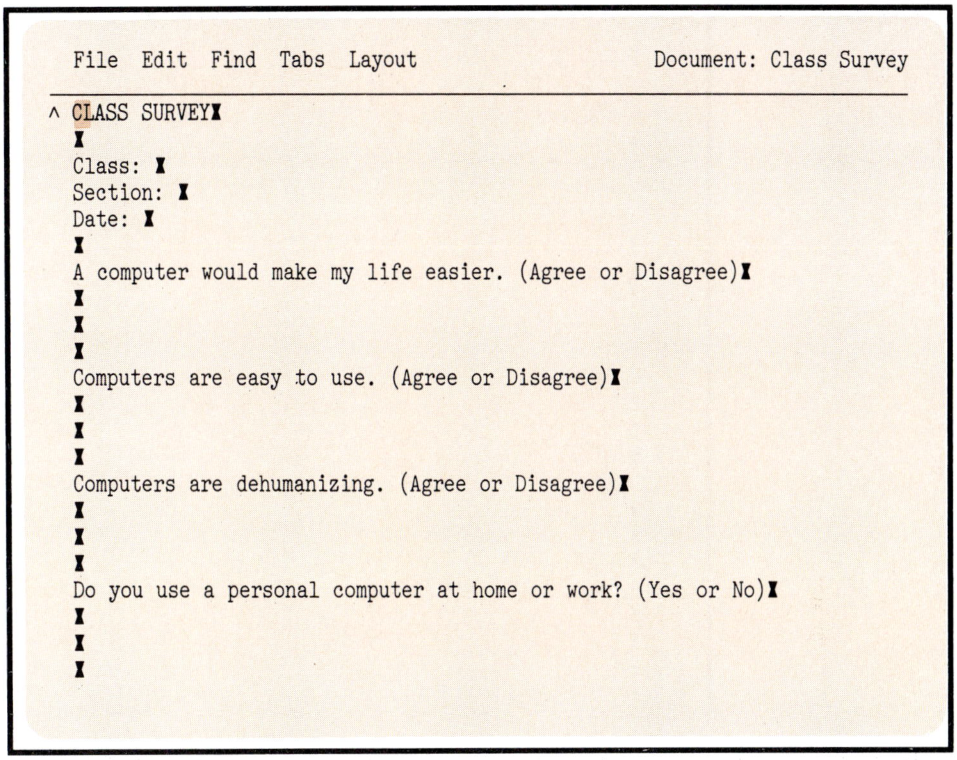

FIGURE 2.17 *The Class Survey.*

Using the Word Processor

In the upper left-hand corner of the workspace, next to the ^, is a blinking rectangular box called a **typing cursor.** The typing cursor provides feedback by pointing to the active location on the screen—the location of the next character you are going to type. Like the pointer, the typing cursor is always movable. You can move it anywhere in the workspace by using the Up, Down, Left, and Right arrow keys. (Try it.)

Use the arrow keys to move the typing cursor to the line where the word Class: appears. Then move the typing cursor so it highlights the paragraph symbol (¶) one position beyond the colon. Take a look at Figure 2.18. Type in your class name and number, just as you would on a typewriter. You do not need to use the Return key when you are finished typing.

Use the Down arrow key to move the typing cursor down one line, to the paragraph sign following the word Section:. If your class is divided into sections, type in your section number or the section leader's name. Then move the typing cursor to the next line, and type in today's date.

If you make a spelling mistake, position the typing cursor over the letter immediately to the right of the mistake. Then use the Delete key to erase the letter to the left of the typing cursor. Then you can type in your correction. Using the Delete key to delete characters allows you to edit anything you see on the display. Be careful, though, since you can easily delete anything on the screen.

```
File  Edit  Find  Tabs  Layout                    Document: Class Survey
------------------------------------------------------------------------
^ CLASS SURVEY¶
¶
Class: ¶
Section: ¶
Date: ¶
¶
A computer would make my life easier. (Agree or Disagree)¶
¶
¶
¶
Computers are easy to use. (Agree or Disagree)¶
¶
¶
¶
Computers are dehumanizing. (Agree or Disagree)¶
¶
¶
¶
Do you use a personal computer at home or work? (Yes or No)¶
¶
¶
¶
```

FIGURE 2.18 *Moving the typing cursor.*

You will notice that there are three paragraph marks (¶) in the left margin below each question in the survey. Use the arrow keys to move the typing cursor to the middle paragraph mark; then type in your answer. When you finish, move the typing cursor to the middle paragraph mark following the next question, and go on.

The survey is too large to display on the screen all at once. To view more of the survey, press the Down arrow key. When the typing cursor reaches the bottom line of the display, the text will move up. The last line of the previous screen will appear at the top of the display. This maneuver, called scrolling, causes a new display to appear at one edge as the previous display disappears at the opposite edge. Figure 2.19 shows the new display of more of the Class Survey. In the word processor, you can scroll up and down by using the Up and Down arrow keys or by holding down the (Apple) key while pressing Up and Down arrow keys. To finish the Class Survey, scroll up one more time.

When you have finished responding to the survey, scan the document for typing mistakes. If you discover a misspelled word, use the arrow keys to position the typing cursor to the right of the mistake. Pressing the Delete key in the upper right-hand corner of the keyboard will cause the character to the left of the cursor to disappear and the space to close up. Type in your correction, and the word processor will insert it in the proper location.

```
File  Edit  Find  Tabs  Layout                    Document: Class Survey
------------------------------------------------------------------------
¶
If yes, what kind is it? (Type the computer's brand name)¶
¶
¶
¶
Do you use a computer more or less than once a week? (More or
Less)¶
¶
¶
¶
Do you think computers are hard to adjust to? (Yes or No)¶
¶
¶
¶
Do you feel comfortable using the computer? (Yes or No)¶
¶
¶
¶
Are you taking this course only because it is required? (Yes or
No)¶
¶
¶
```

FIGURE 2.19 *The Class Survey, scrolled.*

Revert to Last Version

Suppose that you have messed up the Class Survey beyond repair, and you simply want to start over again. The *Revert to Last Version...* command in the File menu provides a way to recover from mistakes by restoring the file to its original version.

To use the command, press the Esc key to toggle to the menu bar. With the pointer highlighting the File menu, press the Down arrow until the *Revert to Last Version...* command is highlighted as in Figure 2.20. Then press the Return key.

```
File  Edit  Find  Tabs  Layout                    Document: Class Survey
------------------------------------------------------------------------
|  Save Document                  |
|  Print Document...              |
| ------------------------------- |
|  Revert to Last Version...      |
| ------------------------------- |
|  Quit Word Processor            |
```

FIGURE 2.20 *The* Revert to Last Version. . . *command.*

A dialog box will appear, warning you that you will lose all the changes you have made since the last save. In other words, the command will destroy all changes to the existing version of the file. You have a choice. Pressing the Esc key will return you to the word processor without altering the current version of the file. Pressing the Return key destroys the current version of the file and loads in the last version of the file. Be sure you want to destroy your work before using this command. There is no way to restore the current version of the file after you execute the *Revert to Last Version...* command.

Saving and Printing the Survey

When you have finished your proofreading and corrections, the first thing you will want to do is to save your document. Press the Esc key to toggle to the menu bar. With the File menu highlighted, press the Down arrow key until the *Save Document* command is highlighted. Then press the Return key. The File menu will retract, and the word processor will spend several seconds copying your Class Survey document to disk. When it is finished, the typing cursor will return to wherever it was before you pressed the Esc key.

To print your document, press the Esc key to toggle to the menu bar. Press the Down arrow key until the *Print Document...* command is highlighted. Then press the Return key.

A dialog box will appear, informing you that the document is single-spaced, and asking you to press the Return key to print page 1 of the document. Before pressing the Return key, check that the printer is connected to the computer and turned on.

Also, the paper should be positioned in the printer so that the top edge is just above the rollers. If you are using continuous form-feed paper, you may have to use the line-feed button or the form-feed button on the printer to correctly position the paper.

Before transmitting your document to the printer, check that the printer is properly connected to the computer. If the printer is improperly connected, or is not turned on, you will have to restart the program.

When you look at the printed version of your survey, or at the version in Figure 2.21, you will notice that the paragraph signs and other user guides do not appear in the document. This is because they are used by the word processor to save space in the file and to indicate where paragraphs and page breaks should appear on a printed document.

After you have finished printing your class survey, press the Esc key to toggle to the menu bar. Press the Down key to select the *Quit Word Processor* command. Then press the Return key. The Application Manager will appear. To quit using the TriPac software entirely, press the Esc key to toggle to the menu bar, press the Down arrow key to select the *Quit TriPac* command, and press the Return key.

The computer will display the following message:

```
You have exited from TriPac. You may turn off the computer or you may
restart the computer by placing any program disk in Drive 1 and press-
ing Return.
```

If you wanted to re-enter the TriPac environment at this point, you could do so by pressing the Return key.

As you become more familiar with the TriPac software, by completing the exercises that follow, you will find that practice translates directly into the ability to use the software to solve problems.

```
CLASS SURVEY

Class: Introduction to Computers
Section: 4
Date: September 15, 1986

A computer would make my life easier. (Agree or Disagree)

Agree

Computers are easy to use. (Agree or Disagree)

Disagree

Computers are dehumanizing. (Agree or Disagree)

Agree

Do you use a personal computer at home or work? (Yes or No)

Yes

If yes, what kind is it? (Type the computer's brand name)

IBM Personal Computer

Do you use a computer more or less than once a week? (More or
Less)

Less

Do you think computers are hard to adjust to? (Yes or No)

Yes

Do you feel comfortable using the computer? (Yes or No)

Yes

Are you taking this course only because it is required? (Yes or
No)

No

(Optional) What is your name? (Type your name below)

Roland Alden
```

FIGURE 2.21 *Sample printed version of the Class Survey.*

REVIEW AND SELF-TESTING

Key Terms

- User interface
- Menu
- Selection
- Dialog
- Reverse video
- Scrolling
- Esc key
- Toggle
- Tab key
- Control key
- Return key
- Cursor-movement key
- Word processor
- Spreadsheet
- Database
- Application Manager
- Directory
- Pointer
- Menu bar
- Pull down menu
- Icon
- Window
- Mouse
- Touch-sensitive screen
- Voice interface
- Natural-language interface
- Typing cursor

Questions for Review and Discussion

1. How do computers differ from other industrial products?
2. How does two-way communication occur between a computer and a user?
3. Name two video techniques that a display uses to make interacting with software more visible.
4. Name the most common use of the Tab key in the TriPac software.
5. What functions does the Application Manager program integrate?
6. In the TriPac environment, what are the names of the two areas that the display is divided into?
7. What is the purpose of the pointer?
8. What command tells the Application Manager to create a new file?
9. What is the purpose of the "untitled" entries in the Application Manager's directory?
10. What is the purpose of a mouse?
11. Outline the steps to open an existing document in the word-processing program.
12. What is the function of the typing cursor?
13. What are the necessary conditions for printing a document?

3

Personal Computers in Perspective

PREVIEW

Computers are usually divided into three categories: mainframes, minicomputers, and personal computers. These three categories are defined by differences of size and power. This chapter will take you on a brief tour of all three types, looking at their uses and their impacts. Seeing personal computers in the context of larger computer systems will give you an overview of their potential.

Although the personal computer is at the small end of the scale, size should not be confused with performance. A silicon chip can contain enough circuits for a powerful computer. From their modest beginnings as do-it-yourself hobby kits, personal computers have grown to encompass simple home computers and powerful business desktop computers. The personal-computer industry is only about ten years old, but its sales have already surpassed those of minicomputers and mainframes.

At the end of this chapter, you will encounter another of the TriPac application programs—the database program.

In this chapter, you'll discover:

- *The three main categories of computers*
- *The convergence of computers and communications*
- *Trends in stand-alone personal computer systems*
- *Trends in multiuser information systems*
- *The role of personal computers in networked systems*
- *The role of the minicomputer*
- *The role of the mainframe computer*
- *The impact of the personal computer on individuals and organizations*
- *The database environment*

What Is an Information System?

To gain some perspective on personal computers, we are going to step back in this chapter and examine the much larger subject of information systems. In Chapter 1 we defined a system as a set of parts that work together to achieve a desired goal. An **information system** is a set of interconnected parts whose purpose is to gather, manipulate, store, transmit, and communicate information.

Information systems range in size from a personal computer system used by one person to massive systems of interconnected computers that support thousands of people. Today, the personal computer plays a prominent role in information systems of all magnitudes. The trend is toward smaller, faster, and cheaper computer systems that deliver more computer power per dollar.

Types of Computer Systems

Computer systems are categorized on the basis of memory capacity and computational power. As we saw in Chapter 1, memory size is measured in bytes. The kilobyte (K) is the equivalent of 210 or approximately 1000 bytes. Because all three categories of computers can have very large memories, we will compare their memory capacities in **megabytes** (MB), the equivalent of 220 or approximately 1 million bytes.

Processing power is measured in **MIPS**, which stands for *million instructions per second.* Keep in mind, when you read these numbers, that the value of any computer system is determined by what serves its users best and most economically, not by its power or speed per se.

Mainframes are room-sized, high-performance computers, capable of running complex programs that would be impractical or impossible on smaller computer systems. They are used by large corporations, government agencies, and universities to process large volumes of information and to perform high-speed processing. A mainframe computer may possess up to 256 megabytes of memory, and operate at speeds of up to 40 MIPS—40 million instructions per second. They are also expensive, and require an air-conditioned environment and trained staffs of operators.

TABLE 3.1 *Three sizes of computers compared*

	Mainframe	Minicomputer	Personal Computer
Model	IBM Sierra	Digital Venus	IBM PC AT
Price	$5 million	$500,000	$5,000
Memory	64 MB	12 MB	1 MB
Price per Megabyte	$80,000	$42,000	$5,000
MIPS	28	4	.5
Cost per MIPS	$180,000	$125,000	$10,000

Three types of computers. From top to bottom: a mainframe, a minicomputer, and a personal computer.

Minicomputers are medium-sized, medium-capacity computer systems, whose performance rivals that of small mainframes. They are typically used as divisional or departmental computers in business, and as the primary computer system in scientific and laboratory applications. A minicomputer has up to 32 megabytes of memory and operates at speeds of up to 4 MIPS. Because of its simpler design, it does not require a special environment or a large staff.

Personal computers, also called microcomputers, are desktop-sized microprocessor-based computer systems. Used in a wide variety of business, professional, academic, and personal undertakings, personal computers possess up to 4 megabytes of memory and operate at speeds up to 1 MIPS.

Table 3.1 compares top-of-the-line computers in each of the three categories.

Computers and Communications

The rapid evolution of information systems has intermixed computers and communications so closely that they have become, for all practical purposes, a single integrated industry.

There are two aspects to computer communications. First, the components of a computer system (the processor, memory, and input and output devices) need to communicate with one another. Second, computers need to communicate with other computers. A group of interrelated computers capable of exchanging information is called a **network.**

The **channels** for transmitting information between computers are direct wiring (if the components of a computer system are close together), telephone lines, cable systems, and satellite systems. Today, most communications traffic is carried on ordinary voice telephone lines. This is made possible by a hardware component called a **modem,** which enables two computers to exchange data over standard telephone lines. Figure 3.1 shows two personal computers, linked by their modems and the phone lines. **Communications** software performs the "behind-the-scenes" operations necessary for hardware devices to communicate with one another.

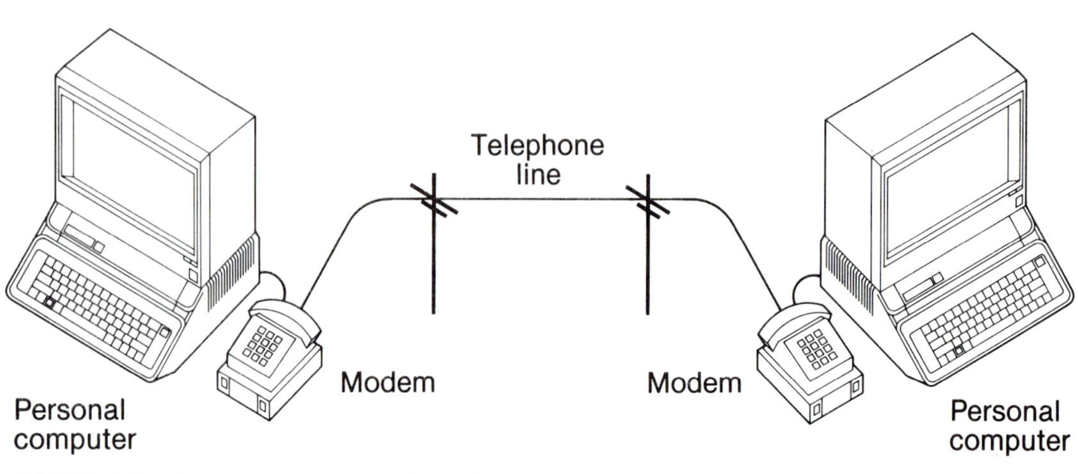

FIGURE 3.1 *Personal computers linked by telephone lines.*

Small Information Systems

In the last five years, personal computers and minicomputers have become powerful enough to perform many of the information-processing tasks that once were reserved for mainframe computers. Users of information systems, in turn, are attracted to the prices of smaller systems, and their ease of use.

The structure of information systems is also changing. In the past, large central mainframe computers were connected to **terminals**—devices without independent computing capability, used only to enter and receive information. Today it is considered more effective to distribute processing among several computers, which may be widely dispersed geographically.

Now let's look at several kinds of information systems, to see what role personal computers are playing in them.

The Single-User System

In business, personal computers have interpersonal functions as well. Personal computers can handle much of the communication businesspeople need to exchange with their associates and customers. By equipping a personal computer with a modem and communications software, one can send and receive **electronic mail.** To send electronic mail, you type a message on a word processor or similar software, and then transmit it—via communications software, a modem, and the telephone lines—to the recipient's electronic mailbox, a storage location in the system's central computer. The recipient accesses his or her mailbox, reads the mail, and sends a reply to your electronic mailbox. Sender and receiver need not be interacting at the same time to use electronic mail.

Personal computers can also access **electronic libraries**, which deliver stock quotes, business news, reference material, and miscellaneous services like airline schedules, hotel reservations, and shopping services. Electronic libraries are stored in a mainframe or minicomputer's disk-filing system, and you can subscribe to one just as you would subscribe to a newspaper or magazine. Figure 3.2 shows a screen displaying daily stock prices, accessed through an electronic information utility.

The Multiuser System

Multiuser systems allow several users to share a computer's processor, memory, disk storage, and software simultaneously. The key to multiuser systems is the ability to share data and program files. For example, computerized accounting systems typically use five general-purpose software packages: accounts receivable, accounts payable, inventory, payroll, and general ledger. If these programs are **integrated**—if they have the ability to exchange data with each other—the information contained in the organization's accounting system can be shared by storing the data and program files on a hard disk, and sharing the files among several personal computers. Multiuser systems come in three types: (1) shared-logic systems, (2) multiprocessor systems, and (3) personal computer networks. Figure 3.3 shows a multiuser system.

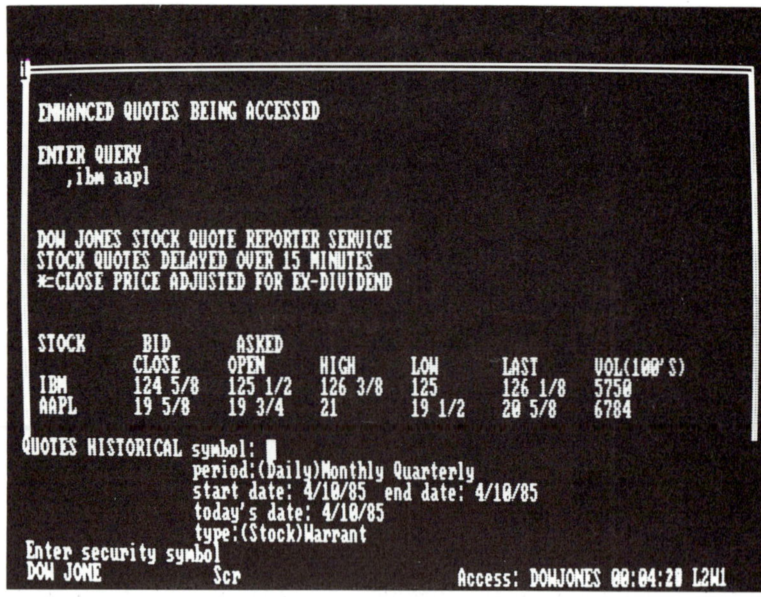

FIGURE 3.2 *With communications software and a modem, personal computer users can access information from an electronic library, such as the Dow Jones Stock Quote shown here.*

Shared-logic systems connect several terminals to a single microcomputer or minicomputer processor. Shared-logic systems work best when all the users are performing the same application. For example, in a small law firm with a shared-logic word-processing system, the legal secretaries share a common set of document files. Each secretary uses a terminal connected to the central

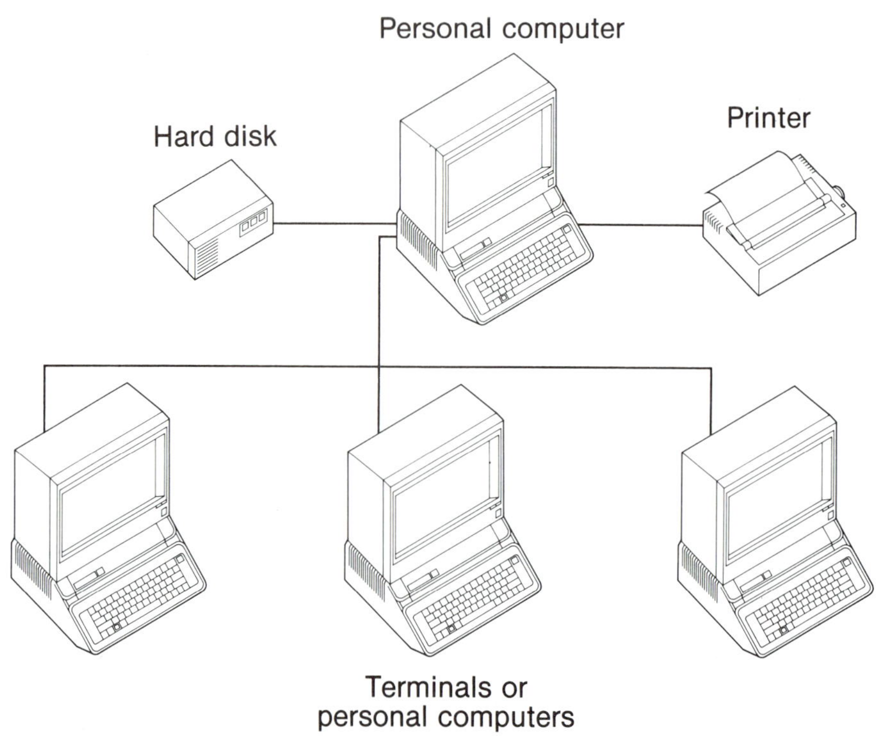

FIGURE 3.3 *A multiuser system.*

processor and disk-storage device. Since the users are all sharing a common processor, adding more users makes the system perform less efficiently for each user. And if the processor fails, the entire system goes down with it.

Multiprocessor systems connect each terminal to its own processor, but place the processors in a central location and assign one processor to control the network and the shared disk. In this configuration, the failure of a single processor does not disable the whole system. However, since the processors share a single central location, they can all be incapacitated by a power failure or other disruption.

Local-area networks link free-standing personal computers for purposes of sharing such resources as a mass storage device and a high-speed printer. Each user can use his or her personal computer without affecting the performance of the overall system, and can also use the network to communicate with other users. The rate at which information is transmitted from one computer to another is determined by the type of communication channel used (usually ordinary wires or cable systems).

Distributed-Processing Systems

Distributed-processing systems are computer systems in which information processing is distributed among physically separate computer systems. For example, each of a nationwide corporation's regional sales offices might have its own minicomputer system. Each sales office is responsible for processing its own customer accounts, and sends only a summary of sales information to the corporate headquarters. Figure 3.4 shows how a typical distributed-processing system is organized.

By distributing information processing and storing among several different locations, large organizations achieve higher performance, faster response times, and a degree of flexibility that is not possible when all data processing is centralized on a single large computer.Another advantage of distributed systems is greater reliability, since the failure of a local system affects only that system.

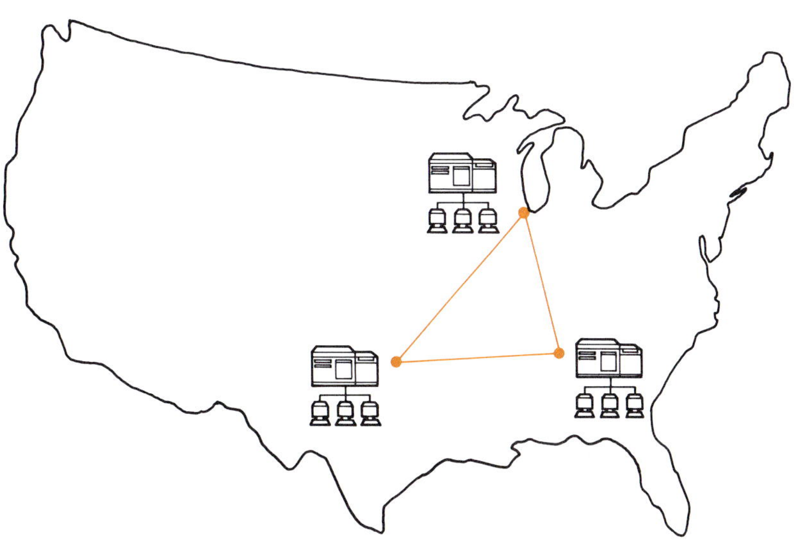

FIGURE 3.4 *Distributed data processing.*

The trend in information systems of all sizes is toward a greater number of small computers, each dedicated to a particular individual, application, or department. This trend is largely responsible for the proliferation of computers in businesses, large and small.

Large Information Systems

Large information systems are those that collect and process information in a single location, on one or more central computers, and distribute the information to far-flung minicomputers and/or personal computers.

Transaction-Oriented Systems

In **transaction-oriented systems**, processing is activated by a distinct input called a **transaction.** An airline reservation system, for example, processes individual requests for flight schedules, reservations, and seat assignments from thousands of terminals throughout the world.

The credit approval systems of major credit-card companies link a central computer to terminals in thousands of retail outlets. At the point of purchase, the clerk inserts the customer's credit card into a magnetic reader. The device reads the number from the card and initiates a phone call to the central computer, where the card number is checked against the customer's credit limit.

These systems are called **on-line systems** because the input is transmitted directly from the point of origin to a central location, where it is processed. Figure 3.5 shows how a typical on-line system is organized. The time it takes an on-line system to process a transaction is called its response time. On-line systems are characterized by their rapid response times. Users of an airline reservation or credit-approval system cannot wait more than a couple of minutes to complete their transactions.

Other transaction-oriented systems include banking systems with automated teller machines, stock-market quotation systems, and hotel reservation and billing systems.

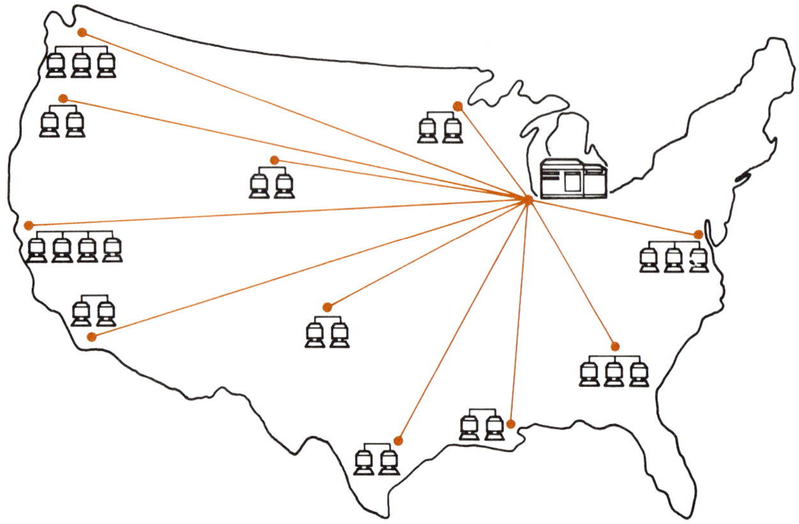

FIGURE 3.5 *A transaction-oriented on-line system.*

Office Automation Systems

Office automation systems apply computer and communication technologies to the enhancement of office functions and procedures. All of the most fundamental office functions—writing, revising, filing, copying, and communicating—have been computerized. Office automation systems also include videoconferencing systems and voice and electronic mail systems. More specialized applications include image processing, typesetting, production text processing, engineering design, graphic design, conference scheduling, and electronic filing.

The typical office automation system is designed to serve the needs of a small (5 to 25) group of people who spend most of their time communicating with each other, and far less time communicating with people in other locations.

There are also similar-sized computer systems that perform similar functions in settings other than offices. Groups of engineers often use networks of specially designed personal computers to design and test new products. Factory automation systems supervise and regulate the manufacturing process. Systems that link information processing with industrial robots actually perform materials and parts handling, production, assembly, inspection, and packaging.

Large-Scale Information Systems

Large-scale information systems are usually linked to large centralized installations of one or more mainframes and/or minicomputers. The volume of information to be processed is large, and the processing tasks are often very complex. A university mainframe, for example, might support administrative functions such as student grading, class scheduling, accounting, library operations, faculty research, and teaching. A staff of professionals manages and operates the

computer system and provides user services such as entering data, running programs, and interpreting output. In the last five years, however, minicomputers and personal computers have begun to supplant this centralized approach.

Large-scale information systems are often organized hierarchically. At the top of the hierarchy are one or more mainframes that serve as a repository for organizational information. This information is stored in databases—the collections of data on which organizations base their activities and decisions. A **database** is a collection of related, structured data. If a database consists of more than one file, software establishes the relation between the files.

A large organization might have large-scale databases for its financial data, personnel data, and inventory data. These databases become so large that mainframe processing speeds and capabilities are needed to structure, maintain, update, and retrieve the data.

Lower on the hierarchy are the minicomputer and personal-computer subsystems found at the departmental and divisional level. In a hierarchical system, minicomputers often serve as **front-end processors.** That is, they collect information from local sources, perform a limited amount of processing on it, and send it on to the mainframe. At the lowest level personal computers serve as workstations for individuals. The workstation is a multifunction device: At times it operates as a terminal under the control of the mainframe or minicomputer; other times it is under the direct control of the user.

Multinational corporations often set up very large **wide-area networks** to link their computer systems and databases even on different continents. A typical multinational, such as an oil company or computer hardware manufacturer, might have a central data-processing facility with several mainframes, regional offices with mainframes and/or minicomputers, and thousands of personal computers on the desks of administrative and clerical workers.

How does such a system serve the diverse needs of a large organization? Personal computers used as stand-alone systems automate office procedures. Personal computers located in the same facility can be connected by a local-area network, for purposes of sharing information. Users who need to access information from the central corporate mainframe databases can use their personal computers as terminals. And any two computers in the worldwide network can communicate via the wide-area communication network.

Another example of a large-scale information system is a large retail chain with thousands of stores distributed throughout the United States. This system combines a wide-area communications network with distributed processing. At each store, sales transactions are recorded by the point-of-purchase terminals that are replacing traditional cash registers. Since it would be impractical for every terminal to be connected to the mainframe computers at the retailer's headquarters, transactions are stored and forwarded daily to regional centers. There they are processed and forwarded to the retailer's mainframe database system.

Organizations of every size and kind are acquiring information and computer systems. Meanwhile, these systems are evolving in response to advances in hardware and software. As a result, our society is heading into an era in which most of the workforce will be creating, processing, and communicating information. What will be the impact on individuals and organizations?

The Impacts of Personal Computers

Computerized information systems are changing the ways people work. In turn, they change the organizations by creating, restructuring, and eliminating departments and divisions. These systems also affect individuals by changing the means of attaining new knowledge and productivity.

Personal computers are descendants of large-scale computer systems, but quantitative and qualitative differences arise from their use. The quantitative differences come about because personal computers make it possible to gather, process, and disseminate high-quality information at very low cost.

Qualitatively, the speed of personal computers tends to restructure power, since personal computers are tools for everyone. Dedicated specialists still use large computers, but they have been joined by millions of people who are more interested in getting a job done than in learning the intricacies of computers.

As we have seen, a personal computer is self-contained, fits comfortably on a desk, and provides enough computer power to meet the needs of a single person. It can also be a node in a network of hundreds of intercommunicating computers.

Impacts on Individuals

Personal computers are an active and participatory medium of expression. As such, they can be used to:

- Express thoughts and ideas more clearly and powerfully
- Interact with other people
- Perform tasks that could not have been accomplished without a personal computer
- Reduce the time-consuming tedium of processing paperwork
- Explore various forms of entertainment and self-education at your own pace

The personal computer promises to do for twentieth-century intellectual work what machines did for nineteenth-century industrial work—eliminate drudgery and free the individual for more creative problem solving.

Impacts on Organizations

Personal computers have directly benefited organizations by providing performance comparable to that of large-scale computer systems, but at lower cost. The economic impact of personal computers has led to a phenomenon known as **end-user computing.** This means that personal computers are controlled by their users, rather than by the organization's data-processing department. End-user computing creates a climate conducive to:

- Decentralizing decision making
- Demystifying information and computer systems
- Greater individual productivity
- Assuming new responsibilities and learning new skills
- Automating routine clerical functions

As personal computers take the mystery out of data processing, and as employees get to know what computers can and cannot do, data-processing departments are shifting their focus from the care and feeding of large-scale centrally managed computers to helping end users develop their own applications.

The Database Environment

We have discussed databases in the context of large-scale information systems, but **database management systems**—the hardware and software that organize and provide access to a database—are also available for personal computer systems.

Shortly, you will gain hands-on experience with the TriPac database program. First, though, let us look at some concepts and terminology that are central to understanding databases.

A database is a collection of related, structured data. In the context of TriPac, the structure consists of records with identical formats. A **record** is a collection of related information treated as a unit: For example, payroll information about one employee is called a payroll record. Figure 3.6 illustrates database fields and records. A record consists of even smaller units of information called fields. A field is the smallest unit of meaningful information in a record. For example, the employee's last name is a field; so are the employee's first name, social security number, address, and pay rate.

What are some everyday examples of databases? A dictionary, an encyclopedia, a telephone book, a card catalog, and an address book all have one thing in common. They contain data that is structured, organized, and presented in a way that makes it easy to find a specific item. Structure is the key to understanding a database.

Database programs are application programs that manage collections of information stored in files; they are often called "database management programs." Database programs consist of procedures for organizing, sorting, selecting, retrieving (often called searching or querying), and printing data in a database.

A Database Example

To illustrate database concepts, we have created a Computer Comparisons database. You are going to use the database program to select and print a list of all the personal computers in the database. To complete the assignment, you will:

1. Select the database called Computer Comparisons.
2. Select all the personal computers in the database.
3. Print and hand in the selected records.

Fields (columns)

	Make	Model	Type	Memory Size	Price	Remarks
Field names →	Make	Model	Type	Memory Size	Price	Remarks
Records (rows) →	Digital	8600	Minicomputer	32000000	970000	Supermini 4.
	HP	3000	Minicomputer	8000000	166100	Traditional

FIGURE 3.6 *Records and fields.*

In the process, you will learn the basic skills of using a database program. First, load your TriPac software. Once you are in the Application Manager program, follow these step-by-step instructions:

1. First, select the database called Computer Comparisons by moving the pointer to highlight its name.
2. Toggle to the menu bar and open the Computer Comparisons database.
3. The Application Manager display will be replaced by the display shown in Figure 3.7.

File Edit Search Layout   Database: Computer Comparisons

Make	Model	Type	Memory Size	Price	Remarks
→ Apple	IIc	Personal	128000	995	Transporta
Atari	520 ST	Personal	512000	995	Home compu
Tandy	Model 200	Personal	72000	1500	Portable
IBM	PC	Personal	640000	1995	Defacto PC
Tandy	1000	Personal	384000	1995	PC compati
Apple	Macintosh	Personal	512000	2495	User frien
Kaypro	2000	Personal	256000	3295	Transporta
Grid	Gridcase 3	Personal	512000	4350	Portable
HP	Integral	Personal	1500000	4995	ROM-based
IBM	PC-AT	Personal	3000000	5795	Latest gen
HP	Touchscreen	Personal	640000	6000	IBM Compat
Compaq	286	Personal	640000	6299	Transporta
AT&T	Unix PC	Personal	2000000	8000	68010 micr
IBM	Series1-4956	Mini	1000000	21650	Traditiona
Wang	VS 90	Mini	32000000	73000	High-end m
Apollo	Domain	Minicomputer	3500000	80000	High-end m
Digital	PDP 11-70	Minicomputer	4000000	89000	Traditiona
Honeywell	DPS6/96	Minicomputer	16000000	130000	High-end m
Burroughs	B 1985	Mainframe	2000000	156400	Small-scal
HP	3000	Minicomputer	8000000	166100	Traditiona
Data General	MV 12000	Mini	32000000	250000	Supermini

FIGURE 3.7 *The Computer Comparisons database.*

Using the Database Program

The database consists of records arranged in a tabular row-and-column format. Each row contains one record; each column contains one field. Make is a field; so is model. You'll notice that the Remarks field is partially hidden from view. Press the Right arrow key briefly to scroll right horizontally. Then press the Left arrow key to scroll back to the left. The database also contains more records than can be displayed vertically on the screen. Use the Up and Down or the Up and Down keys to scroll vertically.

Note that the records are arranged by price from least to most expensive. One of the powerful features of a database program is the ability to sort records.

Sorting is arranging a set of items according to a **key** which determines the sequence of the items. For example, a telephone book is arranged alphabetically. The key that determines the sequence is the customer's last name.

Any field in the database can serve as the key field. Also, you can readily change the key, and re-sort the records into a new sequence by the new key field.

In the Computer Comparisons database, for example, the key could be Make, Model, Type, Memory Size, Price, or Remarks. Suppose you want to sort the records by price, in descending order from highest to lowest. The following instructions explain how:

1. Use the Esc key to toggle to the menu bar. Then move the pointer to the Layout menu. Use the Down arrow key to select the *Sort Records...* command and press the Return key. A dialog box will appear, with the field names on the left-hand side and a list of sort criteria in the middle. The initial dialog box will look like Figure 3.8.

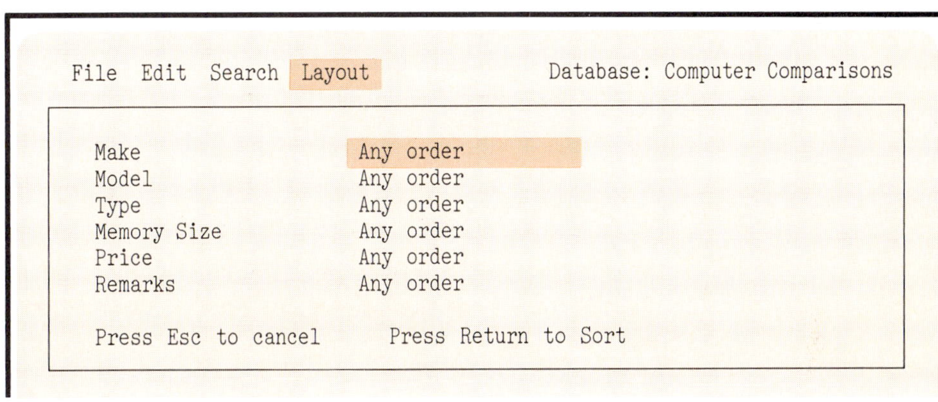

FIGURE 3.8 *Initial dialog box to sort.*

2. The pointer is highlighting the first sort criterion. You can move the pointer by pressing the Tab key. Press it repeatedly until the pointer highlights the sort criterion for Price. If you mistakenly pass the Price field, press the Tab key repeatedly until the the pointer moves back to the Price field.
3. When the pointer is highlighting the sort criterion for Price, press the space bar. The highlighted field will change from Any Order to Ascending Order. When you press the space bar again, the highlighted field changes from Ascending Order to Descending Order. The sort criteria are presented as a hidden list of options, which you can scroll through by repeatedly pressing the space bar. Press the space bar until Descending Order appears again.
4. With Descending Order highlighted for the Price field, as in Figure 3.9, press the Return key. After a few seconds' pause for the program to sort the records, the dialog box will retract and the records will be displayed in descending order by price.

```
File  Edit  Search  Layout                 Database: Computer Comparisons

    Make                       Any order
    Model                      Any order
    Type                       Any order
    Memory Size                Any order
    Price                      Descending order
    Remarks                    Any order

    Press Esc to cancel          Press Return to Sort
```

FIGURE 3.9 *Completed dialog box to sort records by price in descending order.*

A database program enables you to ask questions or **queries** about the data in the database. To answer these questions, the database program searches for the records that meet the selection criteria, and then highlights the selected records for your analysis. In some cases, none of the records might meet the selection criteria you have specified in your search.

Here are some examples of questions you might ask the database program, along with instructions on how to find their answers.

Question: "What models of computers are made by IBM?"

1. Use the Esc key to toggle to the menu bar. Then move the pointer to the Search menu. Use the Down arrow key to highlight the *Search & Select. . .* command, and press the Return key. A dialog box will appear, listing the field names on the left-hand side and selection criteria in the middle. The first of these selection criteria is highlighted. The dialog box will look like Figure 3.10.

```
File  Edit  Search  Layout                 Database: Computer Comparisons

    Make                       any
    Model                      any
    Type                       any
    Memory Size                any
    Price                      any
    Remarks                    any

    Press Esc to cancel          Press Return to Search & Select
```

FIGURE 3.10 *Initial dialog box to search.*

2. As in the Sort Records dialog box, the selection criteria appear as a hidden list of options, which you can scroll through by pressing the space bar. Table 3.2 lists the options in the order you'll see them. To view all the options, continue to press the space bar. Then highlight the = option and press the Tab key.

TABLE 3.2 *Options for Selection Criteria*

Option	Meaning
any	All
=	Equal
>	Greater than
<	Less than
<>	Not equal
< =	Less than or equal
> =	Greater than or equal

3. A highlighted space equal in size to the Make field will appear to the right of the selection criteria. Type in *IBM*, in capital letters. The dialog box will look like Figure 3.11. Then press the Return key.

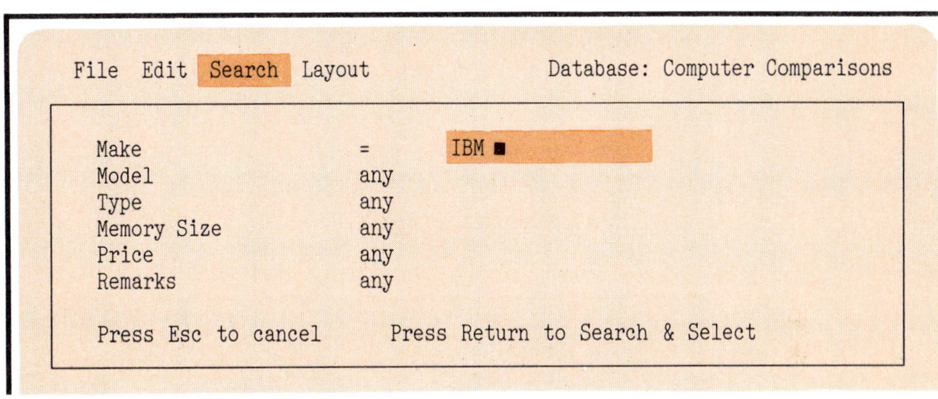

FIGURE 3.11 *Completed dialog box to search for Make = IBM.*

4. All records that meet the selection criteria (Make = IBM) will be selected and highlighted.
5. Now you can use the and Up and Down arrow keys to browse through the highlighted records.

Question: "Which computers have memories of 16,000,000 bytes or more?"

(First, select the *Unselect Every Record* command in the Search menu, and press the Return key. This will return the highlighted records to normal video, in preparation for your next search.)

1. As before, select the *Search & Select...* command in the Search menu. Press the Return key. The dialog box listing field names and selection criteria will appear.
2. You'll see that the selection criteria from the last search remain in the dialog box. Press the space bar to change the Make selection criterion to *any*. Then use the Delete key to erase the highlighted field.

3. Now press the Tab key until the Memory Size selection criterion is highlighted. Press the space bar until the > = option appears; then press the Tab key. Type in 16000000 (without commas or spaces) and press the Return key.
4. All records that meet the selection criterion (Memory Size > = 16000000) will be selected and highlighted.

The Database Assignment

Now, using the searching techniques you have just learned, select all the personal computers in the database. (Before you begin, remember to select the Unselect Every Record command to return the highlighted records to normal video.)

1. Select the *Search & Select. . .* command, and press the Return key. The dialog box listing the field names and selection criteria will appear.
2. The selection criteria from the last search remain in the dialog box. To clear the old settings, press the Tab key until the Memory Size field criterion is highlighted, and use the space bar to set the field to *any*. Then press the Tab key, and use the Delete key to erase the highlighted field.
3. Now press the Tab key until the Type selection criterion is highlighted. Press the space bar until the = option appears; then press the Tab key. Type in *Personal* (with a capital P). The screen will look like Figure 3.12. Then press the Return key.

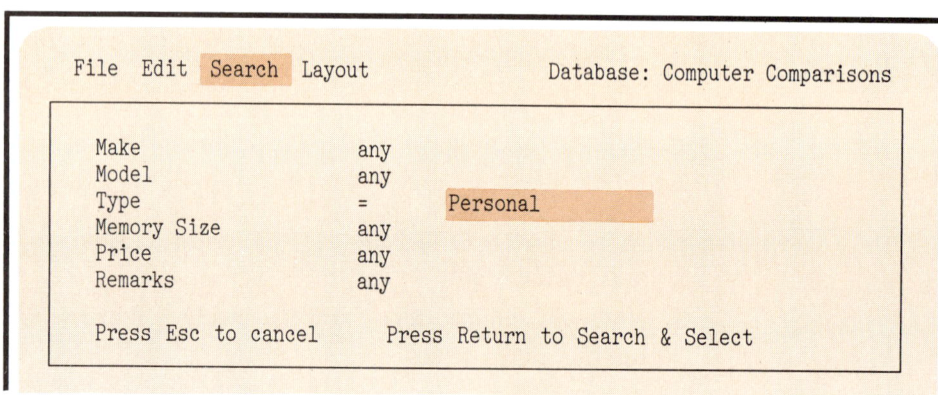

FIGURE 3.12 *Completed dialog box to search for all personal computers.*

4. All records that meet the selection criterion (Type = Personal) will be selected and highlighted.

Printing the Selected Records

To print a copy of the selected records, select the *Print Selected Records. . .* command in the File menu and press the Return key. A dialog box will ask you to press Return to print page: 1. (Remember that the printer must be connected to the computer and turned on, and the paper must be properly positioned in the printer.)

```
Database: Computer Comparisons     Page 1

Make          Apple
Model         IIc
Type          Personal
Memory Size        128000
Price                 995
Remarks            Transportable

Make          Atari
Model         520 ST
Type          Personal
Memory Size        512000
Price                 995
Remarks       Home computer

Make          Tandy
Model         Model 200
Type          Personal
Memory Size         72000
Price                1500
Remarks       Portable

Make          IBM
Model         PC
Type          Personal
Memory Size        640000
Price                1995
Remarks       Defacto PC standard

Make          Tandy
Model         1000
Type          Personal
Memory Size        384000
Price                1995
Remarks       PC compatible

Make          Apple
Model         Macintosh
Type          Personal
Memory Size        512000
Price                2495
Remarks       User friendly

Make          Kaypro
Model         2000
Type          Personal
Memory Size        256000
Price                3295
Remarks       Transportable
```

```
Database: Computer Comparisons     Page 2

Make          Grid
Model         Gridcase 3
Type          Personal
Memory Size        512000
Price                4350
Remarks       Portable

Make          HP
Model         Integral
Type          Personal
Memory Size       1500000
Price                4995
Remarks       ROM-based UNIX OS

Make          IBM
Model         PC-AT
Type          Personal
Memory Size       3000000
Price                5795
Remarks       Latest generation

Make          HP
Model         Touchscreen
Type          Personal
Memory Size        640000
Price                6000
Remarks       IBM Compatible

Make          Compaq
Model         286
Type          Personal
Memory Size        640000
Price                6299
Remarks       Transportable

Make          AT T
Model         Unix PC
Type          Personal
Memory Size       2000000
Price                8000
Remarks       68010 microprocessor
```

FIGURE 3.13 *Printout of selected records from Computer Comparisons database.*

The database program does not print records in tabular form. Your printout will print each record with the field names on the left-hand side of the page and the contents of each field in the middle. Figure 3.13 shows what it will look like.

After you have printed your list of personal computers, press the Esc key to toggle to the menu bar, and press the Down arrow key to select the *Quit Database* command. Press the Return key to return to the Application Manager.

REVIEW AND SELF-TESTING

Key Terms

Information system	Channel
Megabyte	Modem
MIPS	Communications software
Mainframe	Terminals
Minicomputer	Electronic mail
Personal computer	Electronic libraries
Network	Multiuser system

Integrated programs
Shared-logic system
Multiprocessor system
Local-area network
Distributed-processing system
Transaction-oriented system
Transaction
On-line system
Office automation system
Large-scale information system
Database
Front-end processor
Wide-area network
End-user computing
Database management system
Record
Field
Database program
Sorting
Key
Query

Questions for Review and Discussion

1. What trend provides users with more computer power per dollar?
2. What are the two aspects of computer communications?
3. How is most of today's computer-to-computer communication accomplished?
4. Name an example of an interpersonal function for a personal computer system.
5. What is the key to a multiuser system?
6. What is the primary disadvantage to a shared-logic multiuser system?
7. What are the advantages of distributed processing in comparison to centralized processing?
8. List two reasons for using mainframe or minicomputers in a large-scale information system.
9. Why is a dictionary or a telephone book an example of a database?
10. What do database programs consist of?
11. What is the key field in a telephone book?
12. In the database example, how would you sort the Computer Comparisons database by type?

4

Computers and Problem Solving

PREVIEW

No problem can be solved—with or without the aid of a computer—until it is understood and well thought out beforehand. This is so because computers do not solve problems as we do; computers are simply tools with which to perform tasks.

In this chapter, we'll show you a step-by-step method you can use to organize your thinking about problems. Then we'll show you some general-purpose tools that will help you look at problems in a logical and systematic way.

You'll get some hands-on practice by using the TriPac spreadsheet program to help solve a problem. That way, you'll begin to learn how application software can be used as an effective problem-solving tool.

In this chapter, you'll discover:

- *General-purpose tools for problem solving*
- *A method for organizing the flow of problem solving*
- *New points of view for approaching problems*
- *How to break a large problem into smaller, more manageable steps*
- *Approaches to solving problems when writing, calculating, and analyzing*
- *How to get started with a spreadsheet program*

Problem Solving

Problem solving is a **process**—a systematic series of actions aimed at a specific goal. Novices often approach problems in a random, trial-and-error, or hit-or-miss fashion. More experienced problem solvers develop logical and orderly approaches to problems. There are two reasons why this kind of approach is preferable: (1) It helps you to organize your thinking about the problem, and (2) it helps you to visualize a solution.

It's easier to solve a problem when you have a step-by-step method to refer to and apply. Writing, analyzing, and organizing and retrieving information are problem-solving activities for which a logical method is particularly well suited. But before we show you a step-by-step method, let's define what a problem is and what a solution is.

What Is a Problem?

A **problem** is any question or matter characterized by doubt, uncertainty, or difficulty. This broad definition facilitates a positive view of problems as unmet needs, or as the difference between where you are and where you want to be. People often classify problems as personal, economic, social, political, and so on. But whatever the category, calling something a problem implies that it is not the way it should be.

Attitude is a very important aspect of problem solving. Many people view all problems as irritations. Of course, some problems are simply irritating: the car that won't start; the door that sticks; the check that bounces. These are types of problems we tend to avoid if we can.

But another way to look at problems is to view them as opportunities. Entrepreneurs tend to interpret problems as unmet needs, and thus as opportunities to make money. A problem can also be an opportunity to advance your thinking to a new level, or to make a useful contribution to society. If you take a positive attitude toward the problems you are going to be solving in this class, they can be opportunities to further your learning, develop your skills, and gain confidence in your own problem-solving skills.

What Is a Solution?

A **solution** is an answer or explanation to a problem. It is often the result of some course of action taken by an individual or an organization that wants to bring about a change.

It is an interesting exercise to think about your circumstances and the material objects that surround you as "prior solutions to problems." Stop reading for a moment and glance around you. If you are in a dormitory or a classroom, the room you are sitting in is a prior solution to the problem of educating people. The clothes you wear, the house you live in, the car you may drive, the food you eat, the book you are currently reading—all can be perceived as prior solutions to problems.

Like problems, people also tend to classify and categorize solutions. Solutions to social problems are sometimes called laws; solutions to mental or mathematical problems are often called rules or axioms. Solutions to physical problems may be called tools, artifacts, products, buildings, and so on. In the classroom, it is often necessary or preferable to simulate the events in the real world; thus teachers construct models they call case studies, practice sets, exercises, or exams, whose solution takes the form of a written or oral answer.

In this book, you'll learn about problems and their solutions more or less the same way you learned to play sports or games. First, you'll practice with exercises that have already been worked out. As you have already done with the word processor and database programs, you'll learn the rules of the game, and what you can and cannot do. Then, we'll give you some variations on the worked-out problems so that you can practice and explore a little further. Finally, you'll move on to problems that you choose yourself, whose solution hasn't already been found.

Computers as Problem-Solving Tools

A computer is an ideal problem-solving medium, since it is capable of **modeling** or **simulating** almost any kind of event or process that can occur in the real world. A business teacher, rather than giving students a real business to run, can have students practice with a financial model of the business before venturing out on their own. A physics teacher can simulate the effects of a nuclear explosion and leave the actual event to the imagination of the students. General-purpose software that uses word-processing capability, spreadsheets, and databases is an ideal medium with which to practice solving a wide variety of problems. It can teach you important concepts while you learn by doing.

There are many problems that a personal computer won't help solve. It won't help you write creatively, although it may free up time you can use to explore writing. It won't help you remember your relatives' birthdays—although it can store and retrieve a list of birthdays in a database if you want. What kinds of problems are computers good at helping people to solve?

What Computers Do Best

Though a word processor can help you write a love letter or a poem, a personal computer system is particularly well suited to the kinds of problems that yield to rationality and logic. What characteristics of computer systems make them such useful tools for problem solving?

- Speed. A computer system can give you immediate feedback. It can store and organize information, and recall it quicker than you can. It can add a list of numbers, or do other calculations, faster than you can.
- Accuracy. A computer system calculates much more reliably and accurately than you do. In fact, when computer systems are applied to well-thought-out repetitive operations, such as calculating a payroll or processing income-tax returns, they can virtually eliminate the errors that people are prone to when they do repetitive calculating.
- Reduced drudgery. Exploring problems becomes more fun. Because menial tasks like calculating are handled by the computer system, you can concentrate on analyzing alternative solutions.

- Neatness. Writing and calculating by hand usually involves scribbling notes, deciphering illegible inserts, wadding up aborted drafts, erasing, crossing out, and retyping. A word processor can help you polish your reports and term papers for a clearer, cleaner, and perhaps more informative presentation than is possible with other methods.
- Logic. Because a computer system can only perform routine tasks in obedience to your instructions, it requires you to do an orderly analysis of the problem and the relationships between its parts.

What People Do Best

A computer is a useful tool, but it can't think. Computers only do what you tell them to do: no more, no less. Computers don't solve problems; they carry out solutions that people devise. The people who formulate the problem and devise a procedure for solving it are the problem solvers. The key to using a computer as a problem-solving tool is to become familiar with the computer system and figure out what it can do for you. Among the aspects of problem solving that people are best equipped for are:

- Judgment. People know when a problem is outside their sphere of expertise. They know when the best answer is to suggest asking someone else for help. A computer will keep plugging away, processing "the facts," even if the facts don't add up to anything. People know where to look for prior solutions to similar problems, when an imperfect solution is preferable to waiting for a perfect one, and when to hold off and wait for that missing piece of information.
- Flexibility. People are good at anticipating and responding to change. They are not locked into their environment. They might accept it, but they can also change it. They learn that there are many exceptions to any rules. They figure out when to break the rules. On the other hand, the more unstructured a problem becomes, the more difficult it is to use a computer to solve it.
- Intuition. Insight into a problem can take the place of formal logic or reasoning. What we call intuition is actually a kind of condensed reasoning or recognition process, made possible by experience. Card players don't stop to count the spots on the cards; they simply recognize the pattern from past experience.
- Feeling. People approach problems with eagerness, curiosity, competitiveness, tension, excitement, anxiety, love, affection, or hate. These feelings often stimulate creative solutions that are not possible when problem solving is reduced to "the facts."
- Knowledge representation. Computers do not really understand what they are doing. If they did, they could behave in a more intelligent manner. People have a far richer repertoire of representations (or meanings) for ideas, notions, and images, and we store and recall them on demand. We often don't have to think about what it is we are doing; we simply do it.

In Chapter 12, we will look at **artificial intelligence**—the study of computer systems that mimic the behavior of people—and see why it has given rise to the notion that computers can think like people.

To apply a computer system to problem solving, you need to organize the problem to be solved. For this, you need a set of guidelines to help you think about a problem in a systematic, orderly way. This is where a step-by-step method comes in handy. Solving a problem from beginning to end requires you to approach the solution systematically by organizing your thinking about the problem.

A Method for Problem Solving

A **procedure** is a sequence of steps, each of which specifies one or more actions and the order in which they are to be taken. You already use procedures as problem-solving tools in everyday life. You find your way to a new friend's house by following a set of directions. You cook an interesting dinner for a new boyfriend or girlfriend by following a recipe. You pre-register for classes, or assemble a new appliance, by following step-by-step instructions.

The Problem-Solving Process

We can characterize the steps in a general-purpose approach to problem-solving as follows:

1. Get to know the problem
2. Define the problem
3. Identify alternative solutions
4. Choose the best alternative
5. Implement the solution
6. Evaluate the results

These six steps provide you with a consistent procedure for (1) turning problem solving into a systematic series of events, and (2) breaking up a large or complex problem into smaller pieces. It is a method that can be applied to a wide variety of problems.

Of course, some problems are more complex and overwhelming than others. A good rule of thumb is: Complex problems require complex strategies, whereas simpler problems call for less formal tools and strategies. The problem-solving process that we describe in this chapter may not fit every problem you

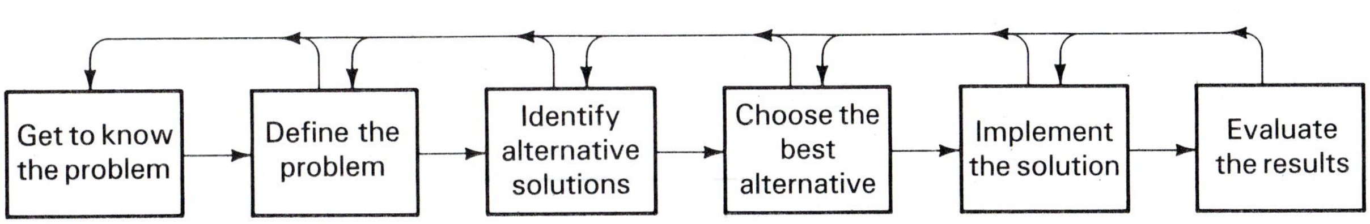

FIGURE 4.1 *Step-by-step problem solving. As indicated by the arrows, the problem solver can go back to an earlier step at any time in light of new developments or new information.*

ever have to solve. It is not meant as a prescription for the right answer. It is a general set of guidelines. Before resorting to a trial-and-error approach, investigate its use to see if it fits the problem.

The problem-solving process is also dynamic; it doesn't always proceed step-by-step from step 1 to step 6. As Figure 4.1 signifies, the process can loop back on itself at any time. For example, suppose that while you are searching for alternative solutions, you discover something that sheds new light on the problem definition. You can, and should, go back to the previous step and incorporate that new information into your problem definition. At other times, you may find yourself working on two or three of the steps at the same time.

Get to Know the Problem

Most problems require you to make assumptions. Information about a problem is often implicit or subtle. For example, if a friend does not return your repeated phone calls, you may assume that something is wrong. Often, the simple analytical technique of asking questions is all you need to solve a problem. At other times, getting to know a problem may mean examining your assumptions about it.

For example, suppose you own a record store and make a small profit at it. How would you know whether you are managing the business well? You might try making a list of your assumptions about the nature of the retail record business, and then asking a consultant about similar stores' pricing policies, advertising, merchandising, promotions, and so on. It may turn out, for example, that your assumptions about merchandising are mistaken. Perhaps you could increase your profit considerably by discounting your prices, staying open at night, or selling compact disks as well.

Sometimes students expect real-world problems to present themselves like the examples in textbooks, clearly organized and articulated and accompanied by a ready-made solution. Problem solving rarely begins this way. If you suspect a problem exists, listing your assumptions about it can help you (1) decide whether a problem actually exists, (2) figure out what you could do about it, and (3) actually do something to solve it.

Checklist for Getting to Know the Problem

- *Does a problem actually exist?*
- *Have you encountered a similar problem before?*
- *Do you know of a similar problem someone else has encountered?*
- *Whom can you ask, and/or what can you read about the problem?*
- *What assumptions are you making about the problem?*

Define the Problem

Formulating a problem is usually the most crucial step in solving it. Defining a problem can be time-consuming. Often what we call problems are only symptoms—the visible effects of an underlying problem. A fever, a runny nose, and an upset stomach are all symptoms of the real problem—the flu. Distinguishing between symptoms and problems is important in accurately defining the problem you want to resolve. Thus a doctor tries to determine the exact reasons for a patient's symptoms because different problem definitions would lead to different treatments.

If you do not understand a problem, you cannot solve it. Take the time to clarify the problem in an unambiguous way. The best way to do this is to ask yourself continually, "What is the problem?" It is easy to overlook that question. Instead, most people jump to the question, "What can I do about the problem?" For example, consider the problem of purchasing a personal computer. Many people begin by asking, "Which computer should I buy?" But they are bypassing a more important question—"What do I want to do with a personal computer?"

If the problem you are trying to solve is particularly difficult—if it involves a lot of ambiguity—it is worth the time to refine the problem definition until you have developed a set of clear, complete objectives, or statements of intent. This does not mean that you need to know everything in advance. It simply means translating your problem into formal statements of intent, which will serve as guidelines for subsequent steps in the problem-solving process.

For example, when a problem calls for designing a system, the problem definition is often called a **functional specification.** It specifies the functions that the system must perform. Suppose your problem is to design a computer-based system to help people prepare their income-tax returns. Your functional specification would probably list the kinds of information that will go into the system (income and expense data, tax regulations, and instructions for calculating the amount of tax due) and the tax-return forms that must come out of the system. By stating clear, complete, definitive functions, the functional specification defines the problem in an unambiguous way. It also serves as a guideline for designing the system.

Checklist for Defining the Problem

- *What facts do you know about the problem?*
- *What exactly is the problem?*
- *What are the pertinent surrounding circumstances?*
- *What are my objectives?*

Identify Alternatives

The first step in identifying alternatives is to clarify your goals. Once you have defined what success would consist of, the available alternatives are the various ways of achieving that goal. At this point, it is a good idea to come up with as many ideas as possible about ways to reach the goal. Then you will have a wide range of alternatives to choose from.

The technique called **brainstorming**—unrestrained thought or discussion, without prejudging or rejecting any ideas—is a good way to generate many different (1) viewpoints on the problem, (2) approaches to the goal, and (3) alternative solutions. Imagine, for example, that you are in Boston and your goal is to get to southern California. Time and money are not constraints. Stop reading for two minutes, and brainstorm all the possible ways you can imagine to get to California.

Did you restrict yourself to conventional forms of transportation such as plane, train, bus, and car? How about walking? Riding the rails? Hitchhiking? Ballooning? Did you consider alternative routes, such as across Canada or via the Panama Canal? What about combinations of alternatives, such as flying to Chicago and then renting a car?

Brainstorming can stimulate some creative ideas that you might not allow yourself if you stick to conventional solutions and common sense. Your list of alternatives may grow and evolve as you explore new ways of seeing the problem.

Checklist for Identifying Alternatives

- *What are the most obvious ways to reach the goal?*
- *Are there any alternative approaches?*
- *Have I left anything out?*

Choose the Best Alternative

How do you choose the best alternative? You evaluate the alternatives, using criteria that enable you to assess various characteristics of each alternative. Then you can rank the list of alternatives from most to least desirable.

Your evaluation criteria should include such constraints as time, money, and personal knowledge of what you can and cannot do. For example, let us restate the problem of the Boston-to-California trip as follows: You attend school in Boston, and you want to go to California for your one-week spring break. You have $300 saved for the trip. Given these constraints, you can rank the alternative modes of transportation rather quickly.

Checklist for Choosing the Best Alternative

- *What are the criteria for choosing?*
- *What are the constraints?*
- *Which criteria should I emphasize most?*
- *How would I rank the alternatives in light of the criteria?*
- *Is the best alternative obvious?*

Implement the Solution

Implementing the solution means taking the course of action (establishing the procedure or process) you have chosen. Later in this chapter, you will solve a budget problem using a spreadsheet, and hand in your answer to the instructor. In real life, however, implementing the solution would mean going out and living on your proposed budget.

In essence, you will be using the computer to model the real world. Real-world problems require you to take a course of action to implement your solution. For example, solving the problem of deciding which personal computer to buy involves trying out different personal computers, comparison shopping, and eventually purchasing the computer of your choice.

Checklist for Implementing the Solution

- *What tasks are involved?*
- *What steps must be taken to carry out the tasks?*
- *How much time will each step take?*
- *How long will the entire implementation process take?*
- *What help do I need?*

Evaluate the Results

In a classroom setting, your instructor gives you feedback in the form of a grade, and perhaps comments or encouragement. But experienced problem solvers learn to look at the strengths and weaknesses of their own finished products, decisions, or solutions, and at the process of arriving there. A good coach goes over each game, evaluating the team's performance and asking such questions as:

"What did they do best?" "What areas need improvement?" "What parts of the game need more work?" Evaluation is a learning tool. It allows you to make the most of the problem you have just solved, so that you can put your experience to use in solving future problems.

Checklist for Evaluation

- *Does the solution work?*
- *Are the results what I hoped for?*
- *Are there any obvious improvements I could make?*
- *Is there time to try out a different approach?*

Variations on Problem Solving

Many different fields have generated valuable strategies and approaches to problem solving. As you enlarge your problem-solving repertoire, you may want to explore these approaches in greater depth.

Decision Making

In business, one of the most valued skills that a good manager can have is decision-making ability. **Decision making** is a problem-solving approach for situations in which only partial information is available about a problem or situation. Decision-making skill is also important in situations in which there may be plenty of information, but the criteria for choosing a course of action are incomplete. Incomplete information introduces the element of uncertainty, and requires the decision maker to form opinions and exercise judgment. Decision making incorporates the following steps:

1. Start the decision-making process by considering any information that sheds light on the problem. How do you know when you have enough information? There is no easy answer. Time is usually a constraint, and a search for all the relevant information could go on indefinitely. For example, suppose you are graduating from college, and you have to make a decision about taking a job. Of course you want the perfect job, but your finances dictate that you find one rather quickly. You will begin the job search by considering the available jobs, applying, and interviewing. You certainly cannot know everything about all of the possible jobs. What jobs should you apply for?
2. Form an opinion; then ask other people what they think. Under conditions of incomplete information, it is important to seek intelligent criticism and

feedback from external sources. For example, if you are making a decision about choosing a job, you might ask classmates who are in a similar situation for their opinions on which job they would take.

3. Identify a list of alternatives. In the case of deciding which job to take, you might make a list of alternative salaries, working conditions, job location, potential for advancement, and potential for creative work.
4. Identify a list of criteria on which the alternatives should be judged. For example, the commute to work should not take more than 30 minutes, the salary should not be below $20,000 per year, or the job should involve some writing skills.
5. Judge how well each alternative meets each criterion. For example, you have two job offers, one of which pays better but has a longer commute, while the other offers more opportunity for advancement.
6. Select the best alternative.

Decision making is essentially the art of dealing with uncertainty. Rarely does a decision maker have all the required information at hand. Often, all the options are less than ideal. Also, the bigger the decision, the greater the risk. With practice, you can develop skill in the art of judging the "right" choices and the "right" risks.

Top-Down Design

Computer programmers, systems analysts, and software engineers often use a top-down approach to solving programming and design problems. In **top-down design**, the solution to a problem is first specified in general terms, and then broken down into finer and finer detail until further detail is unnecessary.

Computer professionals are not the only people who use a top-down approach. Consider the problems an architect faces when designing an office building. Because an office building is a highly complex system, the architect first develops a rough overall solution to guide his or her thinking. This might involve sketches or drawings and a list of specific requirements that the building must satisfy. Then the architect breaks down the problem into subcategories, such as lighting, plumbing, heating and cooling, public spaces (lobbies and halls), and private spaces (offices). The result of this process is a functional specification, which developers and engineers use to construct the building.

Top-down design essentially means starting with the whole and working toward the parts. To put it another way, top-down design takes a big problem and makes a lot of little problems out of it.

The Design Process

The arts and the design professions add the element of creativity to the problem-solving process. Creative problem solvers are usually unafraid of mistakes, because they expect to learn from their mistakes and to incorporate that experience into the solution of the next problem. They are not afraid of being unusual, having been rewarded for unconventionality in the past. Nor are they afraid to take risks, because they associate large risks with large rewards.

As a process of creative problem solving, design can be described as a sequence of events or phases that the problem solver has to pass through. In *The Universal Traveler*, Don Koberg and Jim Bagnall characterize the phases of the creative problem-solving process as follows: (1) Acceptance: stating your initial intentions and seeing the problem as a challenge. (2) Analysis: finding out what the world of the problem looks like. (3) Definition: conceptualizing and clarifying your major goals in addressing the problem. (4) Ideation: searching for all the different ways of getting to the goal. (5) Selection: comparing the goal with the possible ways of getting there. (6) Implementation: taking action or giving physical substance to the alternative you have chosen. (7) Evaluation: charting the progress of the design, and ultimately assessing its effect.

The ability to think creatively about problems is largely a matter of overcoming blocks to creativity. We all bring ingrained habits and attitudes to the problem-solving process. Creative people often expend a lot of effort on examining their own thought processes, to prevent old patterns from becoming obstacles to change and new learning.

It is important to become aware of when and how your habits of thinking operate, and to notice how they affect the way you solve problems. Ingrained mental habits can be useful shortcuts—for instance, there's no need to come up with a fresh approach every time you do your laundry or make a cup of coffee—but you must take care that they do not inhibit or predetermine how you solve important problems.

Writing

Writing is a creative problem-solving process that we all engage in at one time or another. For most people, the problem writing poses is uncertainty about what to say. It is quite useful to view the process of composition as consisting of three broad steps: (1) Prewriting, during which the writer reads, discusses, reflects, and begins to put his or her ideas into the form of jotted notes, informal

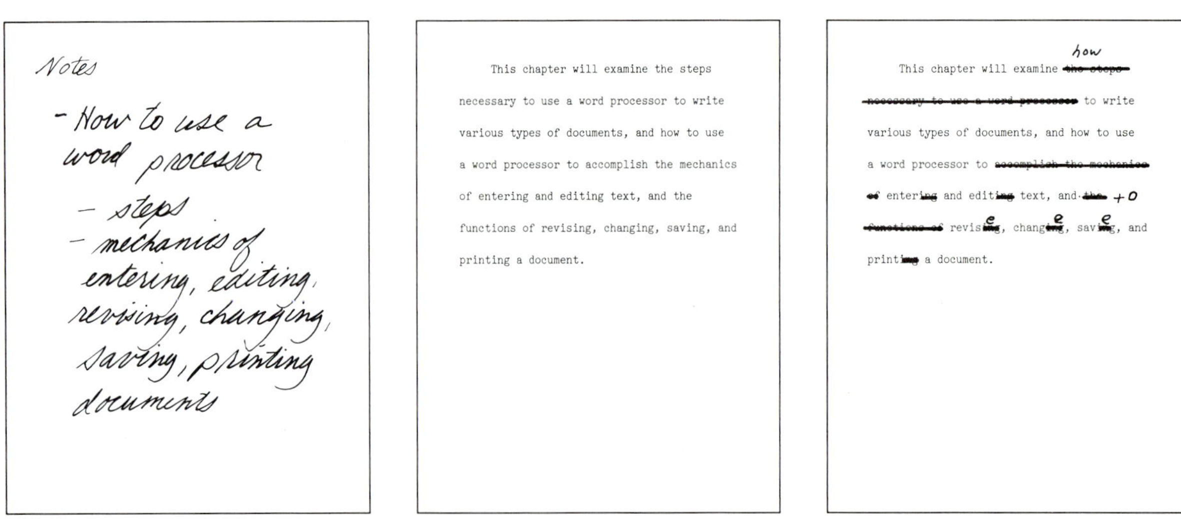

Prewriting Writing Revising

A word processor is a helpful tool when writing is viewed as a problem-solving process.

outlines and memory aids, and short bursts of prose; (2) writing—the actual composition of a sustained narrative; and (3) revising, when the writer reorganizes, condenses, elaborates, polishes, proofreads, and asks other people for their comments.

The Process Applied to Résumé Writing

When you have a problem that calls for writing, you might want to investigate the tools that a word processor offers. In Chapter 2, you used a word processor to fill out a questionnaire. Now let us assume you have just made an appointment with an employment agency to help you find a new job. They have asked you to bring several copies of your résumé with you, for them to distribute to potential employers.

RESUME

Roland Alden
123 Main Street
Anytown, CA 90026
(818) 555-1212

Job Objective: Summer employment or internship in computer programming before attending University of California Irvine in the fall to major in Computer Science.

EDUCATION

1986 Will graduate in June from Altair Community College with an Associate Arts degree.
Major: Computer Information Systems, Minor: Art, GPA 3.76
Activities: President--Student Chapter--Association for Computing Machinery.

WORK EXPERIENCE

Spring, 1986 Lab Assistant, Altair Community College Computer Laboratory. Assisted students in running and debugging programs.

Summer, 1985 Technical Support, Computerworld Computer Store. Assisted with configuring and testing hardware and software for customer systems.

Summer, 1984 Typesetter (intern), Daily Planet. Proofread copy and entered text for advertising copy using a Compugraphic typesetting system.

PERSONAL DATA

Age, 21; height, 5'9"; weight, 165 lbs.; health, excellent; unmarried; hobbies are writing application programs on my Macintosh personal computer and photography.

REFERENCES

Dr. Ellen Goodright
Professor of Computer Information Systems
Altair Community College

Mr. Noel McGinni
Professor of Art
Altair Community College

Mr. George Verant
Owner, Computerworld
Anytown, CA

Sample résumé. The TriPac word processor was used to create this résumé. A tab was set 32 spaces from the left margin to locate the center of the document for the centered text.

A word processor is an ideal tool for creating a résumé, because it enables you to revise quickly and effortlessly. You can try out different formats without retyping. You can create specialized versions to emphasize specific strengths for specific jobs. Later, you can update your résumé without retyping.

The following guidelines will show you how to apply the steps in the problem-solving process to word processing and résumé writing.

1. Get to know the problem. Familiarize yourself with what a résumé is, and what it is supposed to accomplish. Take the time to look at examples of other people's résumés, particularly those of people in the field you want to enter. Notice differences in their formats, and the different impressions that different formats convey.
2. Define the problem. Ask yourself what impression you want your résumé to convey. Think about what you want the output to be. For instance, do you want your résumé to fit on a single page?
3. List the alternatives. There are many different formats for résumés. It could be single-spaced or double-spaced; you could list your previous jobs in retrospective or prospective order; you could use underlining or caps or centering or a combination of elements for headings. You could include or omit a statement of your career goals. You could use full sentences or participles, present tense or past tense, and so forth.
4. Choose the best alternative. The word processor enables you to try out different combinations of style elements and format options. Analyze the different approaches, and select the best combinations based on your goals and possibly the suggestions of the employment agency.
5. Implement the solution. Write and revise your résumé until you are satisfied with it. Then print several copies for the employment agency to send to prospective employers.
6. Evaluate the results. In the case of a résumé, of course, the ultimate test is whether or not you get the job you want. But many other factors can affect that outcome, some of them beyond your control. The number of job interviews your résumé generates may be a better measure of its effectiveness. The employment agency may be able to help you evaluate your résumé.

The Spreadsheet Environment

Although surveys have shown that word processing is the most widely used personal-computer application, many businesspeople begin with spreadsheets. For problems that are mathematical in nature, you might want to investigate a spreadsheet program. It can be extraordinarily useful for problems that involve the analysis of numbers. We are about to do an exercise using the TriPac spreadsheet program.

Like the Application Manager, the word processor, and the database program, the spreadsheet program uses pull-down menus. The information to be processed—the worksheet—is presented in the workspace.

A Spreadsheet Example

Assume that you are about to graduate from college, and have accepted a job in another city. It pays $20,000 per year. You currently live with your parents while attending school, drive a car on which you make $215 per month payments, and pay an annual insurance premium of $425. Your parents are going to give you $1,000 as a graduation present.

Your goal is to move into your own apartment, work hard, live comfortably, save a little money, and become self-sufficient. Your parents have always taught you to be frugal, so you think it would be wise, before striking out on your own, to figure out how much you can afford to pay for your monthly expenses and still have a little left over.

Assumptions:

1. It costs you one month's deposit on the rent, utilities, and telephone to move in.
2. Net income is your gross income of $20,000 a year minus 25% taxes.
3. The annual expenses are calculated by adding the one-time expense to the monthly expense × 12.
4. Savings are net income minus total expenses. If expenses exceed income, the number is negative.

In this example, you are going to modify a spreadsheet. We have already designed and built the spreadsheet, so you can concentrate on exploring the spreadsheet environment before learning to create one of your own. (You will learn those techniques in Chapter 7.) You are going to use the TriPac spreadsheet to:

1. Select and open the spreadsheet called Sample Budget.
2. Use the spreadsheet to perform a "what-if analysis" of the sample budget.
3. Modify the monthly expenses listed in the budget until you have achieved the goal of saving $100 a month.
4. Save the revised spreadsheet on your disk, under the title Sample Budget.
5. Print the completed budget, and hand in a copy to your instructor.

To complete this assignment, and to become familiar with the spreadsheet environment, use the step-by-step instructions that follow. Use the procedure you learned in Chapter 2 to load the TriPac software into the personal computer. From the Application Manager, perform the following steps:

1. Move the pointer to highlight Sample Budget in the SPREADSHEET column.
2. Press the Esc key to toggle to the menu bar. Use the Down arrow key to pull down the File menu and to highlight the *O = Open* command. Press the Return key. You have just instructed the computer to copy the Sample Budget spreadsheet file, and the spreadsheet program, from disk into the computer's memory.
3. The menu will retract, and the display in the workspace will be replaced by the spreadsheet display in Figure 4.2.

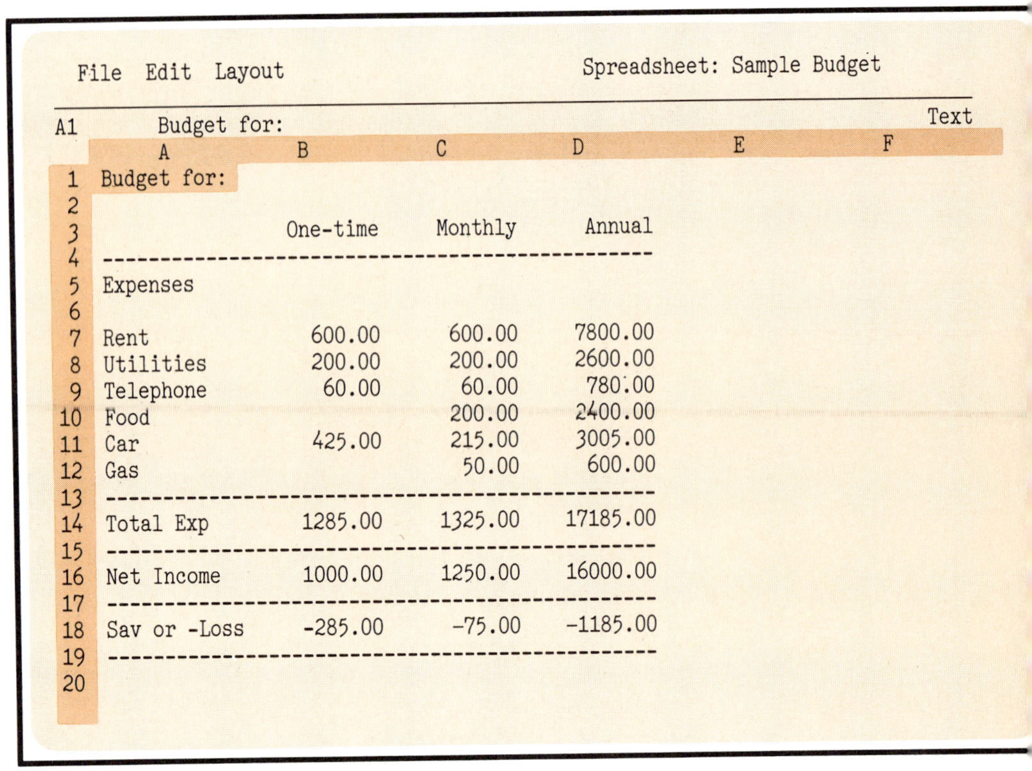
File Edit Layout Spreadsheet: Sample Budget

A1 Budget for: Text

	A	B	C	D	E	F
1	Budget for:					
2						
3		One-time	Monthly	Annual		
4	-------------	-------------	-------------	-------------		
5	Expenses					
6						
7	Rent	600.00	600.00	7800.00		
8	Utilities	200.00	200.00	2600.00		
9	Telephone	60.00	60.00	780.00		
10	Food		200.00	2400.00		
11	Car	425.00	215.00	3005.00		
12	Gas		50.00	600.00		
13	-------------	-------------	-------------	-------------		
14	Total Exp	1285.00	1325.00	17185.00		
15	-------------	-------------	-------------	-------------		
16	Net Income	1000.00	1250.00	16000.00		
17	-------------	-------------	-------------	-------------		
18	Sav or -Loss	-285.00	-75.00	-1185.00		
19	-------------	-------------	-------------	-------------		
20						

FIGURE 4.2 *The Sample Budget spreadsheet.*

What-If Budget Analysis

The first thing you will want to do is to get acquainted with the spreadsheet environment. We have already filled the spreadsheet with numbers and formulas representing assumptions (some correct and some incorrect) about your spending. As you can see, if you followed our optimistic budget, you would be living far beyond your means. Not only would you be unable to pay your monthly bills, you wouldn't have any money left over for large purchases, emergencies, or savings. You'll have to make a few budget cuts to achieve your goal of saving $100 a month.

Before you get started on solving the problem, take the time to familiarize yourself with the spreadsheet. First, notice that it is a grid of lettered columns and numbered rows. The intersection of each column and row on the grid is called a **cell.** Each cell has a name, which consists of the column letter and the row number. The cursor is currently highlighting cell A1. To move the cursor around, use the arrow keys the same way you did with the word processor.

The screen display is 6 columns wide (A through F) and 20 rows deep. The entire spreadsheet is actually 52 columns wide and 254 rows deep. To view other parts of the spreadsheet, you can use various keys to scroll the spreadsheet. For example, to scroll to the bottom of the spreadsheet, press the and Down arrow keys. The entire spreadsheet will shift to the bottom. The and Up arrow keys will return the cursor to cell A1. The arrow keys will also scroll the spreadsheet. Before going on, scroll the spreadsheet back to its original position, with the cursor highlighting cell A1.

Now look at the line directly below the menu bar. It is called an **edit line,** and it begins with the name of the active or highlighted cell. A cell can contain text, numbers, or formulas, or it can be empty. The contents of a cell are indicated on the right side of the edit line. When a cell contains a formula, it displays the results of using the formula; the actual formula itself is displayed in the edit line. For example, move the cursor to cell D7. In the edit line, you will see the following formula:

```
D7  =b7+(12*c7)
```

As in math, operations inside parentheses are performed first. Thus this formula multiplies the contents of cell C7 by 12, and adds the contents of cell B7. The advantage of using **cell references** rather than absolute numbers will become apparent when you begin to modify the budget spreadsheet in the next section. This exercise will not ask you to change or modify any of the formulas. You will only be modifying cells that contain numbers.

Now, stop exploring the spreadsheet and go back to the problem. A spreadsheet is an ideal tool for what is called **what-if analysis.** You can change one cell in the spreadsheet, and watch the results of that change ripple through the entire spreadsheet.

For example, assume that you cut back on your food expenses. You can analyze the effects of lower food costs by asking a "what-if" question: "What if my food expenses decrease to $100 per month?" To try this, move the cursor to cell C10, and type in the number 100. Then press the Return key. The cursor will

```
  File  Edit  Layout                                 Spreadsheet: Sample Budget
D7       =b7+(12*c7)                                                    Formula
             A              B           C             D          E          F
 1  Budget for:
 2
 3                      One-time     Monthly        Annual
 4  ---------------------------------------------------------
 5  Expenses
 6
 7  Rent                  600.00      600.00       7800.00
 8  Utilities             200.00      200.00       2600.00
 9  Telephone              60.00       60.00        780.00
10  Food                              200.00       2400.00
11  Car                   425.00      215.00       3005.00
12  Gas                                50.00        600.00
13  ---------------------------------------------------------
14  Total Exp.           1285.00     1325.00      17185.00
15  ---------------------------------------------------------
16  Net Income           1000.00     1250.00      16000.00
17  ---------------------------------------------------------
18  Sav or -Loss         -285.00      -75.00      -1185.00
19  ---------------------------------------------------------
20
```

FIGURE 4.3 *The edit line is the line directly below the menu bar.*

move down to cell C11, and the program will automatically recalculate all the numbers in the spreadsheet that are affected by the food expenditure. What numbers have changed?

The annual expenditure for food in cell D10 has changed, because the numbers used in the formula for that cell have changed. The total expenditure in cell C14 has changed, since it is the sum of the monthly expenses. The savings or loss in cell C18 has changed, because it is dependent on the number in cell C14. The total expenditure in cell D14 and the savings or loss in D18 also change to reflect the reduction of the monthly food expenditure to $100. If we had used fixed numbers rather than cell references, the program would not have automatically recalculated all the relevant numbers in the spreadsheet.

It should be noted that the Return key is not the only key that causes a cell to be updated. Pressing the Tab key after changing a number updates the cell and causes the cursor to move to the cell immediately to the right of it.

The expenses you probably have the most control over are rent, food, and gas. Experiment with changing those expenses in your budget. As you do so, examine the effects of various changes. The program will automatically recalculate the totals, enabling you to view the results of the various alternatives you try. If you change the monthly rent expense, don't forget to change the one-time rent expense to match it. Try reducing your expenses until you have reached the goal of saving $100 per month (cell C18 should be 100.00 or more).

If you accidentally erase a formula or make a mistake that would make it difficult to continue with the exercise, use the *Revert to Last Version*... command in the File menu to restore the previous contents of the spreadsheet.

After you have successfully completed the exercise, enter your name into cell B1. To do so, move the cursor to cell B1 and type your name. Only twelve characters will fit in a cell; if your name is longer than that, only the first twelve characters of your name will appear in cell B1 when you press the Tab key. With the cursor positioned on cell C1, finish typing your name, starting where you left off in cell B1, and press the Tab key again.

To print a copy of your spreadsheet, press the Esc key, then use the Down arrow key to highlight the *Print Spreadsheet*... command in the File menu. Press the Return key. A dialog box will appear, asking you to press the Return key to print page 1 of the spreadsheet. Press the Return key. (Remember that the printer must be connected to the computer and turned on, and the paper must be properly positioned in the printer.)

After printing, press the Esc key to toggle to the menu bar, and press the Down arrow key to select the *Quit Spreadsheet* command. Press the Return key to return to the Application Manager, and either Quit TriPac or go on to another application.

REVIEW AND SELF-TESTING

Key Terms

Process	Modeling
Problem	Simulating
Solution	Artificial intelligence

Procedure
Functional specification
Brainstorming
Decision making
Top-down design
Cell
Edit line
Cell reference
What-if analysis

Questions for Review and Discussion

1. Give two reasons for treating problem solving as a logical and orderly process.
2. Why do most problems require you to make assumptions?
3. What fields of study might you draw on to aid in learning about problem solving?
4. Describe two behaviors that are typical of creative problem solvers.
5. How is the design process similar to the steps in the problem-solving process?
6. What is the key element in decision making?
7. Why are decision-making skills useful in problem solving?
8. What is the first step in identifying alternatives?
9. Explain one way to choose the best among a list of alternatives.
10. List three advantages of using application software to solve problems.
11. Assume that one of your long-term goals is to communicate more effectively with a wider range of people. How might the software we have been discussing help you accomplish that goal?
12. List two potential uses you might have for a spreadsheet program. Then discuss why they would be good spreadsheet applications.
13. Imagine that you are in charge of preparing the annual budget of the federal government. How might a spreadsheet help you?

Exercise with the Spreadsheet Program

1. In the spreadsheet example, suppose you have been offered a job that pays $22,000 a year. Use the spreadsheet to do a what-if analysis of how it affects the budget calculations.

5

Introducing Word Processing

PREVIEW

A word processor is a computer program that you can use to write, print, and store most of the written communication that you need in your personal and professional life.

In this chapter, you'll learn step by step how to use a word processor to compose, edit, revise, and print documents. This chapter will examine how to write various types of documents, and how to use a word processor to enter and edit text, and to revise, change, save, and print a document.

Along the way, we'll discuss how writing with a word processor differs from writing manually or with a typewriter. We'll also compare the TriPac word processor with commercial word processors, and discuss some of the features that commercial word processors offer.

In this chapter, you'll discover:

- *Word processing as a problem-solving tool*
- *The different types of documents*
- *The process of editing*
- *Selecting, cutting, copying, and pasting*
- *How documents look on the display screen*
- *How to write a sample letter*
- *How to revise text*
- *How to save and print documents*

Word Processing and Problem Solving

Word processing is software that aids in the composition, revision, filing, and printing of text. The term *word processing* was coined at IBM in 1964 to describe the electronic means for handling standard office functions, and to distinguish those functions from data processing. In those days, a word processor was a computer dedicated to the task of word processing. Because of their cost and the special training involved, word processors were largely limited to secretarial use in medium- and large-scale offices.

Although these **dedicated systems** are still found in offices where heavy-volume word processing is the norm, today word processing commonly means software. It has become one of the most popular applications for personal computers. These are some uses of word-processing software on personal computers:

- Authors and editors write articles and books.
- Businesspeople write memos, correspondence, proposals, and reports.
- Scientists and engineers write professional journal articles.
- Teachers write tests, course outlines, and assignments.
- Charities and political organizations write fund-raising proposals and form letters.
- Students write homework assignments and term papers.

Word processing is a general-purpose problem-solving tool. It is used in situations in which the user defines the problem (decides what to write and how to write it), and then prepares a solution (composes the written text), drawing on his or her knowledge and problem-solving skills. As a general-purpose tool,

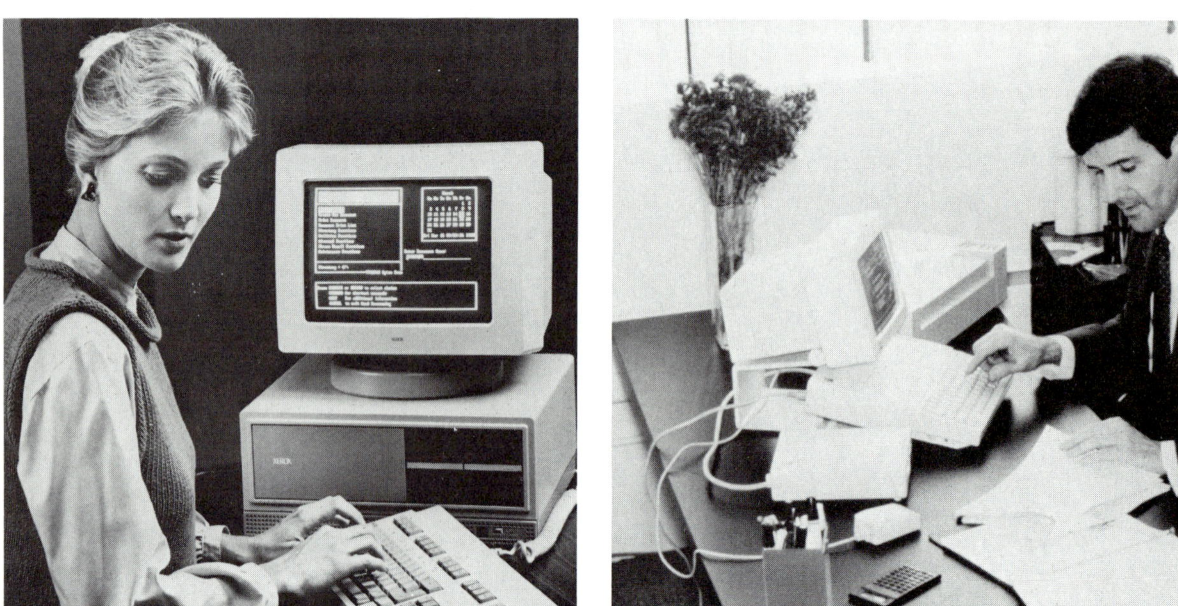

Dedicated word processors, such as the one shown on the left, are often found in offices where there is a heavy volume of word processing. However, personal computers, like the Apple IIe on the right, are becoming increasingly common, and word processing has become one of the most widely used application programs.

word processing is not restricted to any particular kind of writing. It can be used to help make any written communication clear, effective, neat, and error-free, and to streamline the writing process.

Writing is a problem-solving skill whose fundamentals you have already acquired. Whether you write manually or with a typewriter, you will find the transition to word processing relatively easy. The mechanics of using word-processing software are straightforward. The text that you type on the keyboard is temporarily stored in the computer's memory, and displayed on the screen. While the text is in memory, you can change it in any number of ways and immediately see your changes on the display screen. If you are not satisfied with your changes, it is easy to try another alternative.

You can make such changes as:

- Inserting and deleting text
- Copying text from one location to another
- Cutting text from one location and pasting it elsewhere
- Choosing different formats for printing

You can view all these changes on the display screen; you do not have to retype any drafts. Whenever you are ready, you can save the text onto disk. And, of course, you can print it at any time.

Once you become accustomed to using a word processor, its benefits —easier, faster, and neater writing—will become more apparent. Before learning to use a word processor, it is helpful to learn the terminology of the software you are using. Then you can practice the functions and commands that the word processor uses to prepare, revise, format, and print text.

What Is a Document?

The end product of word processing is a printed document. A **document** is any text or collection of characters (letters, numbers, spaces, punctuation marks, and other symbols). The TriPac word processor has a limit of approximately 45,000 characters per document. This means that you can create up to a 15-page single-spaced or 30-page double-spaced printed document. The reason for this length limitation is that the entire document is stored in the computer's memory while the word processor is in operation.

Commercial word processors circumvent length limitations by storing longer documents on disk, and retaining in memory only those portions of the document that are currently being edited. The word processor handles the technical details of swapping portions of the document into and out of memory. The size of a document is thus limited only by the storage space available on the disk.

Types of Documents

It is useful to categorize documents by type, because some word processors place limitations on the types of document they can produce. Broadly, the categories of documents are (as illustrated in Figure 5.1):

- Simple sequential uninterrupted text, such as a letter, note, memo, or rough draft.

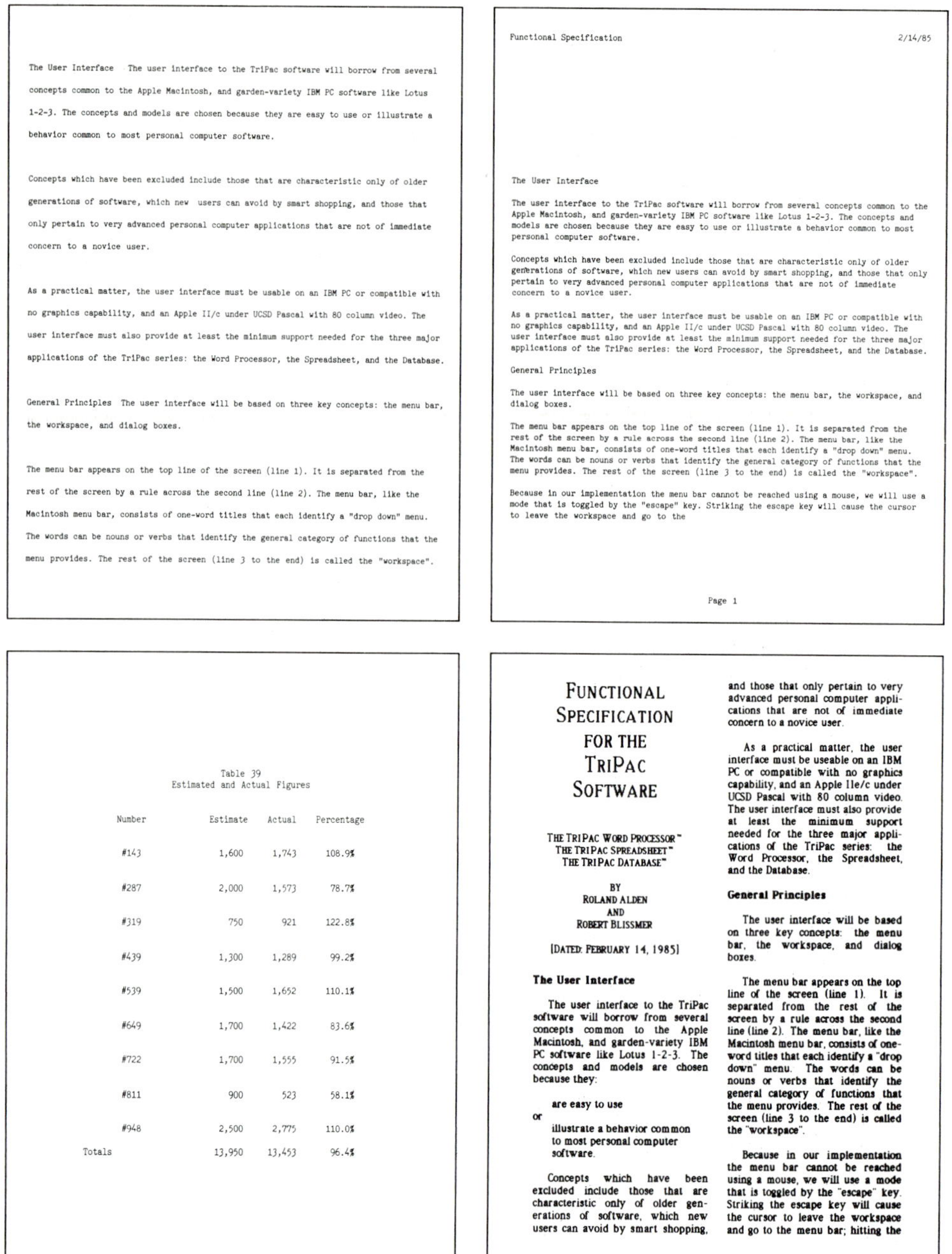

The User Interface The user interface to the TriPac software will borrow from several concepts common to the Apple Macintosh, and garden-variety IBM PC software like Lotus 1-2-3. The concepts and models are chosen because they are easy to use or illustrate a behavior common to most personal computer software.

Concepts which have been excluded include those that are characteristic only of older generations of software, which new users can avoid by smart shopping, and those that only pertain to very advanced personal computer applications that are not of immediate concern to a novice user.

As a practical matter, the user interface must be usable on an IBM PC or compatible with no graphics capability, and an Apple II/c under UCSD Pascal with 80 column video. The user interface must also provide at least the minimum support needed for the three major applications of the TriPac series: the Word Processor, the Spreadsheet, and the Database.

General Principles The user interface will be based on three key concepts: the menu bar, the workspace, and dialog boxes.

The menu bar appears on the top line of the screen (line 1). It is separated from the rest of the screen by a rule across the second line (line 2). The menu bar, like the Macintosh menu bar, consists of one-word titles that each identify a "drop down" menu. The words can be nouns or verbs that identify the general category of functions that the menu provides. The rest of the screen (line 3 to the end) is called the "workspace".

Functional Specification 2/14/85

The User Interface

The user interface to the TriPac software will borrow from several concepts common to the Apple Macintosh, and garden-variety IBM PC software like Lotus 1-2-3. The concepts and models are chosen because they are easy to use or illustrate a behavior common to most personal computer software.

Concepts which have been excluded include those that are characteristic only of older generations of software, which new users can avoid by smart shopping, and those that only pertain to very advanced personal computer applications that are not of immediate concern to a novice user.

As a practical matter, the user interface must be usable on an IBM PC or compatible with no graphics capability, and an Apple II/c under UCSD Pascal with 80 column video. The user interface must also provide at least the minimum support needed for the three major applications of the TriPac series: the Word Processor, the Spreadsheet, and the Database.

General Principles

The user interface will be based on three key concepts: the menu bar, the workspace, and dialog boxes.

The menu bar appears on the top line of the screen (line 1). It is separated from the rest of the screen by a rule across the second line (line 2). The menu bar, like the Macintosh menu bar, consists of one-word titles that each identify a "drop down" menu. The words can be nouns or verbs that identify the general category of functions that the menu provides. The rest of the screen (line 3 to the end) is called the "workspace".

Because in our implementation the menu bar cannot be reached using a mouse, we will use a mode that is toggled by the "escape" key. Striking the escape key will cause the cursor to leave the workspace and go to the

Page 1

Table 39
Estimated and Actual Figures

Number	Estimate	Actual	Percentage
#143	1,600	1,743	108.9%
#287	2,000	1,573	78.7%
#319	750	921	122.8%
#439	1,300	1,289	99.2%
#539	1,500	1,652	110.1%
#649	1,700	1,422	83.6%
#722	1,700	1,555	91.5%
#811	900	523	58.1%
#948	2,500	2,775	110.0%
Totals	13,950	13,453	96.4%

FUNCTIONAL SPECIFICATION FOR THE TRIPAC SOFTWARE

THE TRIPAC WORD PROCESSOR™
THE TRIPAC SPREADSHEET™
THE TRIPAC DATABASE™

BY
ROLAND ALDEN
AND
ROBERT BLISSMER

[DATED: FEBRUARY 14, 1985]

The User Interface

The user interface to the TriPac software will borrow from several concepts common to the Apple Macintosh, and garden-variety IBM PC software like Lotus 1-2-3. The concepts and models are chosen because they:

are easy to use
or
illustrate a behavior common to most personal computer software.

Concepts which have been excluded include those that are characteristic only of older generations of software, which new users can avoid by smart shopping, and those that only pertain to very advanced personal computer applications that are not of immediate concern to a novice user.

As a practical matter, the user interface must be useable on an IBM PC or compatible with no graphics capability, and an Apple IIe/c under UCSD Pascal with 80 column video. The user interface must also provide at least the minimum support needed for the three major applications of the TriPac series: the Word Processor, the Spreadsheet, and the Database.

General Principles

The user interface will be based on three key concepts: the menu bar, the workspace, and dialog boxes.

The menu bar appears on the top line of the screen (line 1). It is separated from the rest of the screen by a rule across the second line (line 2). The menu bar, like the Macintosh menu bar, consists of one-word titles that each identify a "drop down" menu. The words can be nouns or verbs that identify the general category of functions that the menu provides. The rest of the screen (line 3 to the end) is called the "workspace".

Because in our implementation the menu bar cannot be reached using a mouse, we will use a mode that is toggled by the "escape" key. Striking the escape key will cause the cursor to leave the workspace and go to the menu bar; hitting the

FIGURE 5.1 *Four types of documents.*

- A structured document, such as a report, term paper, or chapter of a book. The structure is provided by such elements as headers, footers, page breaks, and page numbers.
- A document whose layout determines its form, such as a résumé, chart, or diagram. The elements of layout include centering, indentation, tabs, and multiple margins.
- A complex arrangement of layout and typographical elements, such as super- and subscripting, **boldface**, *italic*, and underlining, and different styles and sizes of type. This kind of document might also include footnotes, an index, and a table of contents.

The sophistication of the word-processing program determines which types of documents you can produce. The TriPac word processor can prepare the first two types of documents; for more complex documents, you would need a commercial word-processing package with additional features. Typographically complex documents usually also require special hardware devices, such as a graphics printer, a laser printer, or a typesetter.

How to Create a New Document

This is a hands-on exercise. To begin, you should have the TriPac software up and running on the computer. If you are not yet familiar with the Application Manager commands demonstrated in Chapter 2, it would be a good idea to review them before beginning. To create a new document:

1. Move the pointer down to the first untitled document.
2. Press the Esc key to toggle to the menu bar.
3. The pointer will now be on the File menu. Press the Down arrow key to move the pointer to the *O=Open* command. Then press the Return key.
4. A dialog box will appear, asking you to name the new document you are about to open. Type in *Test.* The screen will look like Figure 5.2. Then press the Return key.

```
File  Setup  Info

  Name for new document: Test■

  Press Esc to cancel        Press Return to open new document
```

FIGURE 5.2 *Dialog box to name and open a new document.*

5. The words "Opening Test" will appear briefly in the upper right corner of the screen. The Application Manager is loading into memory the word processor and the document you have just opened. On the first line of the display, you will see the menu bar for the word processor.

What You Will See

Figure 5.3 shows the newly opened document. Below the horizontal line, you will see the empty workspace. The **cursor**—the rectangular blinking box that indicates where the next character will appear on the display screen—is in the upper left-hand corner. To the left of the cursor is a ^ sign, used to mark page breaks. (Its function will be discussed in the next chapter.) The cursor is positioned over a # sign, which marks the end of the document.

When writing manually or on a typewriter, the mechanics of writing begin with a blank piece of paper. In word processing, the equivalent of a blank page is the empty document into which you insert text. In the vocabulary of word processing, the process of going from an empty file to a completed document is

```
File  Edit  Find  Tabs  Layout                              Document: Test
--------------------------------------------------------------------------
^ #
```

FIGURE 5.3 *A newly opened document.*

known as **editing.** Editing includes composing the original text, revising (inserting, deleting, correcting, and formatting text), and periodically saving copies of the document onto disk.

The cursor can be moved to any point in the document by using the cursor-movement keys. However, since your document is empty, you cannot yet move the cursor. Most word processors allow you to begin entering text as soon as you open a document. In some cases, a command to enter text must be activated before you begin to type. To practice using the basic editing features, we will start you off with some exercises that involve the format of the document rather than its content.

Experimenting with Word Processing

When you use a word processor, you will constantly be performing two operations: inserting new text into the document and manipulating the text that is already there. To begin practicing, insert some text into the document. Type

`This is a test.`

Note that the cursor and the end-of-document sign have both shifted to the end of the sentence. Your document is now one sentence long. Since the cursor can be moved anywhere in the document, you can now use the Left and Right arrow keys to move the cursor anywhere in the sentence.

Now move the cursor to the initial *t* in *test* and type the deliberately misspelled words

`word porcessing`

followed by a space. Note that the new text is automatically inserted beginning at the location of the cursor, and that the text that follows it is pushed to the right. You do not have to worry about deleting text by typing over it.

Next, you would like to correct the spelling of *porcessing.* To do that, you must command the word processor to manipulate the text that is already there. (In this case the command will be to delete the *o* in the misspelled word, and then correct the spelling.) To do so:

1. Move the cursor to the letter *r* in *porcessing*, as shown in Figure 5.4, and press the Delete key.

```
File  Edit  Find  Tabs  Layout                              Document: Test
--------------------------------------------------------------------------
^ This is a word porcessing test.#
```

FIGURE 5.4 *Cursor position to delete the letter* o.

2. The delete command erases the character to the left of the cursor. The space held by the deleted character is closed up.
3. To correct the spelling, move the cursor one position to the right (over the *c*) and type the letter *o*. When inserting a character or characters, position the cursor at the point where you want the insertion to begin.

By moving the cursor, using the Delete key, and inserting additional text, you can correct spelling and other errors in a document. Pressing the Delete key several times deletes several characters in sequence. Try positioning the cursor to the right of the *d* in *word* and pressing the Delete key four times. The characters will disappear one at a time, and the space left by the deletions will automatically close up. Then, without moving the cursor, retype the letters *word*.

Selection

Selection is an important principle of word processing. It is used to designate a set of characters to be manipulated, such as by:

- Copying the characters elsewhere in the document
- Moving the characters elsewhere in the document
- Deleting the characters

Note that selection is always used in conjunction with another command. To practice selecting:

1. Move the cursor to the beginning of the document (to the *T* in *This*).
2. Then use the Esc key to toggle to the menu bar. Move the pointer right to the Edit menu, then down to the *S=Start Selecting* command. The screen will look like Figure 5.5. Press the Return key.

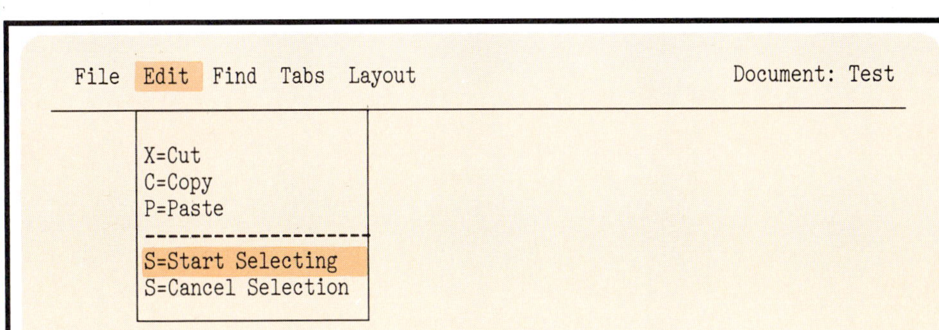

FIGURE 5.5 *The* S = Start Selecting *command.*

3. The Edit menu will retract, and the cursor will reappear where you left it.
4. Press the Right arrow key continuously until you have highlighted the entire sentence, as shown in Figure 5.6. Highlighting will appear on the display screen as reverse video. Note that there is no blinking cursor. This is because the selected sentence cannot be manipulated until the next command is given to the word processor.

```
File  Edit  Find  Tabs  Layout                         Document: Test
------------------------------------------------------------------------
^ This is a word processing test.#
```

FIGURE 5.6 *A selected sentence.*

5. You can cancel any selection by pressing the Esc key to toggle to the menu bar, moving the pointer to the Edit menu and then to the *S=Cancel Selection* command, and pressing the Return key. Try this, and watch the highlighting disappear from the selected sentence.
6. Selection can proceed in either direction. Repeat the steps to execute the *S=Start Selecting* command, but this time press the Left arrow key continuously. The highlighting will proceed to the left. Before going on, execute the *S=Cancel Selection* command.

You should remember the following important points about selection:

- A selection begins at the left edge of the cursor. In other words, when you press the Right arrow key, the highlighting begins on the character where the cursor was last located. If you press the Left arrow key, the highlighting begins on the character to the immediate left of where the cursor was last located.
- A selection will be replaced by an insertion. For example, if you select a sentence and press the Y key, the highlighted sentence will be deleted and replaced by the insertion of the letter *y*.

Now we will show you some commands to use with selection when you want to edit a document.

Copy-and-Paste

Copy-and-Paste is a set of commands used to copy a passage of text from one location in a document to another, leaving the original intact. The **Copy command** copies the selected passage into a temporary storage area called a **clipboard**, until a **Paste command** is executed to reproduce the passage elsewhere in the document. To practice using the Copy and Paste commands to copy the sentence you selected earlier:

1. Move the cursor to the beginning of the document. Repeat the procedure outlined in the last section to select the entire sentence.
2. Press the Esc key to toggle to the menu bar. Move the pointer right to the Edit menu, then down to the *C=Copy* command. The screen will look like Figure 5.7. Press the Return key. The highlighting disappears, and the sentence you selected is copied into the clipboard. The cursor is now positioned on the # end-of-document symbol.

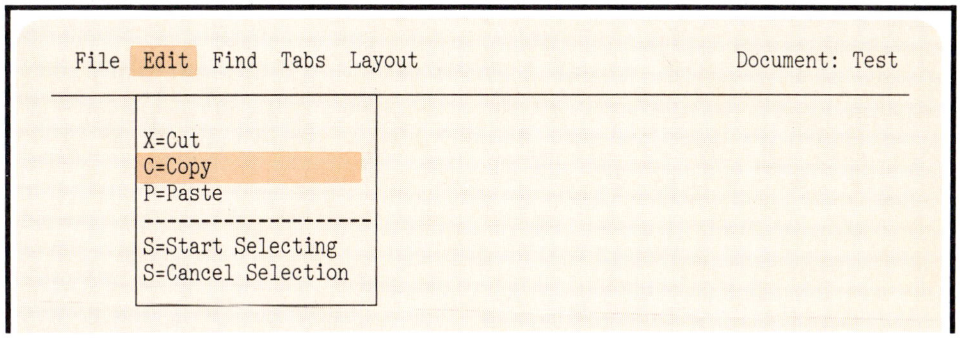

FIGURE 5.7 *The* C = Copy *command.*

3. Toggle to the menu bar. Move the pointer to the Edit menu, then down to the *P=Paste* command. Press the Return key.
4. A copy of the sentence in the clipboard will appear beginning at the position where the cursor was located when you gave the command.

The text is not removed from the clipboard; it is only copied. Try repeating the Paste command without doing anything else. Another copy of the sentence in the clipboard will appear, beginning at the position where the cursor was last located. The clipboard retains its contents until you store something new in it. Type in another sentence or two, and practice the Copy-and-Paste command.

Cut-and-Paste

Cut-and-Paste is a set of commands used to move selected characters from one location in a document to another. The **Cut command** moves the selected text into the clipboard for storage, deleting it from its original location. The Paste command copies the text from the clipboard into a new location.

TABLE 5.1 *Copy-and-Paste versus Cut-and-Paste*

Copy-and-Paste	Cut-and-Paste
1. Selected text is copied to the clipboard.	1. Selected text is copied to the clipboard.
2. The selected text remains unchanged at its original location.	2. The selected text is cut from its original location. The document is reformatted to close up the deletion.
3. The selected text is pasted from the clipboard into the new location. The document is reformatted to accommodate the insertion.	3. The selected text is pasted from the clipboard into the new location. The document is reformatted to accommodate the insertion.
4. The copied text remains in the clipboard until it is replaced by another cut or copy operation.	4. The cut text remains in the clipboard until it is replaced by another cut or copy operation.

As an analogy, imagine that you want to reverse the order of two paragraphs using scissors and tape. You would cut one paragraph out of its original location, and tape it in at the new location. The cut-and-paste function in a word processor accomplishes the same thing. By contrast, copy-and-paste copies a selection but leaves the original intact. Table 5.1 compares the copy-and-paste and cut-and-paste commands.

To practice cutting and pasting:

1. Move the cursor to the beginning of the second sentence in your document. Select the sentence, using the selection process described on page 91.
2. Toggle to the menu bar. Move the pointer to the Edit menu and then to the *X=Cut* command. Press the Return key. The sentence is copied into the clipboard, and disappears from the display screen.
3. Move the cursor to the beginning of the document.
4. Toggle to the menu bar. Move the pointer to the Edit menu, then down to the *P=Paste* command. Press the Return key.
5. The text in the clipboard will appear in the document, starting at the point where the cursor was last located.

As with Copy-and-Paste, the text has not disappeared from the clipboard; if you wish, it can be pasted into the document again. Press the Esc key and move the pointer to the Edit menu; then move the pointer down. Notice that the pointer jumps to the *P=Paste* command. The *X=Cut* and *C=Copy* commands cannot be chosen, because no selection has been made. For those commands to be chosen, you must first make a selection. However, the Paste command can still be chosen, because text is still located in the clipboard. Press the Return key and watch as the sentence is inserted into the document.

Editing Shortcuts

Once you have learned the uses of the commands in the Edit menu, you can use a shortcut method for invoking those commands. The reason why the commands in the Edit menu are preceded by a letter and an equal sign is to provide you with a shortcut way to use them. You can bypass toggling to the menu bar, and instead initiate the commands by holding down the Control key while pressing the specified letter. This shortcut allows you to execute the commands without having to leave the workspace. To practice using the Control key in conjunction with the Edit commands:

1. Move the cursor to the beginning of the second sentence in your document. Then hold down the Control key while pressing the S key. This has the same effect as the *S=Start Selecting* command in the Edit menu. (You will notice that the word *Edit* in the menu bar flashes.)
2. Now use the Right arrow key to select the sentence.
3. To copy the selection, hold down the Control key while pressing the C key. The cursor will momentarily disappear while the selection is copied into the clipboard.
4. To paste the selection, move the cursor to the end-of-document symbol. Hold down the Control key while you press the P key, and watch as the selection is pasted into your document.

5. To cut a selection, select another sentence using the Control and S keys. Remember that selection can proceed in either direction. Try this by moving the cursor one position to the left; then hold down the Control key and press the S key. Now press the Left arrow key.
6. When you have finished selecting the sentence, hold down the Control key and press the X key. The selection will disappear from the screen and be moved into the clipboard.
7. To paste the cut selection at the beginning of the document, move the cursor to that position and hold down the Control key while pressing the P key.

So far, you have only selected sentences. A selection can be a single character, a word, a sentence, a group of sentences, a paragraph, or the entire document. To practice selecting a passage of text that is larger than a sentence:

1. Move the cursor somewhere near the middle of the top line on the display, and execute the *S=Start Selection* command.
2. Now press the Down arrow key. The text to the right of the cursor on the top line, and the text to the left of the cursor on the next line, will be selected.
3. Press the Down arrow key again. Another line of text will be highlighted. Now press the Up arrow key; the previously highlighted line of text will no longer be selected. Now press the Down arrow key twice to select a passage of text.

If you have not deleted it, copy the selected block of text; otherwise, select another block. Then paste it over and over, filling up the display screen with text so you can observe the feature called scrolling.

Scrolling

When a document is too large to be displayed on the screen all at once, **scrolling**—moving text up, down, left, or right on the screen—brings different parts of the document into view. Since the widest possible line (65 characters) fits on the screen, the TriPac word processor scrolls only up and down. Some word processors allow lines wider than 65 characters, and use **horizontal** scrolling to display lines of text that are wider than the display screen.

Pressing continuously on the Down arrow key moves the cursor down the display line by line. When the cursor reaches the bottom line of the display, the entire screen is redisplayed. The bottom line of the previous screen now appears at the top of the display, and the cursor is positioned on the second line of text in the new display. Pressing the Up arrow key causes the same process to occur in reverse. The cursor moves line-by-line up the display; when it reaches the top line, the entire screen is redisplayed with the first line of the previous screen appearing at the bottom of the display, and the cursor positioned directly above that line.

Editing and the Display

The **format** of the text is the way it is physically organized on the display screen. Whenever text is inserted or deleted, the word processor will automatically reformat the display to accommodate the insertion or deletion.

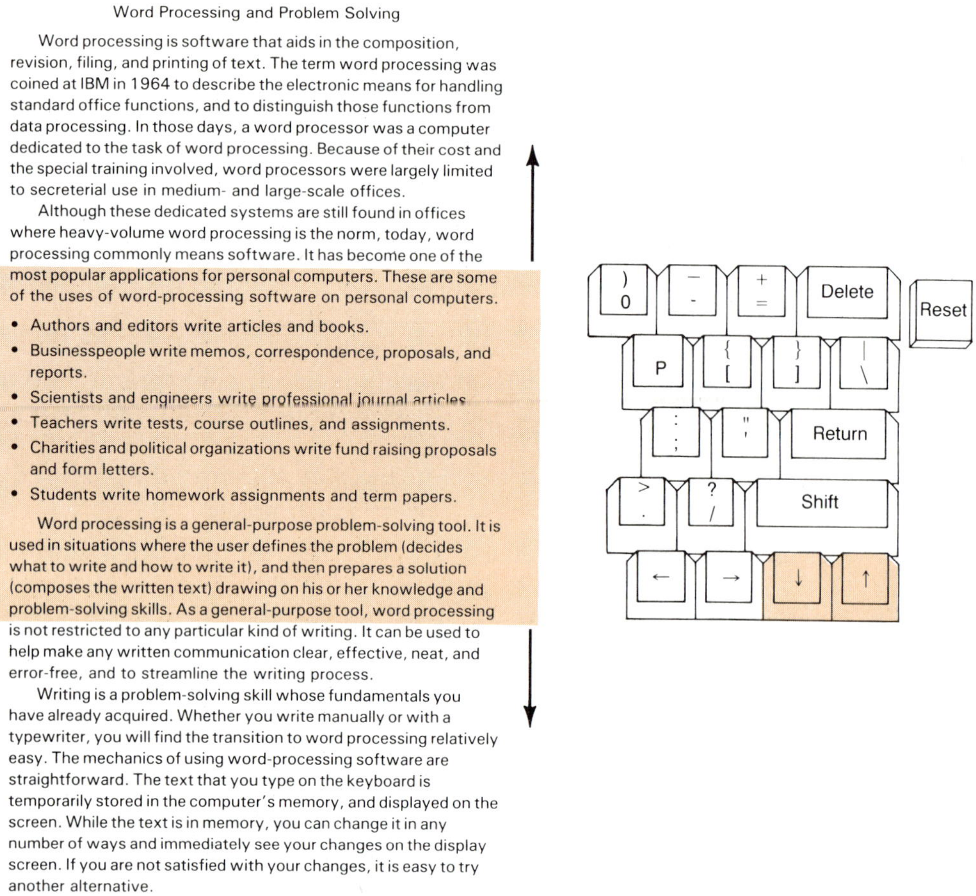
Word Processing and Problem Solving

Word processing is software that aids in the composition, revision, filing, and printing of text. The term word processing was coined at IBM in 1964 to describe the electronic means for handling standard office functions, and to distinguish those functions from data processing. In those days, a word processor was a computer dedicated to the task of word processing. Because of their cost and the special training involved, word processors were largely limited to secreterial use in medium- and large-scale offices.

Although these dedicated systems are still found in offices where heavy-volume word processing is the norm, today, word processing commonly means software. It has become one of the most popular applications for personal computers. These are some of the uses of word-processing software on personal computers.

- Authors and editors write articles and books.
- Businesspeople write memos, correspondence, proposals, and reports.
- Scientists and engineers write professional journal articles.
- Teachers write tests, course outlines, and assignments.
- Charities and political organizations write fund raising proposals and form letters.
- Students write homework assignments and term papers.

Word processing is a general-purpose problem-solving tool. It is used in situations where the user defines the problem (decides what to write and how to write it), and then prepares a solution (composes the written text) drawing on his or her knowledge and problem-solving skills. As a general-purpose tool, word processing is not restricted to any particular kind of writing. It can be used to help make any written communication clear, effective, neat, and error-free, and to streamline the writing process.

Writing is a problem-solving skill whose fundamentals you have already acquired. Whether you write manually or with a typewriter, you will find the transition to word processing relatively easy. The mechanics of using word-processing software are straightforward. The text that you type on the keyboard is temporarily stored in the computer's memory, and displayed on the screen. While the text is in memory, you can change it in any number of ways and immediately see your changes on the display screen. If you are not satisfied with your changes, it is easy to try another alternative.

Scrolling. The Down arrow and Up arrow keys scroll line by line. The and Down arrow and and Up arrow scroll screen by screen.

To visualize this, think of a document as a continuous stream of text that flows from the beginning of the document to the end-of-document symbol. The display screen, meanwhile, is a rectangle consisting of 22 lines, each 65 characters long.

As you type, the cursor continues advancing to the right to indicate the location of the next character. When the cursor reaches the end of a line, it automatically drops to the first position in the next line. If you are in the middle of a word when the cursor reaches the end of a line, the word is carried down to the next line along with the cursor. This feature is called **word wrap.** It allows you to continue typing without using a return key, as you would have to when typing on a typewriter. The Return key has a special function, which we will discuss in the next section.

Word wrap occurs when you insert or delete text, to eliminate crowding or gaps in the stream of text. To see word wrap in action, move your cursor to the middle of the first line of text and add the sentence:

```
This is a test of the word-wrap feature.
```

Watch how the text at the end of the line drops down to the next line. Then use the Delete key to delete part of the sentence you just added, and watch how word wrap works in reverse.

Word wrap also occurs when you hyphenate a word at the end of a line. To observe this feature, choose a line that is filled with text and move the cursor to the last word in the line. If you insert a hyphen in the word, you will see the remainder of the word drop to the beginning of the next line. (The word must end at the last position in the line for word wrap to work.) If you delete the hyphen, you will see word wrap work in reverse.

Paragraphs

Breaks occur in the continuous stream of text only when you create a paragraph. Recall from Chapter 2 that the end of a paragraph is indicated by a **paragraph mark.** In the Class Survey, shown in Figure 5.8, paragraph marks appear at the end of each line and between questions. To create a paragraph in your document, move the cursor to the end of the first sentence. Then press the Return key. A paragraph mark (¶) will appear where the cursor was, and the text to the right of the cursor will move down to the next line. The first line has become a paragraph.

To insert a blank line between paragraphs, you can create a paragraph without any text. Press the Return key again. A blank line will be created, with

```
  File  Edit  Find  Tabs  Layout                    Document: Class Survey
^ CLASS SURVEY¶
  ¶
  Class: ¶
  Section: ¶
  Date: ¶
  ¶
  A computer would make my life easier. (Agree or Disagree)¶
  ¶
  ¶
  ¶
  Computers are easy to use. (Agree or Disagree)¶
  ¶
  ¶
  ¶
  Computers are dehumanizing. (Agree or Disagree)¶
  ¶
  ¶
  ¶
  Do you use a personal computer at home or work? (Yes or No)¶
  ¶
  ¶
  ¶
```

FIGURE 5.8 *Paragraph marks.*

a paragraph mark at the left margin, and the remainder of the text will drop down one line.

In some word processors, the paragraph mark is invisible or optionally visible. In TriPac, it is visible on the screen but not in the printed document. A paragraph mark can also be selected, copied, cut, pasted, and deleted just like any other character.

Exercises with the Word Processor

- Experiment with inserting text by using the arrow keys to move around in your test document and typing in additional text. Then practice using the Delete key to delete text.
- Practice cutting-and-pasting and copying-and-pasting various blocks of text. Try using the editing shortcuts—the Control key in conjunction with the letter keys.
- Use the Return key to create paragraphs in the document. Experiment with deleting sentences, lines, paragraphs, and paragraph marks by selecting and then deleting with the Delete key.

When you feel comfortable using these commands, press the Esc key to toggle to the menu bar. Then press the Down arrow key, move the pointer to the *Quit Word Processor* command, and press the Return key. The software will return you to the Application Manager program. Executing the *Quit Word Processor* command automatically saves the current document onto disk.

To delete the test document, position the pointer over the document named Test. Press the Esc key to toggle to the menu bar, press the Down arrow key, move the pointer to the *Delete*. . . command, and press the Return key. A dialog box will appear, asking if you want to delete the document named Test. Press the Return key and continue with the next lesson.

Writing a Sample Letter

To enable you to apply the editing concepts you have just learned, we have composed a sample letter on which to practice. Move the pointer to the first untitled document. Use the shortcut for the *O=Open* command by holding down the Ctrl key while pressing the O key. A dialog box will appear, asking for the name of the new document. Type in *Business Letter.* Press Return to open the new document.

Then type the letter exactly as shown in Figure 5.9 (including the spelling mistakes). Use the Return key to create new paragraphs. For example, type in the first address line, "123 Main Street," then press the Return key, type in the second address line, then press the Return key, and so on. Also use the Return key to insert a blank line between the date and the recipient's address, and between the address and the salutation. You will find that the letter does not all fit on one screen.

123 Main Street
Anytown, CA 90026
February 15, 1987

Mr. Robert H. Blissmer
Houghton Mifflin Company
One Beacon Street
Boston, MA 02108

Dear Mr. Blissmer:

The blocked paragraph style is widely used in business
correspondance. This version is called a full-blocked style
because each line begins at the left-hand margin. Using full-
blocked style is also the fastest way to type.

New paragraphs are indicated by double spacing rather than
indenting. The format for a blocked letter consists of: the
return address, the date, the recipient's address, then the
salutation. The body of the letter is followed by a complimentery
close, and the sender's name.

Sincerely yours,

John Doe

FIGURE 5.9 *Sample business letter.*

Editing: Correcting Mistakes

After you have finished typing in the business letter, you will want to (1) correct the deliberate mistakes in the letter and (2) proofread the letter for any additional mistakes of your own. Scroll back to the beginning of the letter. The screen will look like Figure 5.10. Use the arrow keys, or the in combination with the arrow keys, to move around in the document.

In the business letter the words *correspondence* and *complimentary* are misspelled. To correct the spelling, first select the character you want to change. Use the arrow keys to position the cursor on the *n* in the misspelled word *correspondance.* Press the Delete key to delete the character to the left of the cursor. Then type in the correct letter *e*. Do the same for the misspelled word *complimentery* by deleting the second *e* and replacing it with an *a*.

```
File  Edit  Find  Tabs  Layout                 Document: Business Letter
^ 123 Main Street
  Anytown, CA 90026
  February 15, 1987

  Mr. Robert H. Blissmer
  Houghton Mifflin Company
  One Beacon Street
  Boston, MA 02108

  Dear Mr. Blissmer:

  The blocked paragraph style is widely used in business
  correspondance. This version is called a full-blocked style
  because each line begins at the left-hand margin. Using full-
  blocked style is also the fastest way to type.

  New paragraphs are indicated by double spacing rather than
  indenting. The format for a blocked letter consists of: the
  return address, the date, the recipient's address, then the
  salutation. The body of the letter is followed by a
  complimentery close, and the sender's name.

```

FIGURE 5.10 *First draft of business letter.*

Revising: Adding New Text

Now you can practice inserting additional words and sentences into the business letter. At the beginning of the second paragraph, add the following text to the first sentence:

```
With this style,
```

Notice how the text to the right of the cursor moves, and how the word processor uses word wrap to reformat the entire paragraph. Don't forget to add a space and to make the upper-case *N* lower-case. Then change the last sentence in the second paragraph to read:

```
After the body of the letter, end with a complimentary close and
your name.
```

You can do this in either of two ways: (1) select the existing sentence and delete it, then type in the new sentence, or (2) type in the new sentence, and then delete the old sentence. You can delete the old text before inserting the new text—but remember that once it is deleted, it is gone. If you are replacing a long passage of text, such as rewriting a sentence, it is safest to add the new text before deleting the old, in case you change your mind. Figure 5.11 shows the revised business letter.

```
File  Edit  Find  Tabs  Layout                Document: Business Letter
-----------------------------------------------------------------------
^ 123 Main Street
  Anytown, CA 90026
  February 15, 1987

  Mr. Robert H. Blissmer
  Houghton Mifflin Company
  One Beacon Street
  Boston, MA 02108

  Dear Mr. Blissmer:

  The blocked paragraph style is widely used in business
  correspondence. This version is called a full-blocked style
  because each line begins at the left-hand margin. Using full-
  blocked style is also the fastest way to type.

  With this style, new paragraphs are indicated by double spacing
  rather than indenting. The format for a blocked letter consists
  of: the return address, the date, the recipient's address, then
  the salutation. After the body of the letter, end with a
  complimentary close and your name.

```

FIGURE 5.11 *Revised business letter.*

For additional practice in deleting and inserting text, make the following changes in the business letter:

- Replace the three address lines with your own home address.
- Replace the date with today's date.
- Replace the name *John Doe* with your own name.

Saving the Document

After you have finished the revisions, you will want to save the document onto disk so you can refer to it in the future and won't have to type it over again. To save the document, press the Esc key and toggle to the menu bar. Move the pointer down to the *Save Document* command. The screen will look like Figure 5.12. Press the Return key to save the file. The red light on the disk drive will go on, and a copy of the document will be stored on the disk.

Particularly if you are working on a long document, there is a very important reason to save copies of it periodically. A document stored in memory is temporary, because memory itself is temporary. If you turn off the power switch, or the plug is knocked out of the socket, the contents of memory will be lost. If something happens to the program while you are editing a document, and you have to restart the computer, the contents of memory will be lost as a result of the restart. This is only a minor annoyance if it causes the loss of a brief

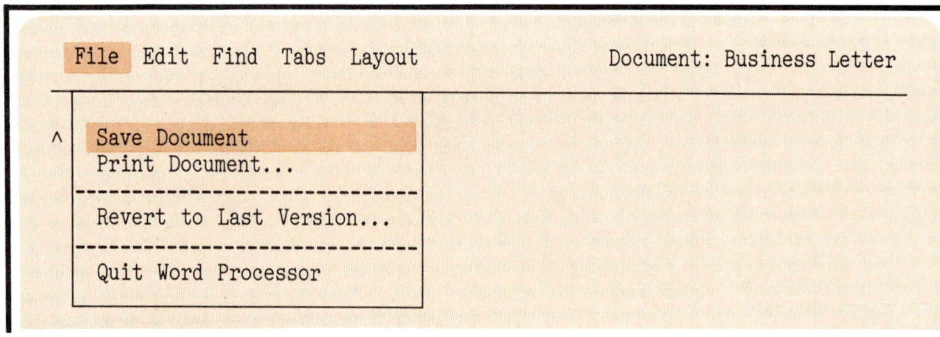

FIGURE 5.12 *The* Save Document *command.*

or unimportant document, but it could mean losing hours of work. A good rule of thumb when working with a word processor is to save your document every fifteen or twenty minutes. That way, if something should happen, only a small amount of work is lost.

Printing the Document

Printing a document also involves deciding on the format or layout of the printed page. Only in the most advanced word processors is what you see on the screen exactly what will be printed. Many word processors require you to specify format commands before printing a document.

Page layout is a matter of page size, left and right margins, page numbering, headers and footers, and single or double spacing. The TriPac word processor specifies the following page layout, illustrated in Figure 5.13. The left and right margins are 1 inch wide, and the line width is 6 1/2 inches with a maximum of 65 characters. The page length is 66 lines, with the first line blank, the next line reserved for a user-defined header, and the next two lines blank. A total of 54 lines are reserved for the document (27 lines in a double-spaced document). At the bottom of the page, two lines are left blank and one line is reserved for a user-defined footer. You will know how to use all of these printing options by the time you finish the next chapter.

Business letters are usually single-spaced, and the TriPac word processor always **defaults** to single spacing. Defaulting means assuming a particular option when none has been specified. Therefore, you do not need to specify any additional layout commands before printing. In the next chapter, you will learn how to change the layout of the document before printing it. To print your Business Letter document without special formatting:

1. Press the Esc key to toggle to the menu bar, press the Down arrow key to move the pointer to the *Print Document...* command, and press the Return key. A dialog box will appear, like the one in Figure 5.14.
2. Make sure the printer is plugged in and turned on, and that the top edge of the paper is positioned underneath the print head.
3. To print the first page of the document, press the Return key.

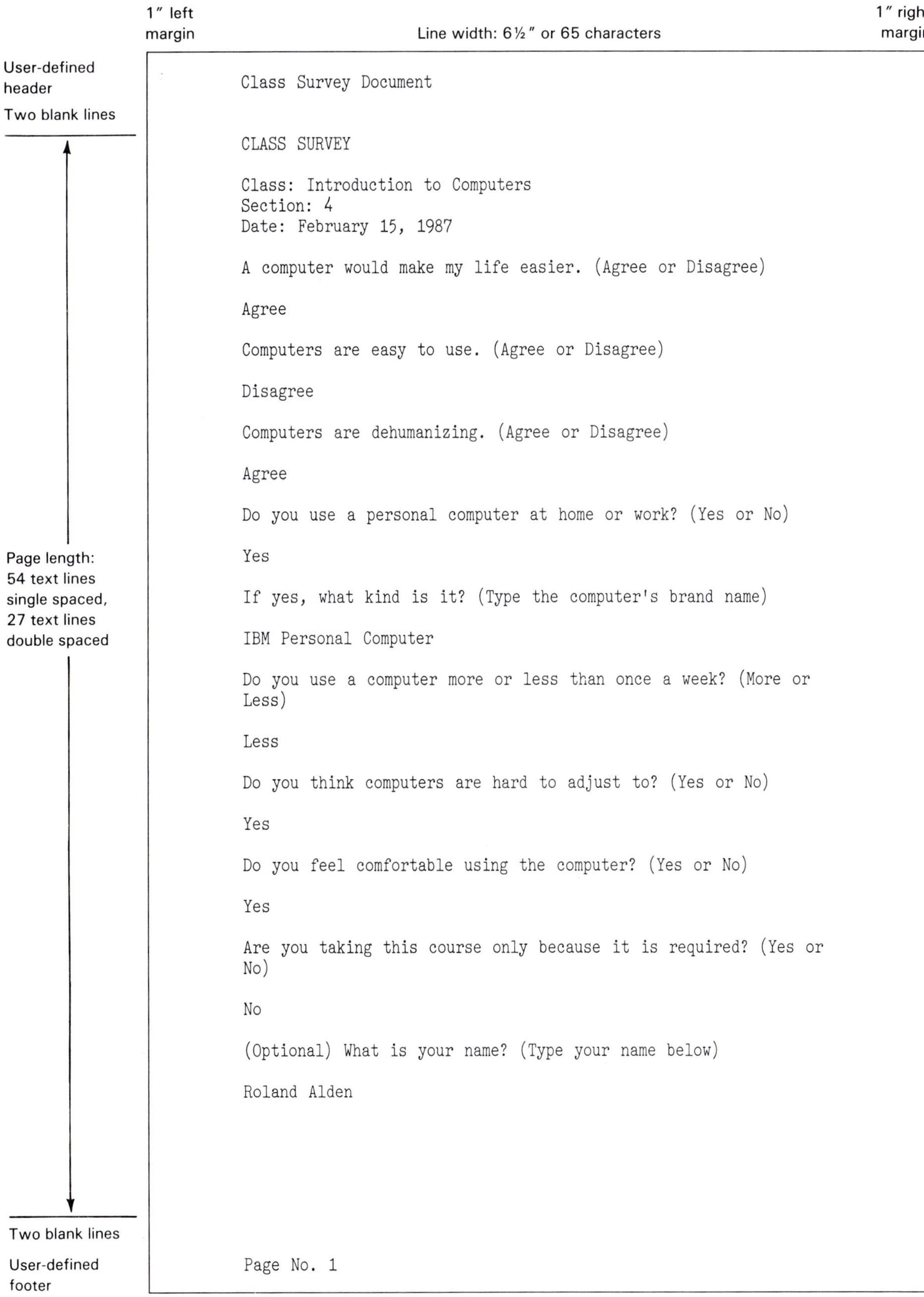

Class Survey Document

CLASS SURVEY

Class: Introduction to Computers
Section: 4
Date: February 15, 1987

A computer would make my life easier. (Agree or Disagree)

Agree

Computers are easy to use. (Agree or Disagree)

Disagree

Computers are dehumanizing. (Agree or Disagree)

Agree

Do you use a personal computer at home or work? (Yes or No)

Yes

If yes, what kind is it? (Type the computer's brand name)

IBM Personal Computer

Do you use a computer more or less than once a week? (More or Less)

Less

Do you think computers are hard to adjust to? (Yes or No)

Yes

Do you feel comfortable using the computer? (Yes or No)

Yes

Are you taking this course only because it is required? (Yes or No)

No

(Optional) What is your name? (Type your name below)

Roland Alden

Page No. 1

FIGURE 5.13 *TriPac page layout.*

File Edit Find Tabs Layout Document: Business Letter

Note: Document is single-spaced

Press Return to print page: 1

Press Esc to cancel

FIGURE 5.14 *Print dialog box.*

Many commercial word processors enable you to change the format of the document. For example, you can move the left and right margins to adjust the width of lines of text. If you include a quotation of five lines or more in a document, it is common practice to indent the entire quotation five spaces from the left margin. Many specialized documents, such as screenplays, poetry, and résumés, have style requirements for which adjustable margins would be a useful feature.

More Exercises with the Word Processor

- After revising the business letter, print a copy and hand it in to your instructor.
- Use the word processor to write a one-page letter to your instructor describing how easy or difficult it was to complete the word-processing exercises.
- Using the sample memo shown in Figure 5.15 as a model, use the word processor to write a memo to another student in the class discussing your plans for meeting to study for the upcoming quiz.

MEMO

To: John Jones

From: Jennifer Smith

Date: February 15, 1987

Subject: Study for Upcoming Quiz

Attached are my class notes from the last two weeks. Note the emphasis on word processing. Also note the focus on special features such as Selection, Copy-and-Paste and Cut-and-Paste.

Please check these notes against your own so that we can most effectively coordinate the study time in our upcoming meeting.

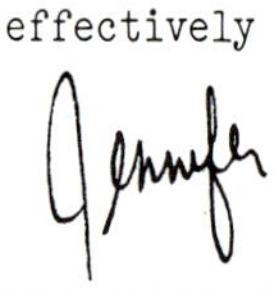

FIGURE 5.15 *Sample memo.*

REVIEW AND SELF-TESTING

Key Terms

- Word processing
- Dedicated system
- Document
- Cursor
- Editing
- Selection
- Copy-and-Paste
- Copy command
- Clipboard
- Paste command
- Cut-and-Paste
- Cut command
- Scrolling
- Format
- Word wrap
- Paragraph mark
- Default

Questions for Review and Discussion

1. What office functions was word processing originally intended to perform?
2. Briefly explain why word processing is a general-purpose problem-solving tool.
3. Briefly outline the mechanics of using a word processor.
4. What does the simplest type of document consist of?
5. What does the most complex type of document consist of?
6. Why should you periodically save copies of the document you are writing on a word processor?
7. What two operations will you continually be performing when using a word processor?
8. Describe the function of the Delete key.
9. What is the difference between Cut-and-Paste and Copy-and-Paste?
10. What function does word wrap perform?

Exercises with the Word Processor

1. Use the word processor to write a one-page single-spaced essay on the benefits of word processing.
2. Research a commercial word processor, by using it or by reading its documentation or articles about it. Use the TriPac word processor to write a one-page report on the best features of the commercial word processor.

6

Writing with a Word Processor

PREVIEW

In this chapter, you'll see how word processing can simplify the creation of more complex documents.

Word processing can help you write research papers, term papers, and reports. You'll learn step by step how to electronically compose, edit, and revise various drafts of a sample report.

At the end of the chapter, we'll discuss some advanced features of commercial word-processing software, and show you how those features can enhance written communication.

In this chapter, you'll discover:

- *How to revise drafts of a document electronically*
- *The use of Find-and-Replace*
- *How to single- and double-space a document*
- *Options for the format of printed documents*
- *The use of headers and footers*
- *Cutting, copying, and pasting between documents*
- *Advanced features of commercial word processors*

Writing the First Draft

In Chapter 4, we discussed writing as a problem-solving process. Word processors have many features that can help you in this process. The best way to show you those features is to practice on a draft document. Begin by opening a new document called Short Report. Then type in the first draft of the report, exactly as shown in Figure 6.1. When you have finished typing, move the cursor back to the beginning of the document.

Revising the First Draft

A word processor is an ideal tool for writing the kinds of documents that you first compose in draft form, then revise several times, and eventually print in final form. A word processor makes it possible to polish draft after draft—making changes, viewing the results of those changes, and occasionally changing your mind and reverting to an earlier draft.

In this chapter, you will see how much of the process of revising can be accomplished electronically, without physically typing draft after draft as you would on a typewriter. We will take you through various drafts of the short

```
The birth of the type-writer

In 1868, Christopher Latham Sholes, with the assistance of
Carlos Glidden, invented the first type-writer. The prototype
model used a piano-style keyboard and was the size of a kitchen
table. The type-writer was redesigned several times, and in
1873, Remington and Sons, gunsmiths, agreed to manufacture and
sell it.

In 1874, the Remington Model I type-writer was introduced. It
had no lower-case letters, and typed words were not visible
until several lines had been typed in. When it was exhibited at
the Philadelphia Centennial Exposition in 1876, many people were
willing to pay 25 cents to type a note to show their friends,
but few were willing to purchase the device.

One of the early problems with the Sholes and Glidden type-
writer was jamming of the keys. Even the earliest typists were
too fast for the machine. The solution was to fix the keyboard
layout in order to get the typists to slow down. By chance, the
keyboard arrangement spelled out Qwerty on the top row of
letters, so the keyboard is often called a Qwerty layout.
Because rearranging the keys placed frequently used letters all
over the keyboard, jamming of the keys was reduced.

In the early years the feeling that correspondence should be
written in longhand, plus the poor quality of the type-writer,
kept sales low. But by the mid 1880s, the type-writer was found
in many modern offices, and the word "secretary" came to mean a
woman at a type-writer. Today, the office type-writer is being
replaced by the word processor, and typing has become a
survival skill for nearly everyone.
```

FIGURE 6.1 *Sample short report.*

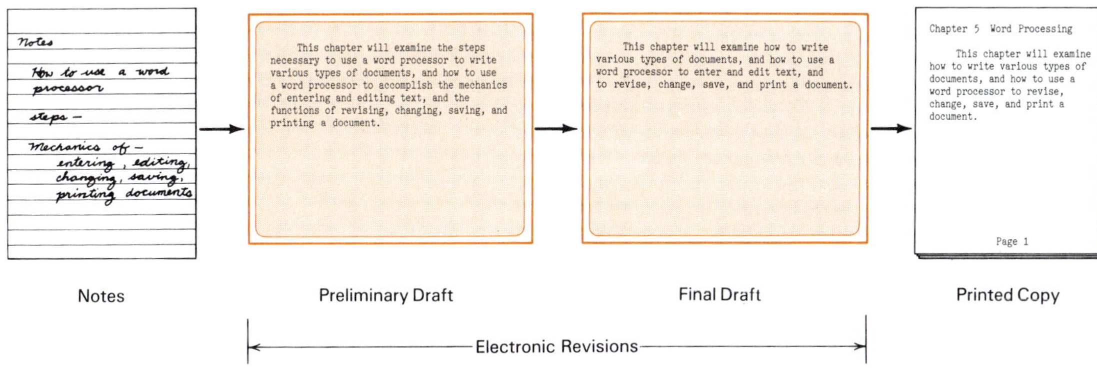

With a word processor, you do not have to retype the entire text in order to change or revise it. Revisions can be accomplished electronically.

report you just typed. You should save the document after each draft. Also remember that you can always use the *Revert to Last Version*. . . command in the File menu if you change your mind.

Find-and-Replace

Find-and-Replace is the capability of a word processor to search a document for a particular word or phrase, and to replace it wherever it occurs with another word or phrase you wish to substitute for it. A common use for Find-and-Replace is to correct a consistently misspelled word. Also, Find used by itself is sometimes more convenient than using the cursor-movement commands to scroll through a document.

Another common use for Find-and-Replace is to reduce the tedium of typing many repetitions of a frequently used phrase. For example, this chapter uses the term *word processor* over and over. In early drafts of the manuscript, we used the abbreviation *wp*. Later we used the Find-and-Replace function to substitute the full phrase for the abbreviation.

In the short report, we purposely used the old-fashioned spelling of the word *type-writer*. To replace it with the more modern spelling *typewriter*, use the following set of instructions:

1. Press the Esc key to toggle to the menu bar. Then move the pointer to the Find menu. Press the Down arrow key and highlight the *Find & Replace*. . . command as shown in Figure 6.2. Press the Return key.

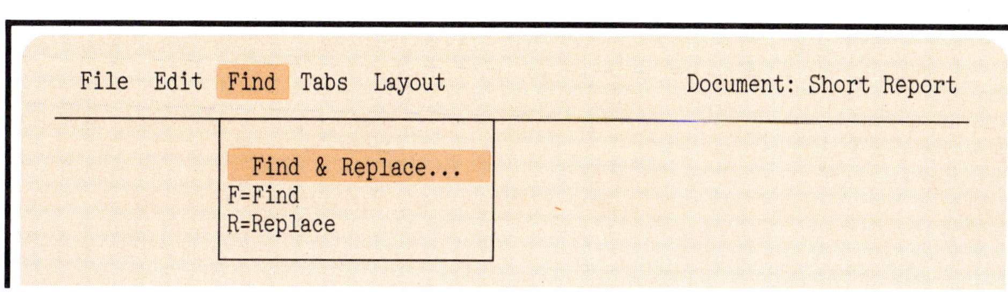

FIGURE 6.2 *The* Find & Replace. . . *command.*

2. A dialog box will appear, asking you to "Find what text?" Type in *type-writer*. The screen will look like Figure 6.3. Press the Tab key.

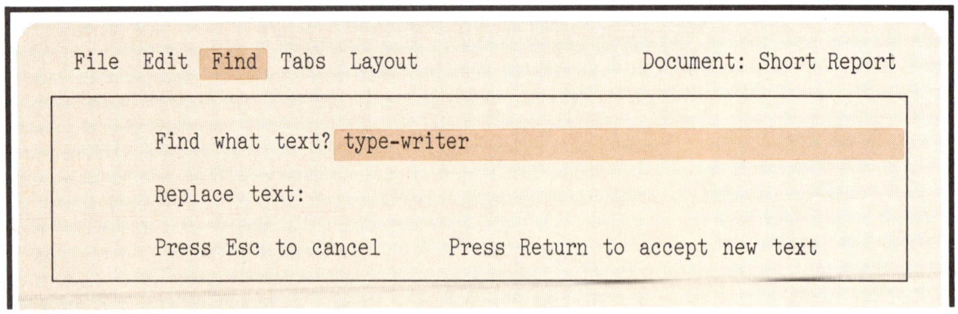

FIGURE 6.3 *Find & Replace dialog box after filling in find.*

3. The highlighted "Replace text:" line will appear. Type in *typewriter*, as shown in Figure 6.4, and press the Return key. The document will reappear on the screen. You have just set up the Find-and-Replace function.

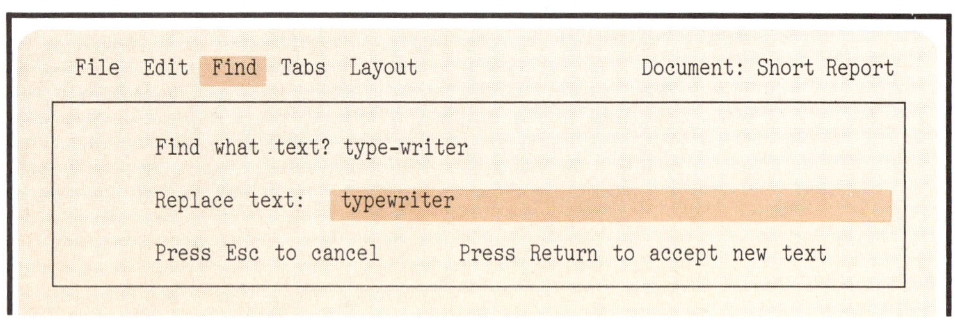

FIGURE 6.4 *Find & Replace dialog box after filling in replace.*

4. To execute the **Find command,** press the Esc key, move the pointer to the Find menu, and press the Down arrow key until the *F=Find* command is highlighted. Press the Return key.
5. The Find command searches forward from the cursor—that is, to the right of the cursor—until it finds the first occurrence of *type-writer*. When that text is found, it is highlighted. Figure 6.5 shows what you will see.
6. To replace the highlighted text, you use the **Replace command.** Press the Esc key, then move the pointer to the Find menu and down to the *R=Replace* command. Then press the Return key. The highlighted text will be replaced by *typewriter*.
7. To replace the other occurrences of *type-writer*, use the shortcut for the *F=Find* command by holding down the Control key while pressing the F key. The next occurrence of *type-writer* is then highlighted.
8. To replace, hold down the Control key while pressing the R key. The highlighted text will be replaced by *typewriter*. If, in a particular spot, you choose not to replace the original version, simply repeat the Find command and move on to the next occurrence.
9. Repeat the process, using the shortcut Find-and-Replace commands, to change all occurrences of *type-writer* to *typewriter*.

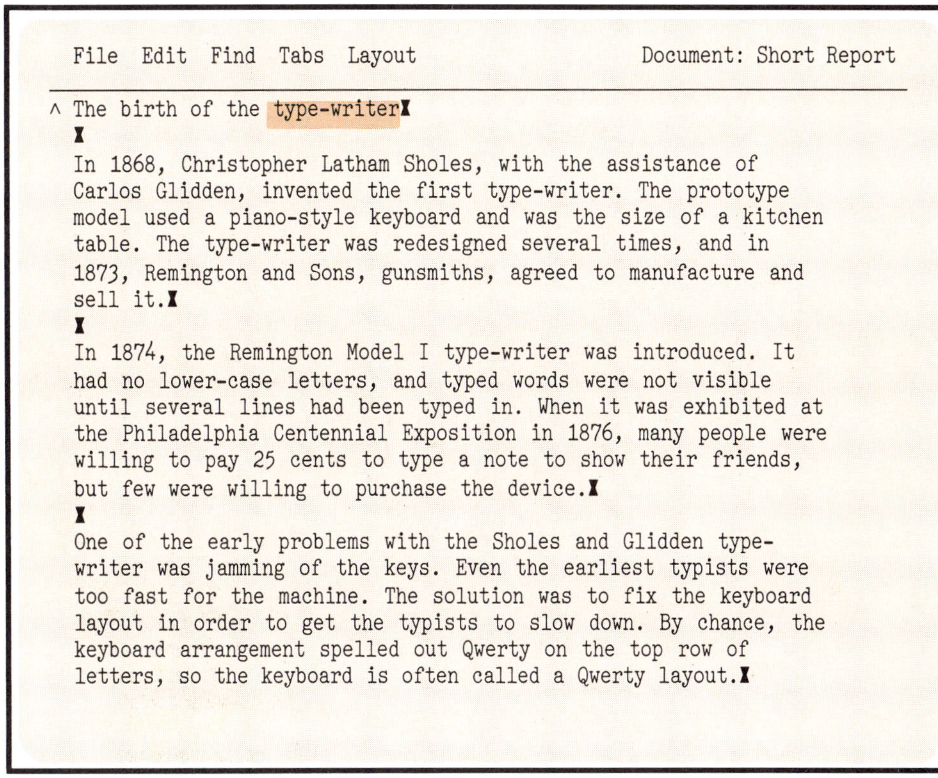

FIGURE 6.5 *Finding the first occurrence of type-writer.*

How will you know when all occurrences of a phrase have been found? You will know the search is complete when you execute an *F=Find* command and the cursor simply blinks and stays in the same spot. (The Find-and-Replace function not only searches forward from the position of the cursor; it also wraps around to the beginning of the document to perform a **global search** through the entire document.)

When the Find command locates a word or phrase, it is highlighted as a selection. This means that you can quit executing the Find command at any time by using the *S=Cancel Selection* command. The highlighting will disappear and the cursor will reappear in the position following the highlighting.

You can also use the Find command to search for a word or phrase, and then simply type in a replacement word or phrase, instead of using the Replace command. Table 6.1 summarizes the options available after the F=Find command has found a match.

TABLE 6.1 *Options after the F=Find command has found a match.*

Cursor location	Options
Cursor highlights the selected text	Repeat the Find command to search for the next occurrence. Quit the Find command by using the S = Cancel Selection command. Execute the R = Replace command. Type in a word or phrase of your choosing.

There are several matching techniques used in Find-and-Replace functions. The TriPac word processor uses a literal matching technique; that is, the text in the Find command must exactly match the text in the document for the command to work. For example, if you typed in *Type-writer* with an upper-case *T*, the Find command would search for that exact form, fruitlessly.

In commercial word processors, the Find command can often:

- Match text despite variations in upper- and lower-case. For example, it can find a word when it is capitalized at the beginning of a sentence, and also when it is lower-case.
- Match text even when it is embedded in another word. For example, if the text to be found is *find*, the Find command will search for any word that contains *find*, such as *finding*, *finds*, or *finder*.
- Match a portion of a word. For example, you might search for *pre** (the asterisk indicates that any valid characters may follow). The Find command would highlight any word that begins with those letters, such as *prepare*, *prepay*, or *presence*.

Writing Additional Drafts

As we said earlier, a word processor makes it easy to rearrange text for purposes of enhancing the document. For example, it is common to write a first draft single-spaced, then double-space later drafts.

Many word processors can display double and even triple spacing on the display screen. The TriPac word processor can print a double-spaced document, but only single spacing can be shown on the display screen. To double-space your short report:

1. Toggle to the menu bar, then move the pointer to the Layout menu and down to highlight the *Double Spaced* command, as shown in Figure 6.6.

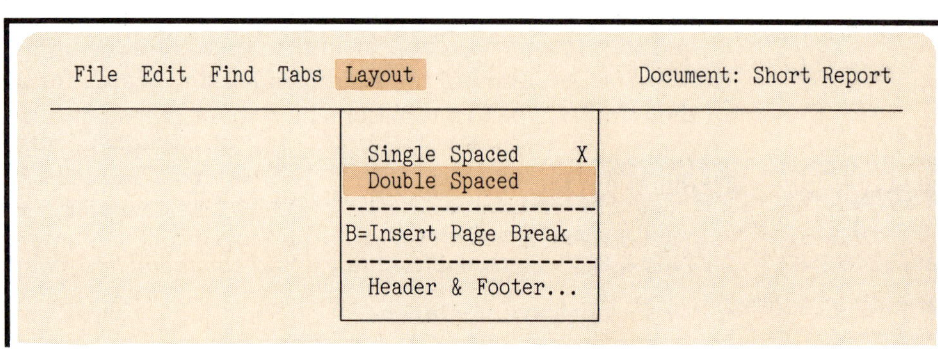

FIGURE 6.6 *The* Single *and* Double Spaced *commands.*

2. Notice that the pointer jumps over the *Single Spaced* command, which has an X next to it. This is an indication that the document is already single spaced, so the command cannot be selected.

3. Press the Return key to select double spacing. The document will not be reformatted on the screen, but the page-break symbol (^) will move to indicate the change in line spacing. When the document is printed, it will be double spaced.

Page Breaks

Most word processors have a fixed-length page, which usually corresponds to the length of a standard 11-inch piece of paper. A **page break** occurs where one page ends and another begins. This occurs automatically when a page is filled unless you override it with a **user-defined page break.**

There are many circumstances in which you will want to begin a new page, rather than filling up the preceding page. For example, in a document that contains chapters, you will want each chapter to begin at the top of a new page. You can do this by inserting a user-defined page break before the chapter title.

Figure 6.7 shows two conditions that sometimes occur when using a word processor, called **orphans** and **widows.** An orphan occurs when the first line of a paragraph falls at the bottom of a page. A widow occurs when the last line of a paragraph falls at the top of a page. User-defined page breaks can eliminate orphans and widows.

After you have double-spaced your short report, you can scroll through it and observe where the page-break symbol occurs. The first page-break symbol always appears at the beginning of a document. When the document was single

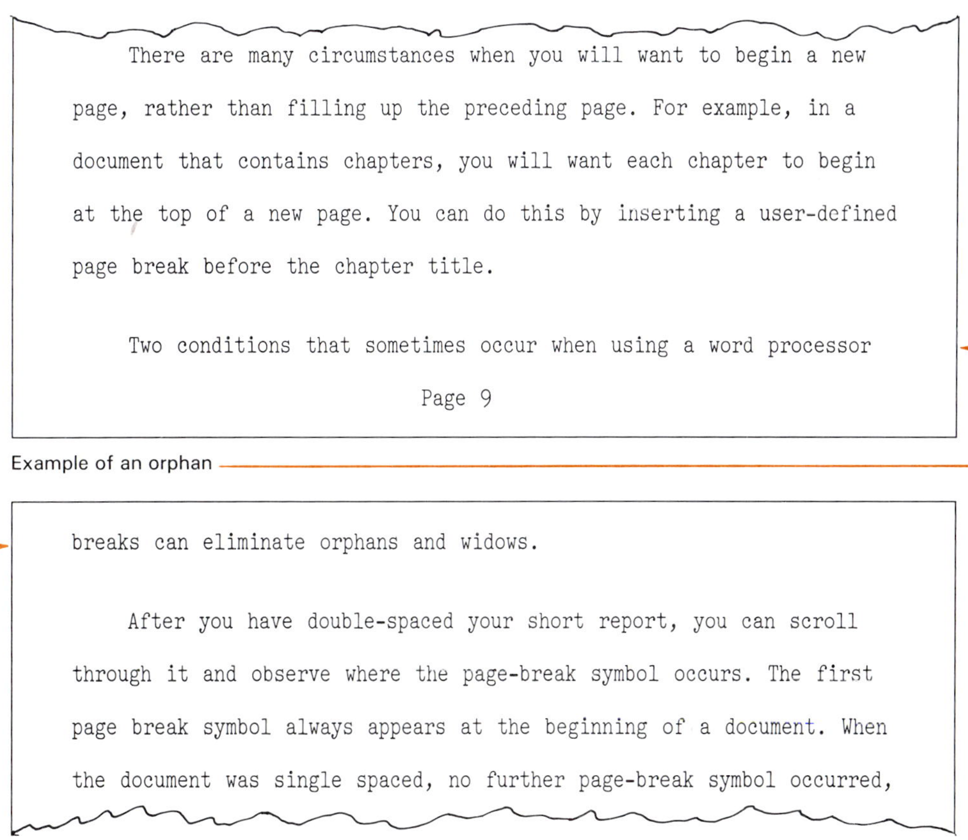

There are many circumstances when you will want to begin a new page, rather than filling up the preceding page. For example, in a document that contains chapters, you will want each chapter to begin at the top of a new page. You can do this by inserting a user-defined page break before the chapter title.

Two conditions that sometimes occur when using a word processor

Page 9

breaks can eliminate orphans and widows.

After you have double-spaced your short report, you can scroll through it and observe where the page-break symbol occurs. The first page break symbol always appears at the beginning of a document. When the document was single spaced, no further page-break symbol occurred,

FIGURE 6.7 *Examples of an orphan and a widow.*

spaced, no further page-break symbol occurred, because the short report was not longer than one printed page. When the short report is double spaced, a page break occurs in the middle of the last paragraph.

The *B=Insert Page Break* command in the Layout menu gives you the option of inserting user-defined page breaks at any point in your document. For example, to insert a page break after the second paragraph of your report:

1. Move the cursor to the paragraph mark that separates the second and third paragraphs of your report. Press the Esc key to toggle to the menu bar. Move the pointer to the Layout menu, then down to highlight the *B=Insert Page Break* command, as shown in Figure 6.8. Press the Return key. The user-defined page break will appear as a hyphenated line on the screen, like the one in Figure 6.9.

```
File  Edit  Find  Tabs  Layout                 Document: Short Report

                        Single Spaced     X
                        Double Spaced
                       ---------------------
                       B=Insert Page Break
                       ---------------------
                        Header & Footer...
```

FIGURE 6.8 *The* B = Insert Page Break *command.*

```
File  Edit  Find  Tabs  Layout                 Document: Short Report

^ The birth of the type-writer
  
  In 1868, Christopher Latham Sholes, with the assistance of
  Carlos Glidden, invented the first type-writer. The prototype
  model used a piano-style keyboard and was the size of a kitchen
  table. The type-writer was redesigned several times, and in
  1873, Remington and Sons, gunsmiths, agreed to manufacture and
  sell it.
  
  In 1874, the Remington Model I type-writer was introduced. It
  had no lower-case letters, and typed words were not visible
  until several lines had been typed in. When it was exhibited at
  the Philadelphia Centennial Exposition in 1876, many people were
  willing to pay 25 cents to type a note to show their friends,
  but few were willing to purchase the device.
  ---------------------------------------------------------------
^ 
  One of the early problems with the Sholes and Glidden type-
  writer was jamming of the keys. Even the earliest typists were
  too fast for the machine. The solution was to fix the keyboard
  layout in order to get the typists to slow down. By chance, the
  keyboard arrangement spelled out Qwerty on the top row of
  letters, so the keyboard is often called a Qwerty layout.
```

FIGURE 6.9 *The results of inserting a page break.*

2. A user-defined page break can be deleted, if you change your mind. To delete a user-defined page break, move the cursor to the line immediately below the line of hyphens. Then press the Delete key. The display will appear as it was before the page break was inserted.
3. The shortcut method for inserting a page break is to position the cursor where you want the page break to occur and hold down the Control key while pressing the B key.

Tabs

Tabs are stopping points along the horizontal dimension of a document. Used in conjunction with the Tab key, they mark the spot where the cursor will stop when the Tab key is pressed. Tabs are used to indent paragraphs, indent outlines, and align columns in a table. When you use these functions repeatedly, the Tab key is faster than the space bar. With the Tab function, you can set up or clear one or many tabs.

The most common application for tabs is indenting the first line of each paragraph. To do this in your short report:

1. Advance the cursor five spaces from the left margin.
2. Toggle to the menu bar. Then move the pointer to the Tabs menu and down to the *T=Set* command, and press the Return key.
3. The menu will retract, and a short vertical mark will appear five spaces from the left margin, on the line that divides the menu bar from the workspace, as shown in Figure 6.10.

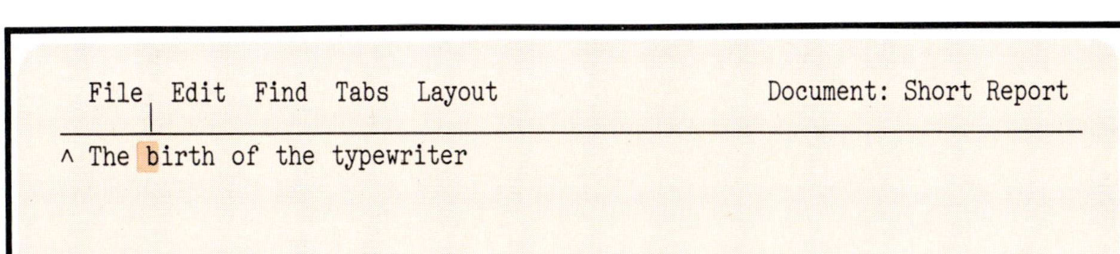

FIGURE 6.10 *A tab set five spaces from the left margin.*

4. Move the cursor to the first character in the first paragraph and press the Tab key. The first line of the paragraph will indent five spaces, and the rest of the paragraph will automatically adjust to reflect the change.
5. Continue indenting each of the other three paragraphs.

The shortcut method for setting tabs is to use the Control key in conjunction with the T key. Any number of tabs can be set in a document. Tabs that have been set can be cleared by moving the cursor to the position at which a tab is set, and either (1) selecting the T=Clear command in the Tabs menu or (2) holding down the Control key while pressing the T key. When you clear a tab, the text remains as it was after it was tabbed. In other words, if you clear the tabs in the short report, the paragraphs will remain indented, but any new paragraphs would not be indented.

The tabs you are using resemble typewriter tabs. Some word processors also have **decimal tabs**, which automatically line up a column of numbers on their decimal points.

Headers and Footers

A **header** is a line of text that appears at the top of each page. A **footer** is a line of text that appears at the bottom of each page. Headers and footers are entered into the document only once. The word processor inserts them on each page when the document is printed. You create headers and footers by using the *Header & Footer...* command in the Layout menu. To create a header for your sample report:

1. Toggle to the menu bar. Move the pointer to the Layout menu, then down to the *Header & Footer...* command. Press the Return key.
2. A dialog box like the one in Figure 6.11 will appear, asking you to type in the text of your header. Type in the name and number of this class. Then press the Tab key.

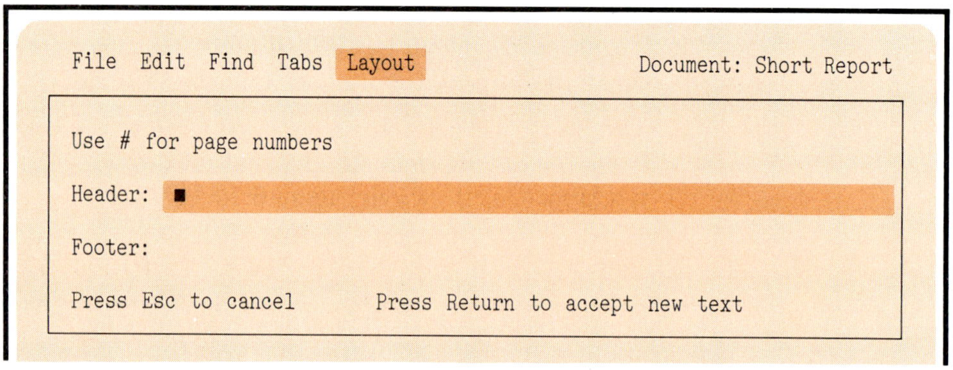

FIGURE 6.11 *Header & Footer dialog box.*

3. The footer line will then be highlighted. It is often sensible to use page numbers as footers. To instruct the word processor to number pages in the header or footer line, type in the word *Page* followed by a space and then the # character (upper-case 3). This tells the word processor to automatically number the pages, beginning with page 1. Then press the Return key.

The headers and footers do not appear in the screen display. They only appear when the document is printed. If you want a header but not a footer, simply press the Return key after typing in the text for the header.

Cutting and Pasting Between Documents

It can be useful when drafting a document to be able to take information from an existing document and paste it into the draft you are currently working on. The Cut-and-Paste and Copy-and-Paste commands can be used to transfer information from one document to another. To take a simple example, suppose you want to copy a name and address from the letter you wrote in the previous chapter, and paste it into the short report. If you are currently working with the Short Report, you must first quit the word processor to save your work, then open the Business Letter to begin copying. To do so:

1. Use the *Quit Word Processor* command to exit from the Short Report and save your work. From the Application Manager, open the document called Business Letter. Select the text to be copied (the recipient's name and address), and execute the *C=Copy* command. The selected text will be placed in the clipboard.
2. Then use the *Quit Word Processor* command to exit from the Business Letter. Re-open the Short Report document.
3. Position the cursor on the paragraph mark of the blank line following the title line, and type the word *by*. Then press the Return key to create another blank line.
4. With the cursor positioned on the paragraph mark of the next blank line, execute the *P=Paste* command. The text will be copied from the clipboard and pasted into the document.

In upcoming chapters, you will see how information can be cut or copied from a spreadsheet or database and pasted into a word-processing document.

Exercises with the Word Processor

- Print a double-spaced copy of the Short Report. Before printing, make sure you have formatted the document so that no paragraphs break in the middle of a page. In other words, look for the page-break symbol. If it appears next to a paragraph of text, move the cursor up to the beginning of the paragraph and insert a user-defined page break.
- Create a table similar to Figure 6.12. Use the Tab menu to set the tab stops for the table.
- Search the Short Report for the term *Qwerty* and replace it with all-caps *QWERTY.*

1990 National Baseball League Batting Averages

Player	Team	Average
Gorzowski	St. Louis	.451
Smith	New York	.406
Jones	Cincinnati	.403
Hopkins	St. Louis	.400
Lombard	Chicago	.391
Ross	Los Angeles	.387
Crichton	Los Angeles	.376
Bateson	Atlanta	.351
Fuller	Milwaukee	.349
Rifkin	Cleveland	.340

FIGURE 6.12 *Sample table with tabs set 5, 20, and 35 spaces from the left margin.*

Advanced Word-Processing Features

So far, we have been discussing the features basic to virtually all word processors. These features provide enough functionality, flexibility, and ease of use to meet the needs of most users. However, there are several advanced features that greatly enhance the process of creating and revising documents:

- Some documents are very complex and require features like automatic footnoting, indexing, proportional spacing, multiple columns, and differing typefaces and styles.
- Other advanced word-processing features are simply conveniences, such as spelling and style checkers, what-you-see-is-what-you-get displays, and windows.

The success with which these advanced features are implemented in various word processors varies enormously. The only way to evaluate how well these features are implemented is to do hands-on tests of the word processors that offer them.

Writing Enhancements

Writing enhancements consist of (1) "electronic proofreaders" that help you produce error-free documents, and (2) programs that automate the production of style elements like footnotes, a table of contents, and an index. Some word processors come with built-in enhancements. If an enhancement is not built-in, it can usually be purchased as a stand-alone program that processes a document after it has been created by the word processor.

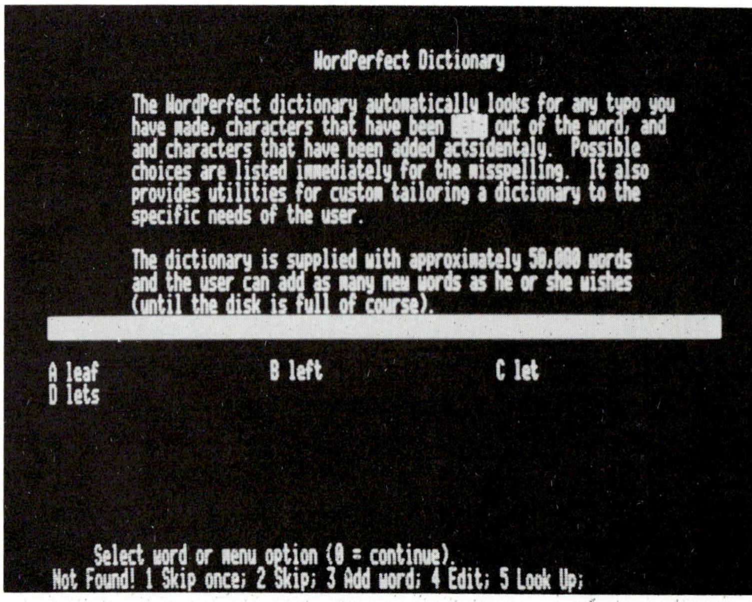

A spelling checker program compares words in a document with words in its own dictionary. Discrepancies are highlighted and the user can change the highlighted discrepancy.

Spelling Checkers

A **spelling checker** or spelling corrector is a program that checks documents for spelling errors. It works by comparing the words in your document with words in its own dictionary. Wherever it finds a discrepancy, it will stop and allow you to decide how to correct the discrepancy.

Some spelling checkers offer immediate correction: The discrepancy is highlighted on the screen, and the user decides whether to change or accept the highlighted discrepancy. In others, you mark the discrepancy and later use the word processor's editing features to correct any mistakes. Either way, quite a bit of manual intervention is involved in using most spelling checkers.

Style Checkers

More sophisticated electronic proofreaders, often called **style checkers,** automatically hyphenate words, point out punctuation errors, and check your writing style for awkward or redundant usage and excessively wordy phrases. These programs work like spelling checkers. They compare your document to a set of style and grammar rules, highlight the discrepancies, and give you the choice of accepting or rejecting the highlighted discrepancy.

Contents, Footnotes, and Indexes

Other advanced writing enhancements enable you to create footnotes, tables of contents, and indexes. Some word processors offer a feature called "floating footnotes." You simply type the number and the footnote as you type the text. The word processor takes care of "floating" the footnote to the bottom of the appropriate page, the end of the chapter, or the end of the document. If you change the document, such as by adding or deleting text, the footnotes are automatically floated to the proper position when the document is repaginated.

A table of contents is a list of the major headings in a document, in order of appearance, along with their page numbers. Some word processors can automatically generate a table of contents, with appropriate page numbers, if you mark the entries you want to include.

An index is an alphabetically arranged list of topics, with page numbers, located at the end of a document. Some word processors allow you to mark words in the text for automatic indexing. Others automatically index every word in the document, and allow you to exclude those that don't belong (such as *a, and, the*, and so on). The latter technique is much faster than marking each word individually.

Printing Enhancements

In the 1960s and 1970s, the design of word processors was strongly influenced by the electric typewriter. In those days, the market for word processors was in business offices; most users were secretaries. A "good" word processor's printed output emulated the output of an electric typewriter. In fact, "letter-quality" printers derive their name from the resemblance of their printing to the output of an electric typewriter.

If you compare typewritten and typeset text (such as the text you are now reading), you will see that typeset words are easier to read and more aesthetically pleasing. Also, a variety of typefaces and sizes can be used to create

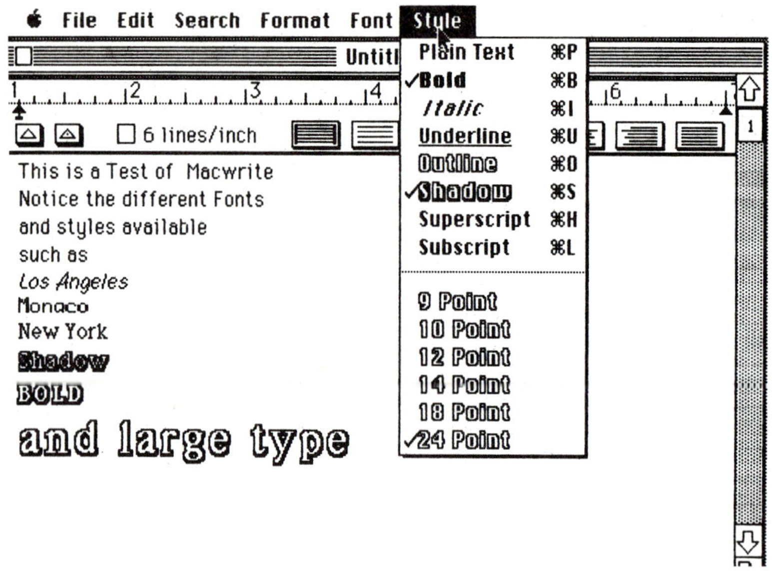

A sample of the different typefaces and sizes available with Apple's MacWrite word processor for the Macintosh.

more interesting and informative written communications. However, typesetting is expensive. It is only economically practical when a large number of copies are going to be printed.

Advances in personal-computer printer technology, first in dot-matrix printers and then in laser printers, have made it possible to approach the quality of typesetting. With a word processor that supports advanced printing features, it is possible to consider the following:

- Proportional spacing, or the use of variable-width letters as in typeset text. For example, because the letter *M* is wider than the letter *I*, it would be allotted more space when using proportional spacing.
- Mixing styles and sizes of type to give greater impact to the printed word.
- Changing the layout of the printed page (printing two or three columns of text, or adding graphics).

When typography, layout, and graphics are combined effectively, the expressive power that is possible with a word processor is far greater than can be achieved with the printed word alone.

Display Enhancements

Though the end product of word processing is a printed document, writing with a word processor involves interaction with the display screen. Most word processors can print such graphic elements as boldfacing and underlining, but cannot yet show these features on the display screen. Advances in graphic-display hardware, such as add-on graphic adapter boards and special video processors, are enhancing display.

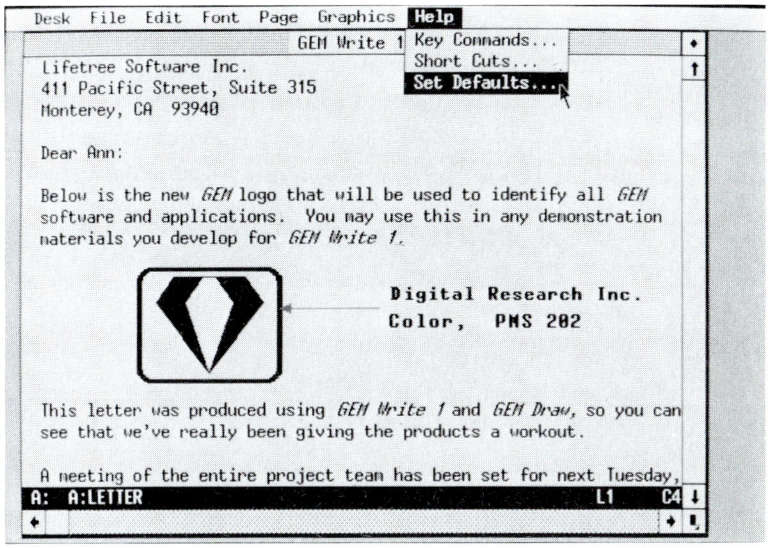

Graphic elements can greatly enhance the display of a document on the screen.

What You See Is What You Get

Some word processors offer **what-you-see-is-what-you-get** or **WYSIWYG** display, which resembles as closely as possible what will eventually be printed. Word processors that use this approach use graphics software to display text. For example, Microsoft Word uses graphics characters to display a true rendition of **boldface,** *italics,* SMALL CAPS, underlining, and superscripts and subscripts on the display screen. MacWrite, a Macintosh word processor, also uses this approach. When formatting a document with one of these word processors, the user sees on the screen an almost exact version of what will appear on the printed page.

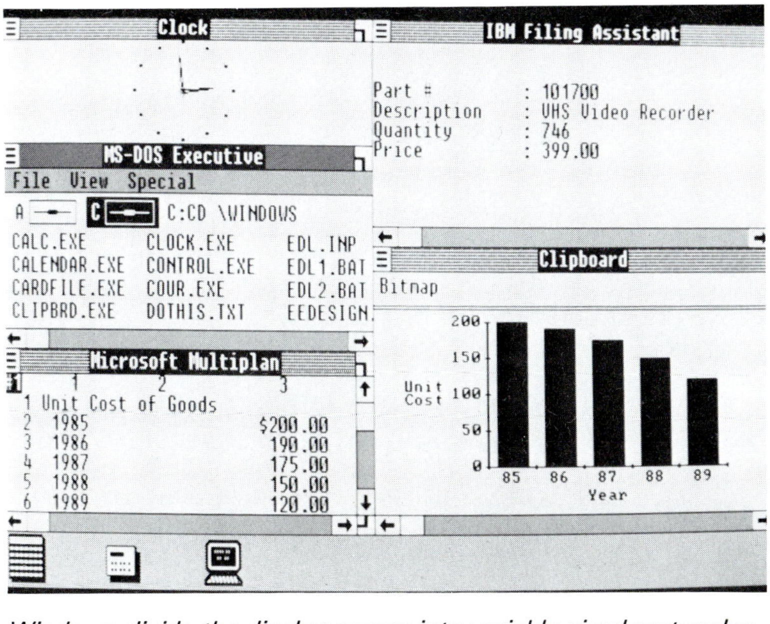

Windows divide the display screen into variable-sized rectangles.

Windows

Windows are a technique that word processors use to divide the display screen into variable-sized rectangles in order to view different parts of a document, or two or more documents, simultaneously. Windows make it easier to use Cut-and-Paste or Copy-and-Paste within a large document. You can look at different parts of a document on the display screen while deciding what to cut or copy. Windows also make it easier to Cut-and-Paste and Copy-and-Paste between two different documents.

REVIEW AND SELF-TESTING

Key Terms

- Find-and-Replace
- Find command
- Replace command
- Global search
- Page break
- User-defined page break
- Orphan
- Widow
- Tabs
- Decimal tabs
- Header
- Footer
- Spelling checker
- Style checker
- What you see is what you get (WYSIWYG)
- Windows

Questions for Review and Discussion

1. Why is a word processor a good tool for revising drafts of documents?
2. Name two occasions when you might use Find-and-Replace while revising a document with a word processor.
3. Name two occasions when you might want to insert a user-defined page break in a document.
4. Where are headers and footers located on a printed page?
5. What is the difference between a spelling checker and a style checker?
6. What advances allow word processors to emulate the printing quality of typesetting?
7. Name some of the ways that printing enhancements give more impact to the printed word.
8. Describe some of the formatting differences in the TriPac word processor between text as shown on the display screen and printed text.

Exercises with the Word Processor

1. Create and print your own résumé. Use the résumé shown in Chapter 4 on page 77 as a style guide.
2. Write and print a two-page double-spaced paper on the benefits of word processing. Include headers and footers.
3. Rearrange the Short Report by cutting the second paragraph and pasting it in following the third paragraph.

7

Introducing Spreadsheets

PREVIEW

As you already know, spreadsheets are software packages that help you perform calculations you would otherwise do with a pencil and paper or a calculator. A spreadsheet is a general-purpose problem-solving tool: It does for calculating what a word processor does for writing. You enter the numbers and formulas, and it shows you the results on the screen and in printed form.

A spreadsheet also gives you instant feedback on the effects of any changes you decide to make. It eliminates the time-consuming part of making revisions, by recalculating the results automatically.

This chapter will show you how to design a spreadsheet, and how to enter numbers, formulas, and text. Then we'll look at how to use the spreadsheet as an analytical tool for solving number-oriented problems.

In this chapter, you'll discover:

- *The concepts embodied in electronic spreadsheets*
- *Some uses for spreadsheets*
- *How to design a spreadsheet*
- *How to build a spreadsheet model*
- *The process of entering numbers, formulas, and text*
- *Editing and correcting mistakes*
- *What-if analysis*

Spreadsheets and Problem Solving

Spreadsheet programs, also called electronic spreadsheets and simply spreadsheets, help solve problems that can be represented with numbers and formulas. An electronic spreadsheet is a computerized version of the traditional accountant's paper worksheet, which organizes numerical information in rows and columns.

A spreadsheet program creates an electronic worksheet, which the user manipulates with the help of the program. The worksheet can store numbers, formulas, and words, and the program can perform automatic calculations and save the results for future reference.

Similar numerical-analysis software has long been available for larger computer systems, but it required a programmer to define the structure of the problem, and to enter the numbers and formulas. This meant that end users such as managers and accountants had to rely on their programming staffs to create and manipulate the programs.

Because spreadsheets are interactive and fairly easy to use, they put analysis back into the hands of the end user. The user can simply run the spreadsheet program and begin solving the problem, without having to learn a programming language.

The first step in solving a problem, whether on paper or with a spreadsheet program, is to structure the problem and its solution. In the case of number-based problems, this involves building a **numeric model** of a real-world situation. For example, to balance your checking account, you gather the existing data—the deposit slips and the cancelled checks—and sort them in sequence. Then you add the amount of the deposits and subtract the amount of the written checks.

Most people do this in a checkbook register, which consists of vertical columns for addition, subtraction, and the balance, and horizontal rows for listing

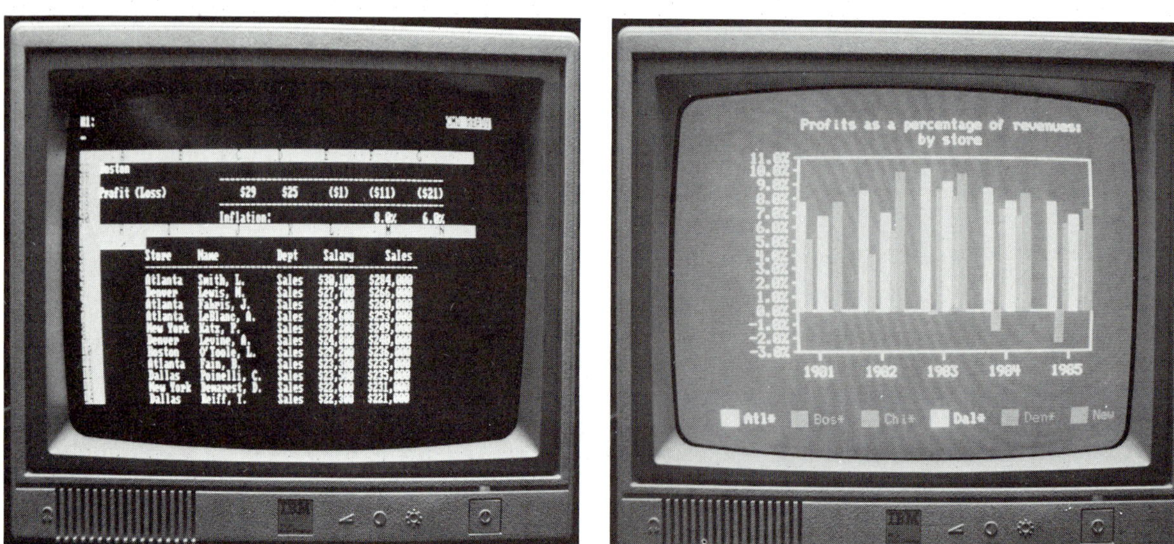

Spreadsheet programs help solve problems that can be represented with numbers and formulas. The results are most often displayed as an electronic worksheet, but in some instances, can be displayed as a graph or chart.

each check and deposit. But you could also build a spreadsheet model of your checking account. To build the model, you type numbers, formulas, and labels into the electronic worksheet. Once the model is built and the data entered, the spreadsheet program will take care of performing the calculations.

What other kind of models might a spreadsheet user build?

- Financial planners use spreadsheets to construct forecasts. For example, a manager could enter this year's sales figures and a formula for projected growth over the next five years. The program could then compute the sales forecast, and adjust cost figures accordingly.
- Managers use spreadsheets to help prepare budgets. As you saw in Chapter 4, alternative budgets can be analyzed by simply changing budget values.
- Accountants use spreadsheets to do tax planning and to compile income statements, profit-and-loss statements, and balance sheets.
- Scientists use spreadsheets to analyze the results of experiments.

A spreadsheet program is a general-purpose problem-solving tool because it is an excellent medium for (1) building a numeric model, (2) asking "What if a value or several values in the model change?" and then (3) entering the new value(s) and watching the program recalculate the model. The interactive nature of the spreadsheet program allows you to compare the results of alternative models.

The Electronic Worksheet

Let's take a look at the worksheet now, to see how the spreadsheet program uses it. This is a hands-on exercise. To begin, you should have the TriPac software up and running on the computer, with the Application Manager visible on-screen. To create a new spreadsheet:

1. Open the first untitled spreadsheet.
2. A dialog box will appear, asking you to name the spreadsheet you are about to open. Type in *Test Spreadsheet*, and press the Return key.

What You Will See

Take a look at Figure 7.1. On the first line of the display, you will see the menu bar for the spreadsheet program. Directly below the horizontal line is the **edit line.** The left side of the edit line contains the **cell reference,** which tells you the location of the **active cell** (in this case, A1). To the right of the cell reference, the line is empty. This means that nothing has been entered into the active cell. On the right side of the edit line, you will see the word *Empty.*

The **electronic worksheet** is displayed on the screen as horizontal rows and vertical columns. The intersection of each row and column is called a **cell.** In most worksheets, like this one, the rows are numbered on the left margin, and the columns are labeled with letters on the top margin. The cell where column A and row 1 intersect is called cell A1. The column letter is always specified first.

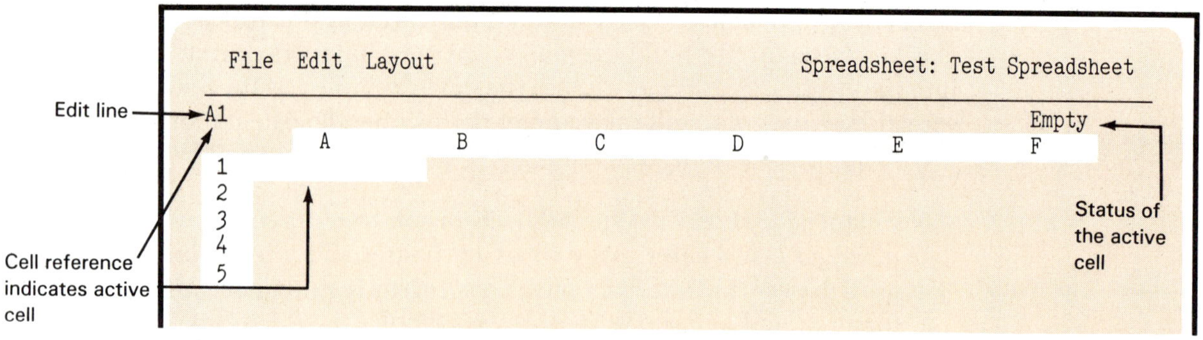

FIGURE 7.1 *The edit line.*

Moving Around in the Worksheet

The TriPac worksheet is 52 columns wide by 254 rows long. Some commercial spreadsheet programs have hundreds of columns and thousands of rows, to accommodate very large models, such as the financial workings of an entire corporation. For instance, the worksheet of Microsoft Excel, a commercial spreadsheet program, has 256 columns by 16,384 rows.

But even a small worksheet is too large to be displayed on the screen all at once. **Scrolling** brings hidden portions of the worksheet into view. The Up, Down, Left, and Right arrow keys move the cursor around the worksheet. The key in conjunction with the Up, Down, Left, and Right arrow keys moves the cursor screen by screen. You can also go to a specific cell in the worksheet by using the *G = Goto Cell...* command in the Edit menu. To see how this works:

1. Press the Esc key to toggle to the menu bar. In the Edit menu, highlight the *G = Goto Cell...* command, and press the Return key.
2. A dialog box will appear, asking you to enter the location of the cell to which you want to go. Enter A254 and press the Return key. The worksheet will scroll vertically down, and the cursor will jump down to the bottom cell in the first column, cell A254.
3. Now use the shortcut method by holding down the Control key while pressing the G key. The Goto cell dialog box will appear. Enter ZZ254 and press the Return key. The worksheet will scroll to the left, and the cursor will jump down to the bottom cell in the last column, cell ZZ254.
4. Repeat the procedure to scroll the spreadsheet to the top cell in the last column, cell ZZ1, and then to the top cell in the first column, cell A1.

When the cursor is located on a cell, that cell is active, meaning that you can enter a number, formula, or text into it. The active cell is highlighted in reverse video.

Entering Information Into the Worksheet

Suppose you want to use a spreadsheet to solve the problem of adding two numbers. A general-purpose solution to this problem would be to place the first number in cell A1, the second number in cell A2, and the sum in cell A3. Cells A1 and A2 would contain the numbers to be added, and cell A3 would contain the formula A1 + A2.

1. Position the cursor to highlight cell A1. Then type in the number *4*, and press the Return key. The cursor will drop to cell A2, and the number 4.00 will appear in cell A1. (Note that numbers default to two decimal places. We will show you how to change the default in the next chapter.)
2. With the cursor on cell A2, type in the number 5, and press the Return key. The number 5.00 will appear in cell A2, and the cursor will drop to cell A3.
3. In cell A3, type an = sign immediately followed by *a1* + *a2*. (It doesn't matter whether the letters are capital or lower-case.) Then press the Return key. The number 9.00 will appear in cell A3, and the cursor will drop to cell A4.

The spreadsheet program automatically calculated the sum, 9.00, and displayed it in cell A3. However, the worksheet is more than just an electronic calculator. It keeps track of the relationships between the various numbers and formulas. If a number changes, the formulas that use that number are automatically recalculated. For example, move the cursor to cell A1. Notice that the number 4 appears in the edit line. Now type in the number 5 and press the Return key. Notice that the number in cell A3 also changes, from 9.00 to 10.00. Changing the number in cell A1 causes the number displayed in cell A3 to change automatically.

Entering numbers into a worksheet creates **static values.** In other words, they don't change unless you manually enter a new number. Entering formulas, by contrast, creates **dynamic values.** Dynamic values change automatically if the values that created them change. Formulas use standard arithmetic operations (+ , − , *, /), numbers, and references to other cells.

We used cells A1, A2, and A3 in the previous example because it is conventional to add numbers in vertical columns. But we could just as well have used cell A2 for the first number, cell B2 for the second number, and cell C2 for the formula A2 + B2. Horizontal arithmetic is often used in worksheets when the data are chronological. For example, a monthly budget might label 12 columns in a worksheet with the names of the months. In fact, horizontal and vertical arithmetic are often used together. To see how this works:

1. Move the cursor to cell B1, and type in the number 5. This time press the Tab key. The number 5.00 will appear in cell B1, and the cursor will move right to cell C1.
2. With the cursor on cell C1, type in the formula = *a1* + *b1* and press the Tab key. The number 10.00 will appear in cell C1, and the cursor will move right to cell D1.
3. Now, using the left arrow key, move the cursor back to cell A1. Type in the number *4* and press the Return key. Note that both cells A3 and C1 are automatically recalculated.

Editing the Worksheet

In most spreadsheet programs, the information you type is not entered directly into a cell. Until you enter it by moving the cursor to another cell, it remains in the edit line. As long as the cell is active, you can edit its contents in the edit line.

If you want to change the information in the active cell, the process is similar to editing with the word processor.

Position the cursor on cell A1. To activate the edit line, toggle to the menu bar. In the Edit menu, highlight the E = Edit Current Cell command. You can now correct an error in the active cell by using the Left and Right arrow keys and the Delete key. Try pressing the Delete key to erase a character.

The shortcut way to activate the edit line is to hold down the Control key and press the E key. Alternatively, you can simply retype the entire contents of the edit line without activating the Edit Current Cell command.

You can erase the contents of the active cell by pressing the space bar. The contents of the edit line will disappear, and when you move the cursor, the cell will be empty.

When you are finished typing, correcting mistakes, or undoing mistakes, press the Return or Tab key to enter the information into the active cell.

Information is entered into the active cell (sometimes called **updating** the active cell) when you move the cursor to select another cell. There are several ways to do this:

- Pressing the Return key causes the cursor to jump down one cell. (When the active cell is A1, pressing the Return key moves the cursor to cell A2.)
- Pressing the Tab key causes the cursor to jump to the right one cell. (When the active cell is A1, pressing the Tab key jumps the cursor to cell B1.)
- Pressing the Up arrow key causes the cursor to jump up one cell. Pressing the Down arrow key causes the cursor to jump down one cell. The Left and Right arrow keys will not cause cursor movement when the editing function has been activated.

Any cell can contain text instead of a number or a formula. Text is used in a worksheet for labels, such as row and column headings; to block off certain areas, such as by inserting a row of dashes between a column of numbers and a total; or to include explanations or other remarks. Typing text in a cell is much more constraining than typing text into a word-processing document. For example:

1. Move the cursor to cell A4, and type in the letters of the alphabet *a* through *z*. Press the Return key. The cursor will drop to cell A5, and only the first 12 letters (*a-l*) will be displayed in cell A4. This is because the column width has been preset to 12 positions. In the next chapter, we will show you how to change the column width.
2. If you move the cursor back to cell A4, you will see that none of the letters you typed in are lost. They are still visible in the edit line.

To leave the spreadsheet, press the Esc key and then the Down arrow key, and select the *Quit Spreadsheet* command. Press the Return key. The spreadsheet will disappear, and the Application Manager will reappear. When the red light on the disk drive goes off, press the Esc key and then the Down arrow key again, and select the *Delete. . .* command to delete the test spreadsheet. A dialog box will appear, asking "Delete the spreadsheet named 'Test Spreadsheet'?" Press Return to delete the spreadsheet.

A Sample Spreadsheet Problem

Now let us use the fundamental operations you have learned to build a spreadsheet model. You are already familiar with receipts that accompany consumer purchases. The general format of such receipts is illustrated in Figure 7.2.

In this example, you will practice the mechanics of entering numbers, formulas, and text into a worksheet; changing the values; watching the program recalculate values; and saving and printing the worksheet.

Designing the Layout

The first step in building a receipt spreadsheet model is to design the layout of the model. Then, by figuring out the relationships within the data, you can specify the formulas in the model. Begin by using a paper worksheet to lay out the model. You can use the paper worksheet in Figure 7.3 if you wish.

Note the empty three lines at the top of the sample worksheet. You will use those lines later to add some more information. Since the layout of the worksheet is already given in Figure 7.3, you can begin developing the formulas to calculate the Amount, Subtotal, Tax, and Total cells.

When working with spreadsheet programs, it is important to distinguish the name of a cell (its column and row coordinates, such as A1) from the value or contents of the cell (such as the number 4). In a cell that contains a formula, the value of the cell is the number that the formula results in. (When a formula references an empty cell or a text cell, the value of the cell is 0.)

Formulas use names of cells, numeric values, and arithmetic operations. Some of the arithmetic symbols they use may be unfamiliar to you. Spreadsheet programs use * instead of × to signify multiplication, and / to represent division.

```
Quantity  Description                         Price      Amount
---------------------------------------------------------------

       2  Box Disks                           29.95       59.90
       1  Box Paper                           39.95       39.95
       2  Magazines                            2.50        5.00

                                          Sub
                                          Total      104.85
                                          Tax (5%)     5.24
                                          ----------------------
                                          TOTAL      110.09
```

FIGURE 7.2 *Sample receipt.*

	A	B	C	D	E	F
1						
2						
3						
4	QUANTITY	DESCRIPTION		PRICE	AMOUNT	
5	------	------	------	------	-----	
6						
7						
8						
9						
10						
11				SUB		
12				TOTAL		
13				TAX (5%)		
14				-----	------	
15				TOTAL		
16						
17						
18						
19						

FIGURE 7.3 *A paper worksheet.*

When working with formulas, it is also important to remember the hierarchy of arithmetic operations. The rules are as follows:

- Operations inside parentheses are performed first.
- Multiplication and division are performed next.
- Addition and subtraction are performed last.

As the following examples show, the order in which operations are performed can affect the outcome:

```
10-5 * 2=0
(10-5) * 2=10
```

If you want an operation or series of operations to be performed first, enclose it in parentheses. When one set of parentheses occurs inside another set of parentheses, the inner set of operations is performed first. Now let's go back to Figure 7.3.

The Amount is determined by multiplying Quantity by Price. For the first item sold, the Amount will appear in cell E6. The formula for cell E6 is = A6 * D6.

(We will consistently use capital letters in cell references, but capital letters in a formula are optional, as is the use of spaces.) Enter the corresponding formulas for Amount into cells E6, E7, and E8.

The Subtotal in cell E12 is determined by adding the individual Amounts. The formula for cell E12 is = E6 + E7 + E8.

The Tax is computed by multiplying the Subtotal by .05, so the formula for cell E13 is = E12 * .05.

Finally, the TOTAL is the sum of the Subtotal and the Tax, represented by the formula = E12 + E13.

Building a Spreadsheet Model

Once you have figured out the layout and the formulas, you are ready to begin building the actual spreadsheet. Use the paper worksheet as a guide in setting up the on-screen worksheet.

1. Move the pointer to the first untitled spreadsheet.
2. Press the Esc key to toggle to the menu bar.
3. The pointer will be on the File menu; move it down to the *O = Open* command, and press the Return key.
4. A dialog box will appear, asking you to name the spreadsheet you are about to open. Type in *Receipt*, and press the Return key.

Entering Text

To begin building the receipt, move the cursor to cell A4. Type in the word *Quantity*. Note that the word appears on the edit line to the right of the cell reference; nothing appears yet in cell A4 itself. A value will only appear in the active cell when you have completed the entry and moved to the next cell.

If you make any spelling errors, you can use the Left arrow key or the Delete key to position the typing cursor over the mistake and type in the correction. When you have finished typing in your first entry, press the Tab key to move the cursor to the right. The word *Quantity* will appear in cell A4, and the cursor will move to cell B4. On the right-hand margin of the edit line, the word *Empty* will reappear.

Type in the word *Description* and press the Tab key. Your entry will appear in cell B4, and the cursor will move to cell C4. Leave cell C4 empty by pressing the Tab key again, and position the cursor on cell D4. Type in the word *Price*. Continue on to cell E4, and type in the word *Amount*.

To insert a dashed line in row 5, move the cursor to cell A5 and type in twelve hyphens. Press the Tab key and repeat the process. Continue until you have filled in cell E5. Then move to cell D11, and finish typing in the layout of the receipt.

Entering Formulas

Move the cursor to cell E6, and type in the formula *=A6 * D6*. This formula tells the spreadsheet program to multiply the contents of cells A6 and D6, and display the results in cell E6. The = sign informs the program that the active cell will contain a formula, not text or a number.

When you have checked the edit line for errors, press the Tab key. Since cell E6 displays the result of the formula (rather than the formula itself), and there are not yet values in cells A6 and D6 to multiply, the value of cell E6 is 0. Type in the formulas for cells E7 and E8; then type in the formulas for cells E12, E13, and E15. Note that the formula for cell E13 is slightly different from the others: It contains the number .05, in addition to a cell reference.

Entering Numbers

Entering a number into a cell is very straightforward. Use the sample data supplied in Figure 7.2. Move the cursor to cell A6 and enter the number *2*. When you press the Tab key, cell A6 will be updated to reflect your entry.

Move the cursor to cell B6 and type in the text *Box Disks*. Then move the cursor to cell D6 and type in the number *29.95*. Press the Down arrow key. Now that enough data has been entered to recalculate the formulas in cells E6, E12, E13, and E15, numbers will appear in the Amount, Subtotal, Tax, and TOTAL cells.

Move the cursor to cell A7 and type in the number *1*. Then move the cursor to cell B7 and type in the text *Box Paper*. Next move the cursor to cell D7 and type in the number *39.95*. When you move the cursor, every dependent cell in the worksheet will be recalculated. Finish typing in the sample data from Figure 7.2. The completed receipt spreadsheet is shown in Figure 7.4.

Recalculating the Worksheet

To see how the worksheet changes when new information is substituted, enter the following data in the appropriate cells in row 6:

```
4 Ribbons  7.95
```

Note that entering a new number in the Quantity cell causes an immediate recalculation of the worksheet. However, the entry is not yet complete, so the recalculation is not correct. When a spreadsheet automatically recalculates, you have to be careful to then finish entering all the new data. In this case, the new Price has to be entered to obtain correct figures in the Amount, Subtotal, Tax, and TOTAL cells. Figure 7.5 shows the recalculated receipt spreadsheet.

Saving and Printing the Spreadsheet

When you execute the *Quit Spreadsheet* command in the File menu, the spreadsheet will automatically be saved on disk, and you will be returned to the Application Manager. However, if you want to save the spreadsheet before quitting the spreadsheet program:

1. Press the Esc key to toggle to the menu bar.
2. Press the Down arrow key to select the *Save Spreadsheet* command.
3. Press the Return key to execute the command.

The cursor will return to the previous position in the spreadsheet. To print the spreadsheet:

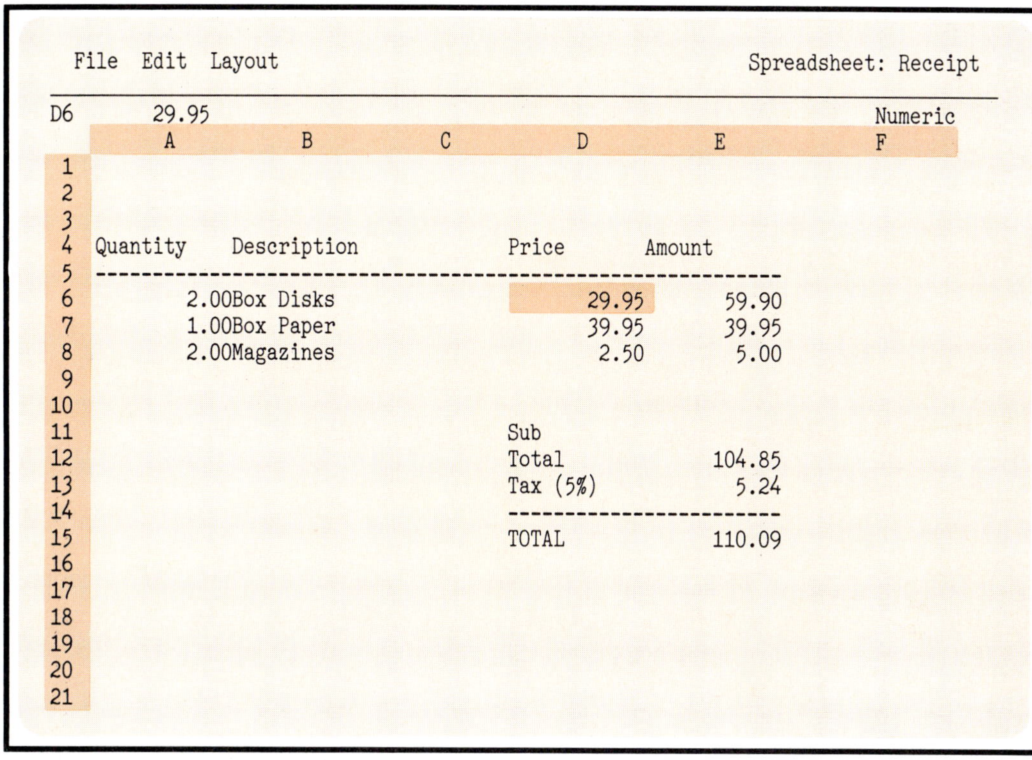

FIGURE 7.4 *Completed receipt spreadsheet.*

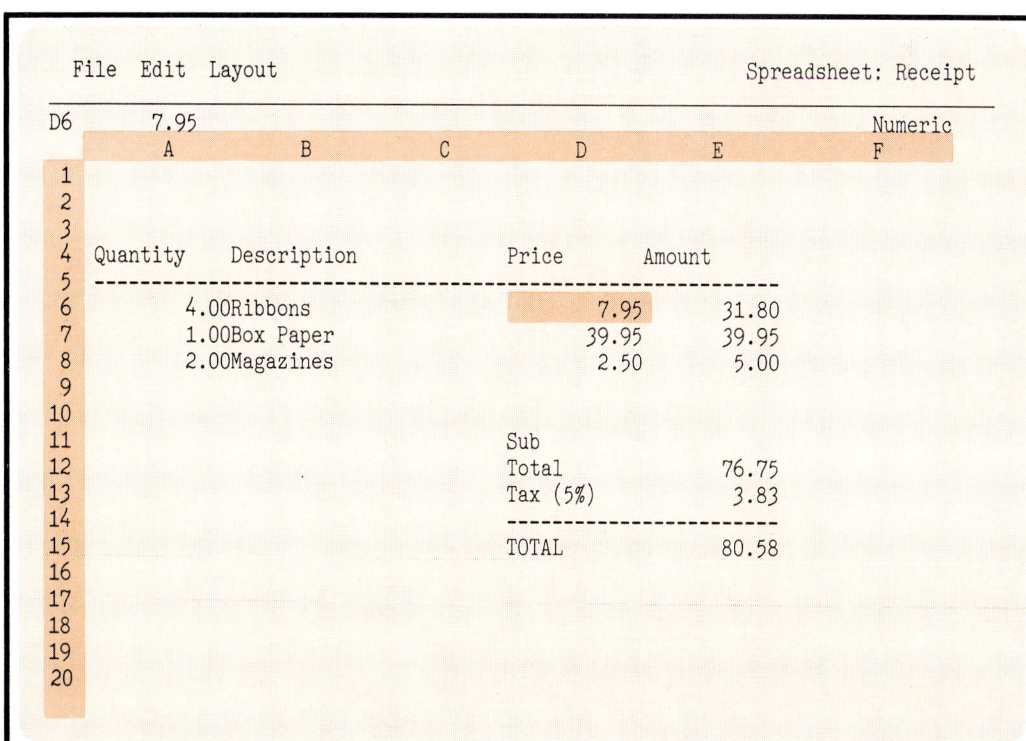

FIGURE 7.5 *Recalculated receipt spreadsheet.*

1. Press the Esc key to toggle to the menu bar. Then press the Down arrow key and select the *Print Spreadsheet...* command. Press the Return key.
2. A dialog box will appear, asking you to press Return to print the first page of the spreadsheet. Make sure that the printer is ready before pressing the Return key.

Exercises with the Spreadsheet

- On the Receipt spreadsheet, add your name on row 1 and the title and number of this class on row 2. Remember that for now each cell can only display 12 characters.
- Change the format of the spreadsheet to calculate a 10 percent discount on all purchases. To do so, replace cell D13 with the text *Less 10%;* then replace cell E13 with a formula that subtracts 10 percent of the subtotal amount. Then change the rest of the spreadsheet so that the tax is calculated on the discounted amount and the TOTAL reflects the discount.
- When you have finished making these changes, print a copy of your Receipt spreadsheet and hand it in to your instructor.

What-If Analysis

Using a spreadsheet to compare alternatives is often called **what-if analysis.** Because the spreadsheet keeps track of the relationships among the numbers in your worksheet, you can forecast alternative outcomes by asking "What if a certain number changes?" and letting the program recalculate your worksheet.

For example, suppose you are given the task of forecasting your company's overall sales-and-profit picture for the next two years. Figure 7.6 shows the results for 1987 and the forecasts for the upcoming two years. According to your boss's best estimates, sales should increase by 10 percent a year for the next two years; meanwhile, the cost of materials, labor, and overhead is estimated to increase by 20 percent a year.

This exercise will show you how to build a spreadsheet to analyze alternative forecasts. You will build a model for the years 1987, 1988, and 1989. The model will project dollar amounts for each year, and you will use it to look at the effects of variations in sales and costs.

As before, building the model begins with figuring out the layout of the worksheet and the formulas. Use the sample layout in Figure 7.6 to begin building the model. First, you want to find out what the dollar amounts of sales, materials, labor, overhead, and profit will be in 1988 and 1989, if the projected increases prove correct. You also want to project the dollar amounts that would result from other rates of increase in sales, materials, labor, and overhead.

More on Numbers and Formulas

For purposes of this exercise, profit equals sales minus the sum of materials, labor, and overhead. In other words, the formula for profits in 1988 (cell C10) would be: cell C5 minus the sum of cells C6, C7, and C8.

	A	B	C	D	E	F
1	THREE – YEAR FORECAST					
2						
3		1987	1988 est	1989 est		
4	------	------	------	------		
5	SALES	10000.00				
6	MATERIALS	4000.00				
7	LABOR	2000.00				
8	OVERHEAD	2500.00				
9	------	------	------	------		
10	PROFIT	1500.00				
11						
12	INCREASES	Percent				
13	SALES	10				
14	MATERIALS	20				
15	LABOR	20				
16	OVERHEAD	20				
17						
18						
19						

FIGURE 7.6 *Paper worksheet for the sample forecast.*

In the last exercise, you learned how to sum a set of numbers by adding each individual cell. There is a shortcut, however, for adding columns or rows of numbers. A **range** is a series of cells. It could be an entire or partial column, or an entire or partial row. A colon (:) is the symbol for a range operation summing a series of cells. It tells the spreadsheet program to sum all the values between the starting and ending cells. For example, to sum materials, labor, and overhead for 1987, we could use the expression = C6:C8. The formula for 1988 profit would subtract that amount from sales. Thus the formula for cell C10 is = C5 – (C6:C8).

The problem also requires you to figure out the result of increasing 1987 sales by 10 percent, and the other 1987 figures by 20 percent. The result of a 10 percent increase over 1987 sales of $10,000 would be $11,000. The formula for deriving that specific result is to multiply the 1987 sales figure by 10 percent, and add the two figures together. But remember that the projected 10 percent increase in sales is only an estimate. What if sales only increased by 5 percent? We need a way to change the projected percentages without having to rewrite the formulas.

Let's store the increase in sales in cell B13. (The particular cell number is not important. We simply want a way to be able to change the number without having to rewrite the formulas.) Then, instead of using an absolute number such as .10 (10 percent) in formulas, we can use a cell reference. This enables us to write a general-purpose formula that can accommodate any projected percentage increase in sales. If we use cell B13 for the percentage increase and cell

B5 for the previous year's sales, the formula for calculating the result of any percentage increase in sales (cell C5) would be:

```
=B5 * ((B13/100) +1)
```

Let's take a closer look at the formula. The expression in the inner set of parentheses converts a whole number like 10 percent into a fraction like .10. The expression in the outer set of parentheses adds 1 to that percentage, producing the number 1.10. Multiplying the original number by 1.10 is a one-step way to add the 10 percent increase to the original number. In other words, multiplying cell B5 (which equals 10,000) by 1.10 produces the same result as multiplying 10,000 by 10 percent and then adding the result to 10,000. But because we've written the formula with a cell reference instead of a specific percentage, we can insert a new percentage without having to change the formula.

To calculate the estimated 1989 sales (cell D5), we simply apply the same general formula to the sales calculated for 1988 (cell C5). So the formula for estimated 1989 sales is:

```
=C5 * ((B13/100) +1)
```

The same general formulas can be applied to forecasting a 20 percent increase in the costs of materials, labor, and overhead for the years 1988 and 1989. Now that you understand the formula for projecting profit, you can complete the worksheet for 1988 and 1989.

Once you have finished the worksheet, use it to build the corresponding spreadsheet model. Call your spreadsheet Sample Forecast.

What If You Change the Forecast?

What-if analysis lets you "play with" the numbers in the worksheet to explore alternative outcomes, such as the best and worst cases. You can ask such questions as "What if sales increase by 20 percent and materials, labor, and overhead only increase by 15 percent?" or "What if sales only increase by 5 percent, but labor increases by 25 percent?" The answers to such questions are simple enough to find out. If the model has been correctly built, you just have to change the percentages of increase. The spreadsheet program will recalculate the sales-and-profit picture for you.

More Exercises with the Spreadsheet

Type your name, and the name and number of this class, in the upper left-hand corner of the spreadsheet. After you finish each of the following exercises, print it to turn in to your instructor. Then Quit the spreadsheet program.

- Revise the model by substituting the following percentage increases: sales, 15 percent; materials, 10 percent; labor, 12 percent; overhead, 15 percent.
- What if sales only increase 10 percent, while labor rises 20 percent? What would be your estimated profit in 1988 and 1989?

- What if sales increase 5 percent, while materials, labor, and overhead increase 25 percent? What would be your estimated profit for 1988 and 1989?
- What if sales drop 10 percent (−10 percent), while costs increase 10, 12, and 15 percent, respectively?

REVIEW AND SELF-TESTING

Key Terms

Spreadsheet program	Scrolling
Numeric model	Static value
Edit line	Dynamic value
Cell reference	Update
Active cell	What-if analysis
Electronic worksheet	Range
Cell	

Questions for Review and Discussion

1. What is the main difference between numerical-analysis programs for large computers and spreadsheet programs for personal computers?
2. Why is a spreadsheet program a general-purpose problem-solving tool?
3. How would you scroll quickly from any cell in the worksheet back to cell A1?
4. What keys would you use to move the cursor to the left after entering data into a cell?
5. What keys activate the editing function in the edit line?
6. Why is a formula said to contain dynamic values?
7. What is the first step in the process of building a spreadsheet model?
8. What is the hierarchy of arithmetic operations?
9. How does the spreadsheet program "know" that a cell contains a formula?
10. What kinds of questions does what-if analysis allow you to ask?

8

Working with Spreadsheets

PREVIEW

In Chapter 7, we explored the basic productivity-promoting features of spreadsheets. This chapter will explore another kind of feature, whose purpose is to enhance how spreadsheets present information.

You'll see how you can vary the layout of rows and columns, and change the appearance of the cells in a worksheet. You'll also see some built-in features that provide more speed and power for spreadsheet users.

At the end of the chapter, we'll discuss some advanced features of commercial spreadsheets, useful for more sophisticated applications.

In this chapter, you'll discover:

- *How to change the layout of a spreadsheet*
- *Variations on the appearance of cells*
- *Copying- and cutting-and-pasting in a worksheet*
- *Transferring information between worksheets*
- *Transferring information to a word-processing document*
- *Uses for functions*
- *Uses for templates*
- *Macros*
- *Graphics*

Layout Features

The analytical and calculating capabilities of a spreadsheet are certainly its most powerful and compelling features. But unadorned columns and rows of text and numbers can be very tedious to look at. Like a letter or a paper done on a word processor, a finished worksheet is meant to communicate information to other people. The ability to create an attractive worksheet is becoming an increasingly important feature for spreadsheet users.

The **Layout commands** of the TriPac spreadsheet give you the means to change the appearance of the worksheet. These commands give you options to:

- Change the width of one or several columns
- Change the alignment (left, right, or centered) of the contents of a cell or several cells
- Change the format for displaying numbers (whole numbers, one decimal place, two decimal places, or dollar format) in selected cells

Layout commands affect how the contents of cells are displayed on the screen and in print.

Variable Column Width

Columns that contain different types of information often need different widths. For example, the leftmost column in a spreadsheet is usually used to identify the rows. If it consists of a list of names, it is likely to require more space than do columns of numbers. Otherwise, you may have to rely on cryptic abbreviations. In the TriPac spreadsheet the default width is 12 characters, but you can vary the widths of individual columns. They must be the same from top to bottom, however; it isn't possible to stagger widths.

To practice using the *Column width*. . . and other Layout commands, open the Sample Budget spreadsheet that you used in Chapter 4. To change the width of column A in the Sample Budget:

1. Position the cursor on any cell in column A. Then toggle to the menu bar. In the Layout menu, move the pointer to the *Column width*. . . command, as shown in Figure 8.1. Press the Return key.
2. A dialog box will appear, informing you of the current column width (12 characters). Type in the number *20*. The completed dialog box is shown in Figure 8.2. Press the Return key.
3. Column A of the worksheet will widen to 20 characters, and the other columns will shift to the right.
4. Notice that the hyphens no longer spread across the entire cell. This is because they were entered as a string of twelve dashes. Later, we will show you how to edit and copy those cells.

You can now use the additional space in column A to type longer names in the text cells; you'll learn how in the next section. First, we'll show you some more ways to enhance the appearance of the worksheet.

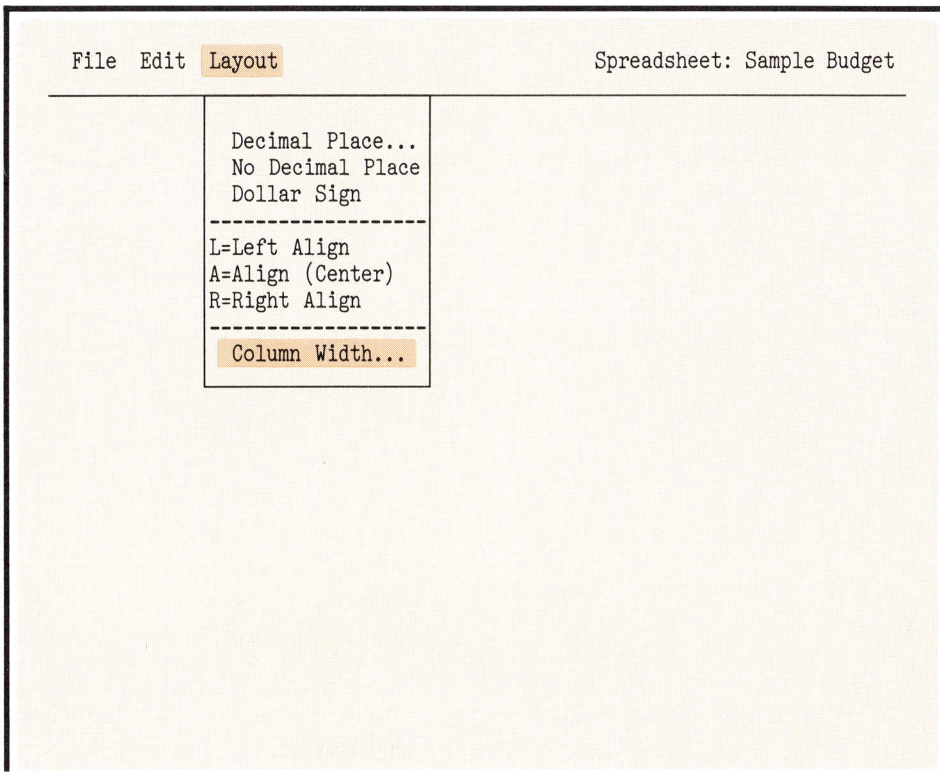

FIGURE 8.1 *Column width command in Layout menu.*

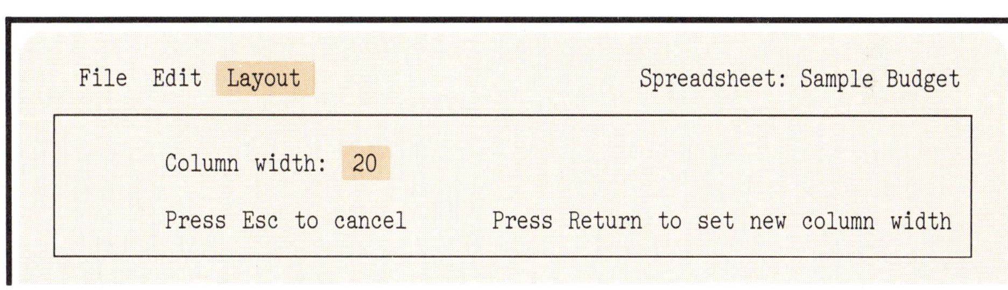

FIGURE 8.2 *Column width dialog box.*

Changing the Worksheet's Appearance

The Layout commands enable you to change the **format** of any cell in the spreadsheet. In the Sample Budget, for example, you could format amounts of money with dollar signs and two decimal places. You could also align column headings and text cells on the right margin of each cell.

1. To change the alignment of the column heading *One-time* in cell B3, position the cursor on cell B3. Then toggle to the menu bar, and move the pointer to the *R = Right Align* command in the Layout menu. Press the Return key. The text *One-time* will be aligned on the right margin of the cell.

2. Now move the cursor to cell C3. Use the shortcut command for *R=Right Align:* Hold down the Control key and press the R key. Then move the cursor to cell D3, and repeat the shortcut alignment command.
3. Now move the cursor to cell B7, toggle to the menu bar, and move the pointer to the *Dollar Sign* command in the Layout menu. Press the Return key.

   Note that the *Dollar Sign* command toggles on and off. To remove the dollar sign, simply issue the *Dollar Sign* command again.

If many format changes are needed, it may save time to deal with a group of cells. By using selection in conjunction with Layout commands, you can manipulate rows, columns, or rectangular arrays of cells.

Selection

Selection is performed the same way as in the word processor. You can execute a *S=Start Selection* command via the menu or via the shortcut method. For example, to align the list of titles in column A on the right margin of the column:

1. Position the cursor on cell A1. Hold down the Control key and press the S key. Then press the Down arrow key to select every cell in the column through cell A19.
2. Now hold down the Control key and press the R key. The entries in the selected cells will align themselves on the right margin of the column. Then hold down the Control key and press the S key to execute the *S=Cancel Selection* command. The highlighted cells will return to normal video, and the cursor will appear on cell A19.
3. To complete the reformatting of column A, we'll edit cells A5, A14, and A18. Move the cursor to cell A5, hold down the Control key and press the E key. Then type in *Monthly,* followed by a space. Press the Return key. Then move the cursor to cell A14, hold down the Control key and press the E key. In the edit line, move the edit cursor to the position following the *p* in *Exp* and type in *ense.* Then move the cursor to cell A18, and add *ings* to the partial word *Sav.* The reformatted sample budget is shown in Figure 8.3.

Selection works with all the commands in the Layout menu. For example, to add dollar signs to the Total cells:

1. Move the cursor to cell B14. Hold down the Control key and press the S key. Press the Down arrow key to select through cell B18. Then press the Right arrow key twice to select a rectangular block of cells.
2. Press the Esc key to toggle to the menu bar. Move the pointer to the *Dollar Sign* command in the Layout menu. Press the Return key. All of the selected cells will be reformatted with dollar signs.

Once a cell or group of cells has been changed by a Layout command, it will retain the new format. For example, if you erase the text in a right-aligned cell and type in a new entry, the new text will also be right-aligned.

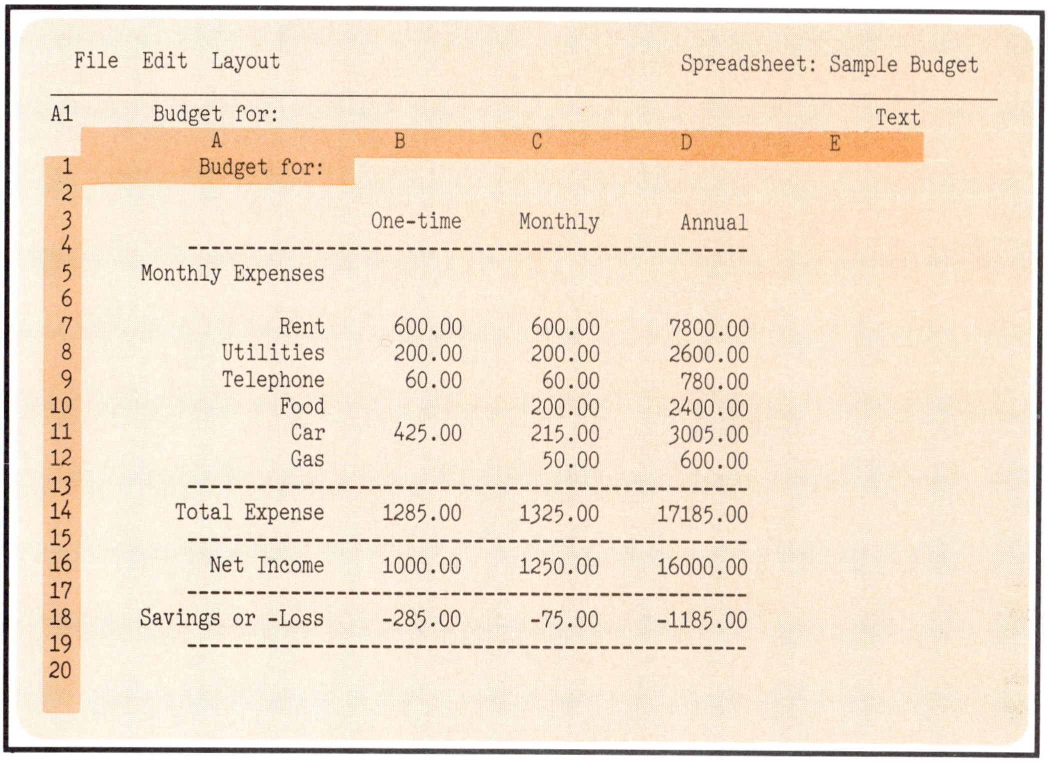

File Edit Layout — Spreadsheet: Sample Budget

A1 Budget for: — Text

	A	B	C	D	E
1	Budget for:				
2					
3		One-time	Monthly	Annual	
4	----------------	----------	----------	----------	
5	Monthly Expenses				
6					
7	Rent	600.00	600.00	7800.00	
8	Utilities	200.00	200.00	2600.00	
9	Telephone	60.00	60.00	780.00	
10	Food		200.00	2400.00	
11	Car	425.00	215.00	3005.00	
12	Gas		50.00	600.00	
13	----------------	----------	----------	----------	
14	Total Expense	1285.00	1325.00	17185.00	
15	----------------	----------	----------	----------	
16	Net Income	1000.00	1250.00	16000.00	
17	----------------	----------	----------	----------	
18	Savings or -Loss	-285.00	-75.00	-1185.00	
19	----------------	----------	----------	----------	
20					

FIGURE 8.3 *Reformatted sample budget.*

Copy-and-Paste and Cut-and-Paste

The TriPac spreadsheet allows you to cut or copy information from a worksheet and paste it elsewhere in the same or another worksheet, or in a word-processing document. Both operations are the same as in the word processor.

The *C = Copy* command copies a selected block of cells and moves them to a clipboard. The *X = Cut* command removes a selected block of cells from the worksheet and moves them into a clipboard; the resulting space is left empty. The *P = Paste* command pastes the selected cells from the clipboard into a worksheet or word-processing document, beginning wherever the cursor is positioned. When pasting a block of cells, the cursor should be positioned at the upper left corner of the new location. Cutting is also a handy way to erase a large segment of a worksheet.

In the Same Worksheet

To practice copying-and-pasting within the same worksheet, move the cursor to cell A4. Edit the cell by filling in the remainder of the 20-position cell with hyphens. When you have finished editing the cell:

1. Hold down the Control key and press the S key. Then hold down the Control key and press the C key to make a copy of cell A4.
2. Position the cursor on cell A13. Hold down the Control key and press the P key. The contents of the clipboard will be pasted into cell A13. Repeat the Paste command for cells A15, A17 and A19.

Important: When pasting near the bottom or right edge of a worksheet, you may not be able to paste all the cells in the clipboard into the desired locations. For example, if you copy or cut cells A1 through A10, and try to paste them beginning in cell A250, only the contents of the first five cells will be pasted into cells A250 through A254. The same condition holds true at the right border of the worksheet, and when trying to paste a rectangular block of cells into the lower right-hand corner of the worksheet.

Important: When cutting- or copying-and-pasting formulas, remember that the formulas retain their original cell references. If you want the formula to refer to a new cell, you must edit it accordingly.

Between Worksheets

The procedure for cutting or copying cells from one worksheet and pasting them into another worksheet begins in the same way. The difference arises when you complete the Cut or Copy command and are ready to paste into the destination worksheet.

Once the Cut or Copy command is complete, execute the *Quit Spreadsheet* command and return to the Application Manager. Open the destination worksheet, and position the cursor in the cell where you want the paste to start. Then execute the Paste command. See Figure 8.4.

(Remember that formulas retain their original cell references when they are pasted into a new worksheet. Make sure that this is what you intend, or that you edit them appropriately.)

Between Worksheet and Word Processor

When a worksheet cell or group of cells is pasted into a word-processing document, numbers and formulas are converted into text. Also, you cannot paste a row or block of cells wider than 65 characters into a word-processing document. If you try to, the word processor will break it into two consecutive blocks of text and stack them on top of each other.

Pasting into a word-processing document is just like pasting into a destination worksheet. Close the source spreadsheet, open the destination document, position the cursor where you want the cells to begin, and execute the *P=Paste* command.

Exercises with the Spreadsheet

- Modify the Sample Forecast spreadsheet as you did the Sample Budget, by adding dollar signs in the appropriate places and adding one decimal place to the percentages.
- Create a new spreadsheet called Sample Budget II. First, copy all the information from the Sample Budget spreadsheet. Then create an additional column showing expenses as percentages of total income. For example, if rent is $600 and income is $1,000, rent will be 60 percent of income.

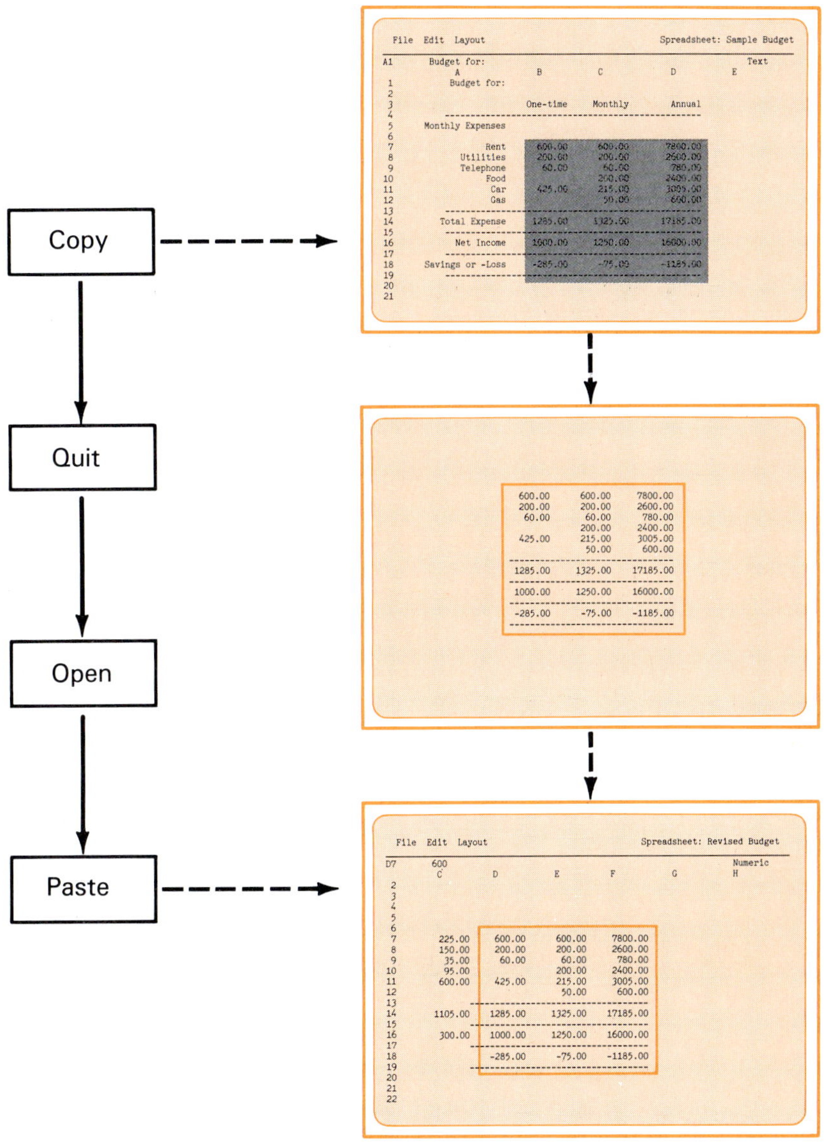

FIGURE 8.4 *Steps in Copy-and-Paste between worksheets.*

- Modify the Receipt spreadsheet as follows. Make the Quantity column 8 characters wide. Make the Description column 24 characters wide. Add dollar signs to the Price and Amount columns. Add the text *Sold to:* in cell A1, and type in your name and address in cells B1, B2, and B3.
- Copy cells A4 through E16 in the Sample Invoice into a new word-processing document called Invoice. Add the text shown in Figure 8.5 to the document and print the invoice.

Additional Spreadsheet Features

At this point we have covered the basic fundamentals of spreadsheets. But commercial spreadsheets often have several additional features that can enhance more complex spreadsheets.

```
                    I N V O I C E

Date:     (today's date)

Sold to: (Your Name)
         (Your Street Address)
         (Your City, State, Zip)

---------------------------------------------

Data from Receipt Spreadsheet pasted here.

---------------------------------------------

Terms: Payable upon presentation of invoice
```

FIGURE 8.5 *Data for word processing document invoice.*

Copying Relative Formulas

You will recall that cell references remain unchanged when they are copied into other cells. Most commercial spreadsheets offer the ability to make a **relative copy** of a formula. This means that the cell references in the formula are adjusted in accordance with its new location. For example, suppose you want to create a series of twelve months of data, in which a number is to increase by 10 percent per month. In other words, you want the formula for the number to be 1.1 times the previous month's figure.

By using a relative-copy command, you can specify that the cell reference in each formula vary with the position of the cell in which it is located.

Or take the case of a five-year plan. You can enter a column of numbers for the first year, and then replicate it across the five-year range without having to retype or edit any of the formulas.

But some cell references should not change, of course, when a formula is copied from one cell to another. For example, if you decided to add another column to the Sample Forecast, for 1990, you would want the references to the percentage increases to remain unchanged. A cell reference that does not change is often called an **absolute cell reference.**

Functions

A **function** is a predefined routine or formula used in a spreadsheet. The TriPac spreadsheet uses a sum function to add a series of numbers and display the total in a cell. Thus, you can instruct the spreadsheet to sum consecutive entries in a column or row by using a colon (:) between the names of the first and last cells in the series (for instance, = A1:A5). Other examples of common functions include:

- *Average*, which averages a range of cells
- *Count*, which counts the number of nonblank numbers in a given range of cells

- *Maximum*, which finds the largest number in a range of numbers
- *Net present value*, which calculates the present value of a series of payments
- *Payment*, which calculates monthly payments on a loan
- *Mathematical functions*, such as Sin, Cos, Log, and Exponent, which are used to construct mathematical models
- *Logical functions*, such as conditional IF-THEN statements, which are used to build conditional models
- *Lookup functions*, which allow you to retrieve numbers from a table of values

Functions are often used in formulas. For example, the average function might be used in a formula as follows: A10 = AVG(A1:A9). This formula computes the sum of the cells A1 through A9, divides that sum by the count of nonblank entries in cells A1 through A9, and places the result in cell A10.

Built-in functions serve as shortcut ways to perform common statistical, mathematical, financial, and logical operations. Using them makes it much easier to construct complex formulas without having to write them yourself.

Templates

A **template** is a partially completed worksheet containing text and formulas but not data. Templates are often designed by specialists for use by nonspecialists. For example, a tax accountant might construct an IRS Form 1040 spreadsheet template to help novice users compute their income taxes. The tax-form template would take care of planning the worksheet and deciding what formulas to enter. The user would simply purchase the template, copy it into the spreadsheet program, and begin solving the tax-calculation problem.

Because there are so many potential applications for spreadsheets, many special-purpose templates have been created. You can obtain packaged templates on disk for such applications as budgeting, bookkeeping, investment analysis, and real-estate transactions. Also, many books about specific applications supply designs for templates that you can type in to your spreadsheet program.

Some templates are specially designed to be used by people unfamiliar with how a spreadsheet works. These templates hide the formulas, and use built-in prompts and forms to guide the user through the process of entering data. For example, a data-entry template can automatically move the cursor to the proper locations for data entry; when all items have been entered, it automatically saves and prints the completed worksheet without any intervention by the user.

Advanced Spreadsheet Features

Every spreadsheet is a grid of rows and columns displayed on a screen. However, some have refined the user interface, added more rows and columns, and added performance-improving enhancements. Several spreadsheet programs use a pointing device, such as a mouse, to simplify their user interface. Multiplan, for example, has a mouse interface for the Macintosh computer and a version for Hewlett-Packard's Touchscreen computer that lets you select cells by pointing with your finger.

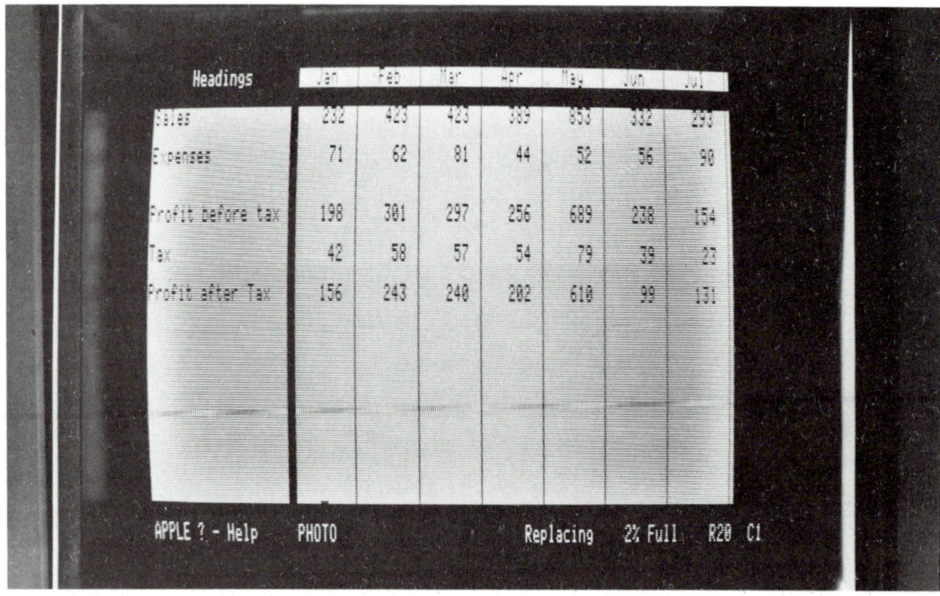

PFS:Plan allows the user to type directly in the spreadsheet itself. Formulas use English words instead of row and column designations.

Some spreadsheet programs have eliminated numbered rows and lettered columns. Instead of row and column cell references, you can use label names in formulas. In PFS:Plan, for example, there are no cell numbers; formulas use the names of column and row headings. Also, information is typed directly into the worksheet instead of on an edit line.

Very Large Spreadsheets

As spreadsheets have evolved, they have become larger. For example, the original personal-computer spreadsheet VisiCalc had 254 rows. Another popular spreadsheet, 1–2–3, raised that number to 2,048 rows. Next, SuperCalc III offered 9,999 rows. Recently, Microsoft's Excel raised the number of rows to 16,384.

Working with a very large spreadsheet differs in several ways from working with a small spreadsheet. One difference is the manner in which recalculation is handled. In the TriPac spreadsheet, recalculation is automatic. Whenever a new value is entered, every formula in the worksheet is immediately evaluated and, if necessary, recalculated.

In large commercial spreadsheets with hundreds of rows and thousands of columns, evaluating and recalculating formulas can take considerable time. When making new entries, the time spent waiting for recalculation between entries can become unacceptably long. For this reason, large spreadsheets offer a **manual recalculation** option. With this option, formulas are evaluated and recalculated only when you enter a command to recalculate.

Another feature of large spreadsheets is the ability to freeze titles, so that they remain in view when you scroll through the worksheet. This feature is often implemented as a **title command.** With a title command, you can fix or

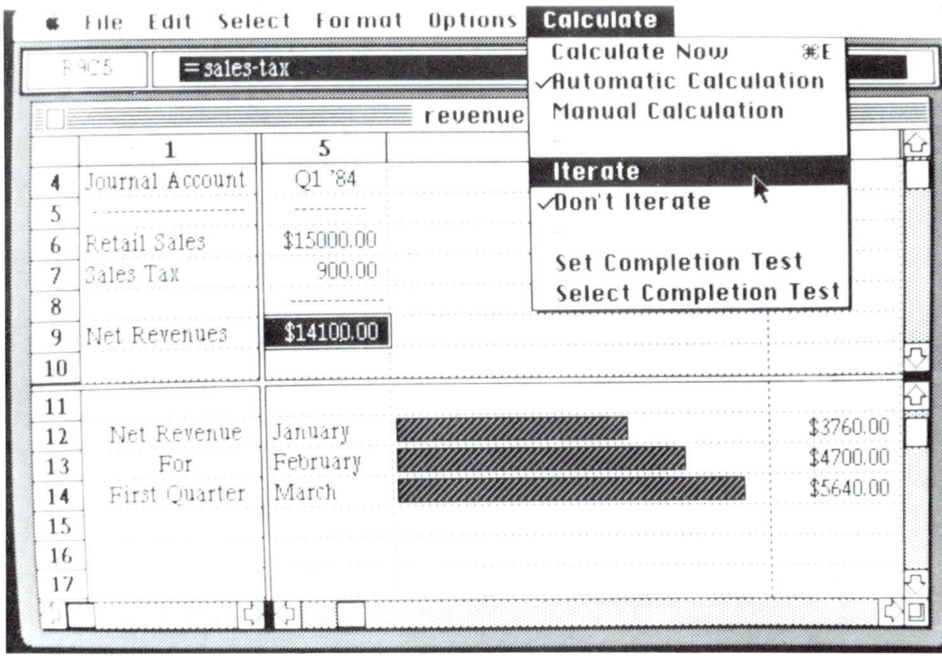

A common feature of many spreadsheets is the ability to divide the screen into windows so that you can view different portions of the worksheet simultaneously.

freeze row 1 so that the column titles stay visible for reference purposes while other rows scroll in the normal manner. Similarly, in a worksheet with several hundred columns, you can freeze column A to keep the row titles visible while you scroll horizontally.

A similar feature of many large spreadsheets is the ability to split the screen so that you can view different portions of the worksheet simultaneously. This feature is often called **windowing.** For example, suppose you wanted to compare the data in rows 2 through 4 with data in rows 256 through 258. The split-screen feature allows you to divide the worksheet horizontally at a specified row. Splitting the screen vertically is also possible.

In some spreadsheet programs, windows enable you to view two or more spreadsheets simultaneously. Some can accommodate as many as eight windows at once.

Linking Multiple Spreadsheets

Often, one spreadsheet will use information derived from another spreadsheet. **Linking spreadsheets** is a technique for consolidating information from two or more spreadsheets, to avoid having to continuously re-enter or copy-and-paste information.

This feature is slightly different from pasting information into another spreadsheet. Linking establishes a relationship between two or more spreadsheets. When data changes in the source spreadsheet, the target spreadsheet is automatically updated as soon as it is opened. The only way to change the contents of a linked spreadsheet is to change information in the source spreadsheet. This is because the target spreadsheet is dependent on the source spreadsheet for its information.

For example, suppose several departments are revising their budgets. Each department creates a spreadsheet. Then, a consolidated budget linked to each departmental budget spreadsheet is created. Linking solves the problem of updating the consolidated budget to reflect the changes in the department budgets.

Macros

A **macro** is a single command or instruction that invokes a sequence of operations. Whenever the sequence is to be performed, a macro can be substituted. Macros are used to automate repetitive tasks. Spreadsheet applications often involve repetitive sequences of commands. For example, when preparing budgets, you might have to enter the same heading across the top of every budget worksheet. In this case, you could use a macro to avoid typing the headings over and over.

More complicated macros can be used to customize a spreadsheet application with **user-defined functions.** Many spreadsheets contain a **macro language** facility, which resembles a programming language. Users can employ the macro language to create macro programs of lengthy and complicated instructions, which are embedded in the spreadsheet program and called up by a single keystroke. For example, a user might have the weekly task of transferring information from one spreadsheet into a company-wide model, and printing a report of the results. The entire procedure could be customized by using an interactive macro, which would not only perform the tasks but also prompt the user for input and make decisions based on the input.

Graphics

The presentation of numeric data usually has more impact if the data are converted into graphs or charts. A large and complicated spreadsheet can be difficult to interpret. It can also be dull, since most spreadsheets have no visual variety. A graph or chart, on the other hand, transforms a set of numbers into a simplified picture.

As people began to use spreadsheets to present information to other people, they began to want better ways to present numeric data. For purposes of analysis and presentation, graphics allows you to:

- Communicate quickly and precisely
- Represent relationships among data more concretely
- Discover possibilities that may not be apparent in numeric form
- Assimilate and remember data more easily

A graphics module in a spreadsheet program automates the production of charts and graphs. Typically, the user begins by selecting or highlighting the data to be graphed. For example, if you are working on a financial projection, you might highlight the projected monthly sales figures. Once the data have

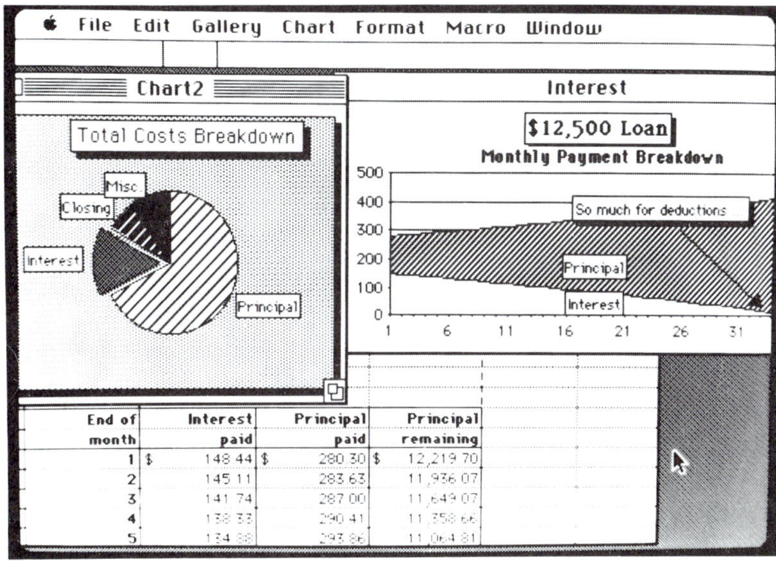

Microsoft Excel contains a built-in graphics program to automate the production of charts and graphs.

been selected, you would execute a graphics command or open a graphics window and select the type of graph or chart you wish to view. For example, you might wish to treat monthly sales as a bar chart. Once you have selected the type of chart, the chart is displayed on the screen.

Most graphics modules allow you to try out different kinds of graphs or charts. If you decide that a bar chart is not appropriate, for example, you could try a line graph.

Once you have selected the type of graph or chart you want, you can enhance the graphic with titles, legends, and variations of scaling.

Computers with graphic-oriented displays, such as the Macintosh, also allow the appearance of the spreadsheet itself to be enhanced. Selected cells can be highlighted in various ways, such as by drawing borders around them; and different styles and sizes of type, such as italic and boldface, can be used to accentuate cells.

In color displays, color can be used to accentuate meaning. Negative numbers could be displayed in red, for instance, or particular parts of a worksheet (such as totals versus ordinary figures) could be displayed in contrasting colors.

More Exercises with the Spreadsheet

1. Grade book. Create a sample grade book, using the data in Table 8.1. Figure 8.6 shows the partially completed grade book. Fill in the data, column by column, and keep a running average score. The count cell keeps track of the number of test scores recorded. Use it in writing the formula to calculate the running average for each student. Be sure to vary it, depending on how many scores have been recorded.

TABLE 8.1 *Grade Book Data*

Pat Abbot	73	89	96
Michael DeLuca	98	96	76
Silvia Ramos	66	76	73
Anthony Smith	67	87	98

File Edit Layout Spreadsheet: Grade Book

B10 Empty

	A	B	C	D	E
1		Test1	Test2	Test3	Average
2	Pat Abbot	73	89		81.00
3	Michael DeLuca	98			
4	Silvia Ramos	66			
5	Anthony Smith	67			
6					
7	Average	76			
8					
9	Count	2			
10					
11					
12					
13					
14					
15					
16					
17					
18					
19					
20					

FIGURE 8.6 *Partially completed Grade Book spreadsheet.*

2. Savings account. Build a savings-account spreadsheet, using the data in Table 8.2. Assume an interest rate of 5 percent per year, compounded annually. Calculate various interest rates for various initial deposits. Can you add a column comparing two interest rates?

A9 Empty

	A	B	C	D	E
1	Interest Rate	0.05			
2	Initial Deposit	100.00			
3					
4	After 1 year	105.00			
5	After 2 years	110.25			
6	After 3 years	115.76			
7	After 4 years	121.55			
8	After 5 years	127.63			

Table 8.2 *Sample savings account data.*

	A	B	C	D	K	L	M	N
1								
2								
3		January	February	March	October	November	December	Total
4								
5	Monthly Expenses							
6								
7	Rent	600.00						
8	Utilities	200.00						
9	Telephone	60.00						
10	Food	100.00						
11	Car	425.00						
12	Gas	50.00						
13								
14	Total	1435.00						
15								
16	Net Income	1250.00						
17								
18	Savings or -loss	-185.00						
19								

FIGURE 8.7 *Sample twelve-month budget data.*

3. Twelve-month budget. Build a monthly budget spreadsheet for a twelve-month period, using the data in Figure 8.7. Then project a month-by-month budget, starting with January. The Total column represents the sum of the monthly items. Print the completed budget and turn it in to your instructor.

REVIEW AND SELF-TESTING

Key Terms

- Layout commands
- Format
- Relative copy
- Absolute cell reference
- Function
- Template
- Manual recalculation
- Title command
- Windowing
- Linking spreadsheets
- Macro
- User-defined function
- Macro language

Questions for Review and Discussion

1. Why is an attractive worksheet important to spreadsheet users?
2. Name three appearance-enhancing commands that the TriPac spreadsheet offers.

3. Briefly describe how you might go about changing the format of a group of cells.
4. How do you indicate where a cut or copied group of cells is to be pasted?
5. What is the major difference between (1) cutting and then pasting to a spreadsheet and (2) cutting and then pasting to a word-processing document?
6. What happens to a formula when you paste it into a new cell?
7. What is the difference between relative and absolute cell reference?
8. Why would you use a function in a formula?
9. What advantage does a template offer a novice spreadsheet user? An experienced user?
10. Why do some spreadsheets offer a manual recalculation command?
11. What is the purpose of a title command?
12. What is a source spreadsheet? A destination spreadsheet?
13. What is the purpose of a macro?

9

Introducing Databases

PREVIEW

The ability to store information is one of the most powerful features of today's computer systems. Databases are a computerized solution to the problem of storing collections of information. In the broadest sense, they are computerized record-keeping systems. Just as word processors improve on the typewriter, and spreadsheet programs extend the principle of a manual ledger, database programs are an elaboration on the filing cabinet.

But storage alone is not enough. Anyone whose desk is cluttered with books and stacks of papers knows that storing information does not guarantee being able to find a particular piece of information later on. For that, you need structure. Database programs provide the means to structure and organize information.

Finally, there is not much point in organizing information unless it can be easily manipulated and retrieved. A database program also takes advantage of the computer's ability to sort data, make comparisons, and select specific information.

In this chapter, you'll discover:

- *How database programs help you solve problems*
- *The functions of a database program*
- *How to design a database*
- *How to create a record structure*
- *How to enter and edit data*
- *How to search and select records*
- *How to sort a database*
- *How to print selected records*

Database Programs and Problem Solving

A **database program** is software that stores, organizes, manipulates, retrieves, and summarizes data. In short, it is a computerized record-keeping program. As you know from Chapter 3, a **database** is a collection of various types of data, organized according to a logical structure.

In the late 1960s, centralized computers in large organizations processed data for all of the organization's departments or divisions. It turned out to be wasteful and time-consuming to maintain separate and often duplicate sets of files for different applications. The database approach made it possible to create a centralized data repository, which each department or division could draw on for its needs. Database management software was developed to create and maintain the database, and to link it to the application programs that used it.

At first database programs needed a technical support staff. Also, their output was limited to sophisticated but static reports. With the advent of on-line systems, they began to evolve into highly interactive end-user tools. When databases for personal computers came on the market, nontechnical end users (such as small business owners) began to develop their own database applications. No longer was it necessary to hire programmers, or even to learn how to program.

Database programs are applicable to any kind of project that involves creating a repository of data and then manipulating that data to create information. For instance, some typical uses of database programs on personal computers include:

- Salespeople keep track of sales leads, prospects, customers, orders, and payment records.

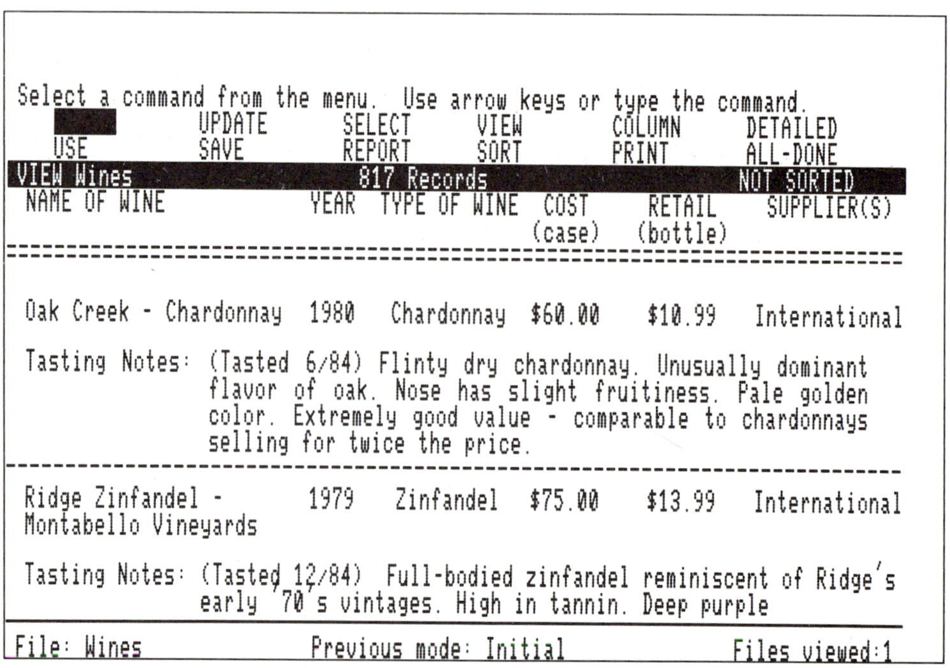

Hobbyists can use database programs to keep track of their collections. Shown here is a display from a database of a wine collection.

- Hospitals keep track of patients' histories, symptoms, test results, doctors, and diets.
- Writers create bibliographies and indexes for books and papers.
- Real-estate agents match property listings to potential clients.
- Hobbyists keep track of their collections of such things as coins, stamps, record albums, and wine.
- Magazine publishers maintain lists of subscribers and advertisers.

Database programs manage information by allowing the user to structure the data, add and delete items as needed, manipulate the data, and select particular information from the database. These functions make databases a useful tool for almost any problem that involves retrieving and analyzing past and current data.

A Sample Database Application

One of the most common applications for database programs is to keep track of an inventory. An inventory might be as simple as a stamp collection, or as extensive as the merchandise in a retail department store or the thousands of parts used to build an automobile or an airplane.

Assume that you are going to lend a hand to your uncle, who repossesses cars and sells them to dealers and individuals. His inventory of cars is not large, but business is brisk and turnover is rapid. Your uncle has a good reputation, and dealers call daily with requests for specific makes and models of cars. He receives inquiries like "Do you have any late-model Cadillacs in stock?" or "I need a 1980 Volvo with standard transmission. Have you got any?"

You are going to design a database to keep track of your uncle's inventory of used cars, and to help answer customers' questions about the cars in stock.

To create and use the database, you will use all four functions of the database program:

- Design the database.
- Enter and edit data.
- Search, sort, and select data.
- Display, print, and save the selected data.

Designing a Database

The starting point for any database application is to design the database. First, we must think about what the used-car database should look like. The TriPac database structures data in the form of a table, with horizontal rows and vertical columns. Each row holds a **record**; each column designates a particular **field.** Take a look at Figure 9.1.

Designing a database means deciding on the **structure** of the records within it. The process includes the following steps:

- Determining what categories of information (fields) the records should contain.
- Determining the order of the fields.

Each column holds a field—a particular category of information.

Each row holds one record—a set of related fields pertaining to the same subject.

The headings provide field names.

NAME	ADDRESS	CITY	STATE	ZIP
Berglund, Steven	85 Summer St	Keene	NH	03431
Conte, Joyce	195 Granite Ave	Sioux City	IA	51104
Garcia, George	1225 Pond Rd	Seattle	WA	98102
Kahn, Stanley	203 East Main St	Aurora	NY	13026
MacAdam, Joan	9 School Ln	Ashland	KY	41101
Pacella, Nicholas	400 Broadway	San Diego	CA	92110
Palmer, Anthony	16 Summit Ave	Orlando	FL	32856
Richardson, Paula	1440 Riverside Rd	Stamford	CT	06902
Sumner, Chris	56 Edge Hill Ave	Chicago	IL	60604
Woods, Emily	42 Acorn Ln	Peoria	IL	61625

FIGURE 9.1 *Data structured in rows and columns.*

- Naming each field.
- Specifying the length of each field.
- Describing the type of data in each field (text or numbers).

We want the Used Car database to answer the kinds of questions people typically ask about buying a used car. Each record should contain all the relevant data about a particular car. But specifically, what should that data be?

Reviewing your uncle's records of past phone requests, you find that potential buyers want to know the make, model, color, year, price, mileage, and a few other details about each car. Each item in that list will become a field in the car record.

Next, decide the order in which the fields should appear. Since we are accustomed to reading from left to right, the most important data should be on the left. Let's make the order of fields in the record the same as your informal list, above, of the things potential buyers want to know. To name the fields, we will give each field a short descriptive heading (as in Figure 9.1).

The best way to show you how to create a database is to give you step-by-step instructions, which you can follow along using the TriPac software.

Starting the Database Program

Move the pointer to the first untitled database, and execute the *O* = *Open* command. When the dialog box asks you to name the database, type in *Used Cars* and press the Return key.

To create the structure of your new database, toggle to the menu bar, move the pointer to the Layout menu, and select the *Define Record Structure*... command. Then press the Return key.

```
File  Edit  Search  Layout                             Database: Used Cars

   Field  1   Name: ■                    Type:            Text 20
   Field  2   Name:                      Type:            Text 20
   Field  3   Name:                      Type:            Text 20
   Field  4   Name:                      Type:            Text 20
   Field  5   Name:                      Type:            Text 20
   Field  6   Name:                      Type:            Text 20
   Field  7   Name:                      Type:            Text 20
   Field  8   Name:                      Type:            Text 20
   Field  9   Name:                      Type:            Text 20
   Field 10   Name:                      Type:            Text 20

   Press Esc to cancel     Press Return to create database
```

FIGURE 9.2 *Empty dialog box to define a record structure.*

The dialog box that will appear asks for the name and **data type** (text or numbers) of each field. Figure 9.2 shows the dialog box. The highlighted space on the first line equals the maximum length of the field's name.

TriPac allows you to specify two types of data: text or numbers. The program puts the following limits on the size of the database itself, and on each of its components:

- 100 records in total
- 10 fields per record
- 20 characters per text field
- 11 characters per numeric field

You can designate the length of a text field as 2, 4, 8, 12, or 20 characters. The length of a numeric field is fixed at 11 digits and cannot be changed, but you can specify zero, two, or three decimal places.

Following the word *Type:*, you will see the term *Text 20.* This is one of the options for the Type specification. All the options are built into the program; you can see them all by scrolling through a list. Press the Tab key to highlight the term *Text 20.* Then press the space bar. The type specification changes to *Text 12.* Each time you press the space bar, a new option will appear. Keep pressing the space bar to view all the options until the list wraps around to the beginning. Table 9.1 lists the options in the order you'll see them.

TABLE 9.1 *Options for the type specification*

Text 20
Text 12
Text 8
Text 4
Text 2
#######
#####.#
####.##
###.###

These built-in option lists are an important feature of the TriPac database program. Instead of having to remember the options, you can just scroll through a list. Built-in options also cut down on the amount of typing you have to do.

Specifying the Record Structure

The pointer should be highlighting the position just to the right of *Field 1 Name:*. If it isn't, use the Tab key to move the pointer back to that location. The fields in the Used Cars database should be named and entered in the following order:

```
Field 1    Name: Make      Type: Text 8
Field 2    Name: Model     Type: Text 8
Field 3    Name: Color     Type: Text 8
Field 4    Name: Year      Type: Text 4
Field 5    Name: Price     Type: #######
Field 6    Name: Mileage   Type: #######
Field 7    Name: Remarks   Type: Text 20
```

Type in *Make* at Field 1. Then press the Tab key. Next, the pointer will highlight the word *Text 20* following Type:. Press the space to advance from Text 20 to Text 8, then press the Tab key. Type in *Model* at Field 2. Press the Tab key again. Continue using the Tab key to advance through the list. DO NOT PRESS THE RETURN KEY YET. If you make a typing mistake, use the Delete key to correct it. To select the no-decimal-place option for the numeric fields Price and Mileage, press the space bar and scroll through the option list until *#######* appears. Then press the Tab key to move on.

When you reach the end of the list, check it over. If you discover an error, use the Tab key to move to and correct it. You can edit a name field by using the Delete key.

Accidentally pressing the Return key or the Esc key before you've finished entering and editing your record structure means you will have to toggle to the menu bar and select the *Define Record Structure*. . . command in the Layout menu again.

When you've finished defining your record structure, the dialog box should look like Figure 9.3. Press the Return key. The program will store the structure and display the structure as a heading line directly below the menu bar. Figure 9.4 shows what it will look like. Now you can begin to enter data into the database.

Tips on Database Design

Because it's easy to create a database with TriPac, you may be tempted to set one up without thinking ahead much. But it always pays to think through your record structure in advance. Use a pencil and paper to consider various sequences for the fields, and various names, lengths, and types.

Here are some pointers on designing a database and specifying a record structure:

Enter the most frequently used fields first. Even though you can scroll horizontally, it is best to have as much information as possible on the screen at once.

The name of any field can be up to 20 characters long, though we have chosen shorter names. TriPac displays the database with the column widths set at

```
File  Edit  Search  Layout                            Database: Used Cars

  Field  1   Name: Make                 Type:          Text  8
  Field  2   Name: Model                Type:          Text  8
  Field  3   Name: Color                Type:          Text  8
  Field  4   Name: Year                 Type:          Text  4
  Field  5   Name: Price                Type:          #######
  Field  6   Name: Mileage              Type:          #######
  Field  7   Name: Remarks              Type:          Text 20
  Field  8   Name: ■                    Type:          Text 20
  Field  9   Name:                      Type:          Text 20
  Field 10   Name:                      Type:          Text 20

  Press Esc to cancel      Press Return to create database
```

FIGURE 9.3 *Completed dialog box to define a record structure.*

```
File  Edit  Search  Layout                            Database: Used Cars
|Make    |Model   |Color   |Year|Price      |Mileage    |Remarks
```

FIGURE 9.4 *Heading line.*

11 for numeric fields, and 2, 4, 8, 12, or 20 for text fields. A name can be longer than the column width, but it will not be completely displayed on the screen. It will, however, be complete when it is printed.

Often, what appears to be a numeric field should be designated as a text field. For example, Zip codes should be designated as text fields even though they are all numbers. This is because TriPac always eliminates the leading zeros in a numeric field. Thus the Massachusetts Zip code 01907 would be displayed and printed as 1907. Also, numeric fields don't allow dashes (-) or slashes (/); therefore, dates like 01-01-87 or 01/01/87 should be designated as text fields. In our sample database, the Year field has been designated as a 4-character text field because it takes less space than an 11-character numeric field.

Use as many fields as you need to sort or select information. For example, if you are planning to sort names alphabetically according to the last name, use separate name fields for first name and last name.

Entering and Editing Data

Once the record structure has been displayed as a header line, you can add data to the database. You'll do this by filling in the blanks in a record-structure dialog box. TriPac adds new records to the database in the order in which you enter them. Records do not need to be complete: You can add a partial record to a database, and fill in the empty fields later.

Entering Data

To enter new data into your database, you will use the *N = Add New Record...* command in the Edit menu. You can activate this command through the menu bar, or by holding down the Control key while pressing the N key.

When you execute the *N = Add New Record...* command, a dialog box resembling Figure 9.5 will appear. Each field occupies a separate line, with the field's name on the left-hand side. A highlighted space corresponding to the field's length appears on the first line.

This list of fields is often called a **form.** The form helps you visualize the structure of the record, and the correspondence between field names and sizes and the data itself.

The data for the Used Car database is in Table 9.2 on page 165. For now, you'll just enter the first 20 records.

Enter the data for the first field. Then press the Tab key to move to the next field, and so on. Use the Delete key to correct typing mistakes, and the Tab key to move from field to field.

When you have finished entering an entire record, press the Return key. The dialog-box form will retract, and the data will be entered in the database and displayed on the screen in the tabular format. Continue entering data until you have entered 20 records.

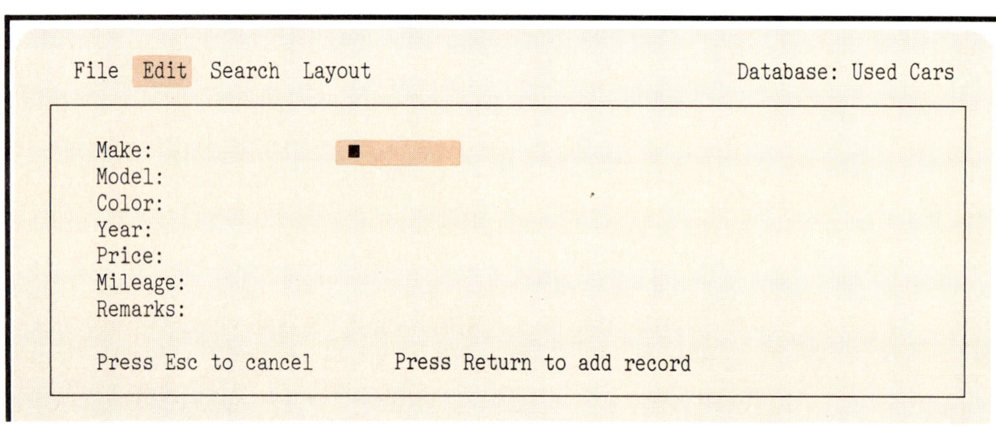

FIGURE 9.5 *Dialog box to add new record.*

Editing Data

As you enter records into the database, an arrow-shaped **current record pointer** on the left-hand side of the screen will point to the current record. You can scroll the arrow cursor up and down to point to any record in the database. By using the *E = Edit Current Record...* command in the Edit menu, you can display the contents of the current record in a dialog-box form, modify any or all of its fields, and replace it in the database.

Editing data serves two purposes. The first is to correct errors; the second is to **update** or replace the contents of a record with more current information.

In the Used Cars database, the field most likely to be updated is the price. For example, your uncle's sales strategy might be to lower the price of a car if it

TABLE 9.2 *Data for the Used Car database.*

Make	Model	Color	Year	Price	Mileage	Remarks
Mercedes	380SL	Blue	1983	37999	14000	One owner
Volvo	244DL	Brown	1977	4100	65000	Sunroof
Porsche	944	Red	1984	22950	13800	Power windows
Ferrari	308GTS	Silver	1980	32500	29000	Luxury trim
Ford	Mustang	Green	1976	375	102000	Running well
Dodge	Colt	Silver	1981	1250	42000	4 speed AM/FM radio
Honda	Civic	Blue	1984	7200	16000	Hatchback
Porsche	928	Red	1983	33900	16600	Leather interior
Audi	4000S	White	1984	13950	12000	Full fact equipped
Jaguar	XJ6	Green	1985	31895	5000	Leather interior
Honda	Accord	Silver	1979	2100	50000	4 door
Buick	Park Ave	Green	1982	9500	30000	Velour interior
Buick	Skylark	Brown	1982	4800	18500	Air conditioning
Saab	900S	Blue	1983	11000	30000	Sunroof
Volvo	242DL	White	1983	9985	21000	Air conditioning
Audi	5000	Black	1981	8877	42000	Alloy wheels
Mercedes	380SL	Grey	1982	32900	38000	Perfect condition
Buick	LeSabre	Blue	1983	8995	38000	One owner
Saab	900S	Silver	1983	10000	19000	5 speed 4 door
VW	Rabbit	Beige	1980	1600	84000	Sunroof
Dodge	Colt	Red	1978	2500	48000	Excellent condition
Ford	Mustang	White	1982	3300	26000	Very clean
Porsche	911	Red	1982	24900	22000	Sunroof
Cadillac	Eldorado	Blue	1984	18900	8000	Leather interior
VW	Jetta	Silver	1984	7200	12000	Deluxe interior
Honda	Accord	Grey	1983	8000	30000	Electric roof
Ford	Granada	Red	1975	1500	120000	New paint
Volvo	244DL	Tan	1980	6950	53008	Air conditioning
Buick	Century	Ivory	1974	2200	90000	Mint condition
Jaguar	XKE	Grey	1964	7000	175000	6 cylinder
Buick	Regal	Grey	1982	6300	30000	Air conditioning
Audi	5000S	Silver	1981	5495	44000	Sunroof
Mercedes	280	Red	1985	26000	10000	Climate control
VW	Rabbit	White	1982	6500	32000	Rustproofed
Saab	Turbo	Red	1983	11500	60000	4 door
Ferrari	380GTB	Black	1977	28000	40000	Velour interior
Jaguar	XJS	Silver	1983	23000	30000	AM/FM stereo
Honda	Civic	Black	1983	5600	16000	5 speed
Buick	Park Ave	Maroon	1982	6950	34000	Mint condition
Saab	Turbo	Grey	1983	11900	21000	Alarm system

doesn't sell in a certain amount of time. You can update a price by pointing to the record with the cursor, executing the *E=Edit Current Record...* command, changing the price, and replacing the record in the database.

Removing Data

Removing data—often called deleting data—is accomplished with the *X=Cut* command (Figure 9.6). The command removes selected records from the database. Unlike the *X=Cut* command in the word processor and spreadsheet

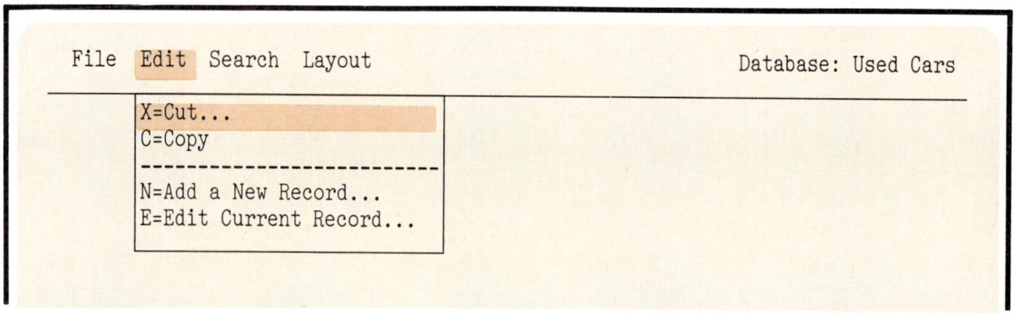

FIGURE 9.6 *The* X = Cut *command.*

programs, cut data are permanently removed. There is no Paste command in the database.

For example, suppose the first three cars in the database were sold. Move the arrow cursor to each record, and use the *S = Select Record* command to highlight them. Then use the *X = Cut...* command to remove the records from the database. Be careful; once the records are removed, you cannot retrieve them.

Searching, Selecting, and Sorting Data

Database programs can perform several kinds of **data manipulation.** The usual reason for manipulating data is to answer a question. The user puts the request for information in the form of commands that cause the appropriate data manipulation to occur. The two most common types of data manipulation are:

- Searching for and selecting records that match certain criteria, and highlighting those records.
- Sorting records, according to one or more keys.

Search and Select

A database program enables you to ask questions, or **queries,** about the contents of the database. This is called **searching,** because questions are phrased as criteria for searching through the database. **Selecting** means highlighting (in reverse video) the records that are found in response to your questions. Let us consider searching and selecting in the context of a customer calling in with some questions.

Starting the Search

Suppose someone calls your uncle's car lot and asks, "Do you have a Porsche 928 in stock?" You are going to translate that request into a command to search the Used Cars database. To translate the customer's request into a command, you have to tell the database program what criteria to use in the search.

Press the Esc key to toggle to the menu bar, move the pointer to the Search menu, and select the *Search & Select...* command. A dialog box will appear, listing the field names on the left-hand side and selection criteria in the middle.

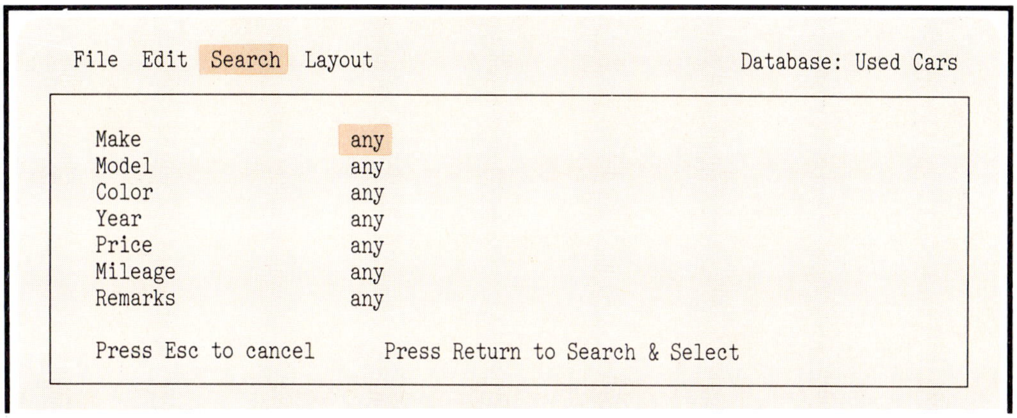

FIGURE 9.7 *Empty dialog box to search and select.*

The first of these selection criteria will be highlighted. The dialog box will look like Figure 9.7

As in the Edit Record Structure dialog box, the selection criteria appear as a hidden list of options. You can scroll through the selection criteria by pressing the space bar repeatedly. Table 9.3 lists the options in the order you'll see them. Stop when the option = appears, and press the Tab key. A highlighted space representing the Make field will appear to the right of the selection criteria. Type in the word *Porsche* and press the Tab key.

The next criterion we are interested in is the Model. With the pointer highlighting the Model selection criterion, press the space bar until the = option appears. Then press the Tab key. In the highlighted space, type in the number 928. Press the Tab key again.

You have just translated the customer's question into a search command. The dialog box will look like Figure 9.8. Now press the Return key to search the database. The dialog box will retract, and any records that meet the search criteria will be highlighted in reverse video, as shown in Figure 9.9. If the database were too long to appear on the screen all at once, you could use the Up and Down arrow keys to scroll through the database for selected records. You will discover that there is one Porsche 928 in stock.

TABLE 9.3 *Options for selection criteria*

Option	Meaning
any	All
=	Equal
>	Greater than
<	Less than
<>	Not equal
< =	Less than or equal
> =	Greater than or equal

```
File  Edit  Search  Layout                               Database: Used Cars

    Make              =        Porsche
    Model             =        928
    Color             any
    Year              any
    Price             any
    Mileage           any
    Remarks           any

    Press Esc to cancel      Press Return to Search & Select
```

FIGURE 9.8 *Completed dialog box to search and select.*

File Edit Search Layout — Database: Used Cars

	Make	Model	Color	Year	Price	Mileage	Remarks
→	Mercedes	380SL	Blue	1983	37999	14000	One owner
	Volvo	244DL	Brown	1977	4100	65000	Sunroof
	Porsche	944	Red	1984	22950	13800	Power windows
	Ferrari	308GTS	Silver	1980	32500	29000	Luxury trim
	Ford	Mustang	Green	1976	375	102000	Running well
	Dodge	Colt	Silver	1981	1250	42000	4 speed AM/FM radio
	Honda	Civic	Blue	1984	7200	16000	Hatchback
	Porsche	928	Red	1983	33900	16600	Leather interior
	Audi	4000S	White	1984	13950	12000	Full fact equipped
	Jaguar	XJ6	Green	1985	31895	5000	Leather interior
	Honda	Accord	Silver	1979	2100	50000	4 door
	Buick	Park Ave	Green	1982	9500	30000	Velour interior
	Buick	Skylark	Brown	1982	4800	18500	Air conditioning
	Saab	900S	Blue	1983	11000	30000	Sunroof
	Volvo	242DL	White	1983	9985	21000	Air conditioning
	Audi	5000	Black	1981	8877	42000	Alloy wheels
	Mercedes	380SL	Grey	1982	32900	38000	Perfect condition
	Buick	LeSabre	Blue	1983	8995	38000	One owner
	Saab	900S	Silver	1983	10000	19000	5 speed 4 door
	VW	Rabbit	Beige	1980	1600	84000	Sunroof

FIGURE 9.9 *Results of a search.*

The last selection will remain highlighted until you unselect it. (This is because it is possible to perform multiple searches, which we will discuss in the next section.) For now, you want to unselect this record. Move the arrow cursor to the selected record and hold down the Control key while pressing the S key. The record will return to normal video display.

The next question the customer asks is, "Do you have a Porsche for less than $30,000?" Return to the Search & Select dialog box. Notice that the dialog box still contains the selection criteria for the last search. Make = Porsche is still the first selection criterion, but the Model criterion needs to be changed to *any* and the Price selection criterion should be changed to < = 30000. After you enter the criteria, press the Return key.

Only one highlighted record meets these criteria. You can answer the customer's question by describing the one Porsche that sells for under $30,000. Be sure to unselect the record before going on.

When searching for data, keep in mind the following rules:

- Search operates on the principle of exact matching. If there is any variation between the search criterion you type in and the contents of the field, no records will be selected. For example, if you had entered *porsche* instead of *Porsche*, no records would have been selected.
- When multiple selection criteria are specified, only records that meet all the criteria are selected. For example, if three criteria are specified, a record is selected only if the first *and* the second *and* the third criteria are met.

Multiple Searches

Sometimes more than one search is required to answer a question. For example, suppose a customer asks, "What cars do you have between $20,000 and $30,000?"

In order to select all cars that fall within this price range, two searches must be performed. This process is called a **range search.** First, return to the Search & Select dialog box. The search criterion *Price* <= 30000 is already selected. All the other search criteria should specify *any*. When you press the Return key, all the records that have a price less than or equal to $30,000 will be highlighted.

Now return to the Search menu, and select the *Search & Unselect*. . . command. Then change the search criterion to *Price* <= 20000. Press the Return key. This command will cause all records with prices of $20,000 or less to be unselected. The result is the selection of the cars whose prices fall between $20,000 and $30,000.

Multiple searches can also be used to answer questions such as "Do you have any Volvos or Audis?" The clue is the word *or*. Since both criteria refer to the same field (the Make field), two searches must be performed to select the records that meet both criteria.

To answer this question, return to the Search & Select dialog box and specify the criterion *Make* = *Volvo*. (Be sure to unselect the records from the previous search and change the Price criterion to *any*.) Once you have selected all records that meet that criterion, return to the Search & Select dialog box and specify the criterion *Make* = *Audi*. The result will be the selection of records that meet either the first *or* the second search criterion.

Sorting Records

Sorting records means arranging them in a particular order. Examples of sorting include arranging records alphabetically by name, numerically by price, or chronologically by date.

Sorting can greatly reduce the effort involved in searching. For example, consider a list of names sorted into alphabetical sequence, such as the telephone book. If the names were not ordered alphabetically, you would spend a great deal of time trying to find a particular name. When items are sorted in a familiar sequence, you can rapidly (1) find a particular name, (2) determine whether a particular name is present or absent, and/or (3) scan or retrieve a group of similar names.

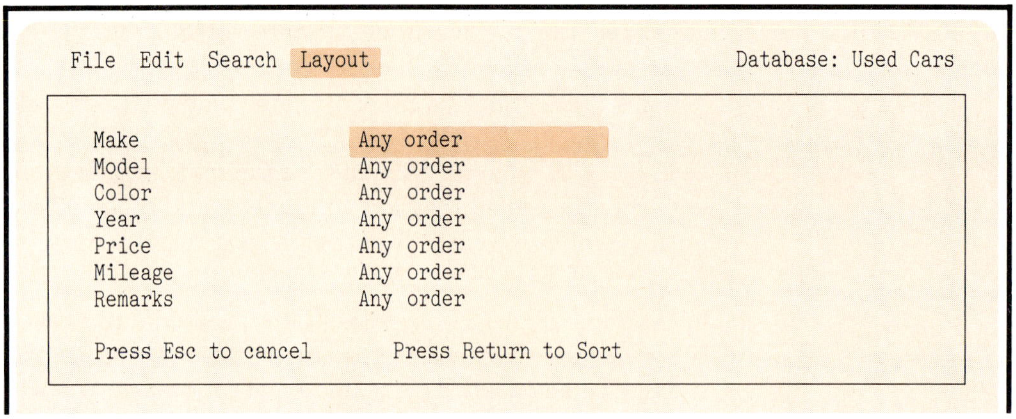

FIGURE 9.10 *Dialog box to sort records.*

Sorting is often the best technique for answering general questions like "Do you have any low-priced cars?" or "Do you have any low-mileage cars?"

Sorting uses the *Sort Records*. . . command in the Layout menu. For practice, we will sort the records in our Used Car database to answer the two questions above.

A question like "Do you have any low-priced cars?" is rather broad, so you would like to provide the customer with the broadest possible answer. Press the Esc key to toggle to the menu bar, move the pointer to the Layout menu, and select the *Sort Records*. . . command.

A dialog box like Figure 9.10 will appear, listing field names and sort criteria. To answer the question, you want to sort the records by Price in **ascending order.** Press the Tab key until the pointer highlights the sort criterion for Price. Press the space bar until the *Ascending Order* sort criterion appears. Then press the Return key.

The dialog box will retract, and the database will be displayed with the lowest-priced car listed first, the next least expensive second, and so on.

To answer the question about low-mileage cars, first, change *Ascending Order* in the Price field to *Any Order;* then sort the database by Mileage in ascending order. The database will be displayed with the lowest-mileage car listed first, and so on.

Sorts can also be nested—sorted on more than one field at a time. Suppose you want the Used Cars database to be listed alphabetically by Make, and within each Make to be arranged by price in ascending order.

First execute the *Sort Records*. . . command. Then specify that Make is to be sorted in ascending order, *and* that Price is to be sorted in ascending order. The resulting display will be grouped by the car's make. Within each make, cars will be listed by price in ascending order.

Rules of Sorting

When sorting data, keep in mind the following rules:

- Sorting can be done in ascending (lowest to highest) or **descending** (highest to lowest) **order.**
- Sorting occurs from left to right.

- Sorted characters are arranged according to the following sequences:

  Punctuation characters (.,#$)
  Numbers (0–9)
  Capital letters (A–Z)
  Lower-case letters (a–z)

- In order to sort chronologically, dates must be written in a year-month-day format instead of the usual month-day-year format. For example, the two dates January 4, 1981, and June 28, 1984, would be written as 81-01-04 and 84-05-28.

Printing Selected Data

To print selected records, use the *Print Selected Records*. . . command in the File menu (Figure 9.11). Make sure at least one record is selected, or the cursor will jump over the command.

Records are printed with field names on the left and field contents on the right. The entire database can be printed by activating the *Select All Records* command in the Search menu.

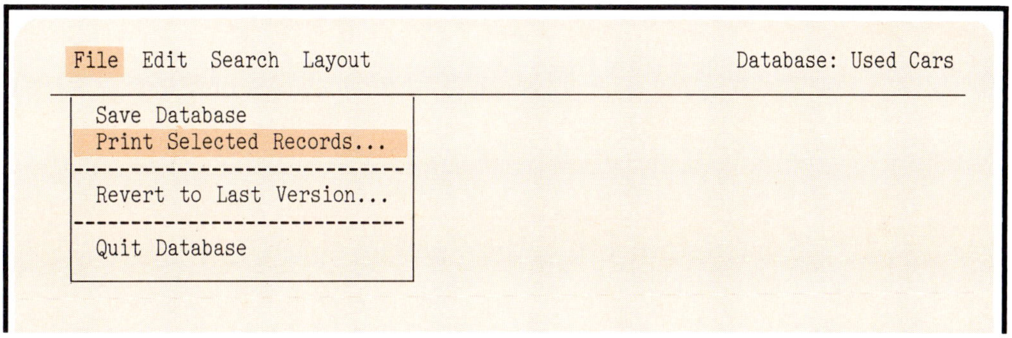

FIGURE 9.11 *The* Print Selected Records . . . *command.*

Exercises with the Database Program

- Enter 20 more records from Table 9.2, for a total of 40 records.
- Use the Search commands to answer the following questions, and the Print command to print the results:

  "Do you have any Saabs for under $12,000?"
  "What do you have in the way of Jaguars or Ferraris?"
  "Do you have any 1981, 1982, or 1983 Hondas?"
  "Do you have any Buick Park Ave's for under $7,000?"

- Use the Sort command to answer the following questions, and the Print command to print the results:

  "What do you have in the way of high-priced Ferraris?"
  "I don't care what it is, as long as it's black!"
  "Do you have any low-mileage, inexpensive cars?"

- Using the guidelines listed on pages 159–163, design and create a database to keep track of your music collection. Your collection consists of albums, cassettes, and compact disks. You like to select sets of music by the same artist, no matter what the medium. Your tastes run the gamut of rock, jazz, classical, and reggae. You like to select groups of cassettes to take with you on long car trips. Create a database that would allow you to do all this. Enter four sample records, print them, and hand the results in to your instructor.

REVIEW AND SELF-TESTING

Key Terms

Database program
Database
Record
Field
Structure
Data type
Form
Current record pointer
Update
Data manipulation
Query
Searching
Selecting
Range search
Sorting
Ascending order
Descending order

Questions for Review and Discussion

1. For what use were databases originally designed?
2. Why are database programs useful for keeping track of inventory?
3. Name the four functions of a database program.
4. In terms of content, what does a record consist of?
5. What are the two main considerations in naming a field?
6. Why should numeric fields sometimes be treated as text fields?
7. What are the two purposes of editing data?
8. How do Search & Select and Search & Unselect differ?
9. Why is sorting useful for answering questions of a general nature?
10. What must be taken into consideration when sorting chronologically?

10

Working with Databases

PREVIEW

In this chapter, you're going to use the TriPac database program to create a class-schedule database for Altair Community College. In the process, you'll learn how to systematically analyze, design, and implement a database application. Then we'll talk about how more advanced database software handles similar scheduling and registration tasks.

This chapter introduces a systematic problem-solving procedure for developing a database system. It also offers some guidelines to orient you to systems analysis and design.

With TriPac, you can learn the basics of developing applications through hands-on experience (though you can't build a full-fledged workable application). There are many commercial database packages designed specifically for developing your own applications, and we'll point out some of their advanced features.

In this chapter, you'll discover:

- *How to develop a database application*
- *How to analyze a database problem*
- *How to specify requirements*
- *How to create a database*
- *How to copy data to the word processor*
- *Relational databases*
- *Advanced data-manipulation techniques*
- *Report generators*
- *Security issues*
- *Data integrity issues*

The Application Development Process

Application development is a problem-solving process that begins with the needs of the user, and ends with a system that does what the user wants it to do. In between come the tasks of analyzing the need, designing the system, and implementing it.

There are several ways to implement an application. You can buy a ready-made off-the-shelf solution in the form of packaged application software. But a packaged program might not fit your needs exactly. You can develop your own custom computer program, to meet the exact requirements of your application. But this solution requires proficiency at designing and writing programs.

In between these two extremes is the database program. It too might not fit your needs exactly, but it is an alternative worth examining. Because database programs are general-purpose programs, they can be excellent tools to develop applications.

Using a database program to develop an application draws on the problem-solving method that we discussed in Chapter 4. In this case, getting to know the problem means getting to know the application, and defining the problem is a matter of specifying the functional requirements.

Getting to Know the Application

The application you are going to develop is a course-registration system for a college. When you register each semester, you select a schedule of classes. In this case, you will select your classes from a class-schedule database that you will first design and create. Then you will enter a set of test data that represents a hypothetical schedule. Your system will equip you to (1) select classes from a class-schedule database, (2) fill out a registration form by copying those classes to a word-processing document, and (3) print the registration form.

As a **builder-user**, you will design and develop the system, enter the data, and be its end-user. Often a **systems analyst** interprets the user's needs in sufficient detail to develop the requirements, and then turns them over to a programmer who builds the system for the end-user.

Later, you will see how this systematic method is used to develop large-scale scheduling applications.

Specifying the Requirements

After you get to know the application, and the user's needs and wants, the next step is to **specify the requirements**—to define the problem in a sufficiently well-organized way to guide the development of an appropriate system. The formal output of specifying requirements is often called a **functional specification.** The steps in specifying requirements for a database application are as follows:

- Identify the outputs.
- Identify the inputs.
- Identify the types of searches and sorts to use to question the database.
- Define the database.

For each step, you should assemble some documentation. In this case, that means writing down your thoughts, ideas, forms, and lists of questions and data fields. Under more formal circumstances, documenting the process is crucial in the design and development phases. When more than one person is involved in the process, written documentation serves as a communication tool among the people involved. That way, the specifications can be reviewed and challenged.

The output of our system will be a printed registration form listing titles, a date, the student's name and address, and a schedule of classes. Figure 10.1 shows what it will look like. To produce such a form, you'll need information from various sources besides the database.

Identifying inputs involves thinking about the overall flow of data in the system. What data is entered into the system? Where does that data come from? The student's name and address and the date, for example, will be entered by the student using the system. The class titles, times, dates, and so on will be derived from the class-schedule database.

Deciding what kinds of searches or sorts will be needed involves anticipating the kinds of questions you will want to ask about the schedule. Here are some examples of questions that can be answered by selecting records or sorting the database:

> "What if I can only go to classes on Monday evening?"
> "I've heard Professor Smith is a great teacher. How do I find out what classes she teaches?"
> "My work schedule limits me to Monday, Wednesday, and Friday morning classes. What classes can I take?"
> "I'm only interested in Communication. What classes can I take?"

```
Registration Form

Altair Community College

Date:

Name:
Address:
City:
State Zip:

Course   Description          Day and Time       Credits
----------------------------------------------------------



----------------------------------------------------------
                                    Total Credits:
```

FIGURE 10.1 *Sample registration form.*

Analyzing the output, input, and questioning requirements helps you decide what fields the database ought to contain. First, look at the sample output in Figure 10.1. It contains **fixed information**, such as the titles and headings, and **variable information**, which changes on each registration form. Variable information includes the date, the student's name, and the class schedule.

The variable information that is entered by the student isn't included in the database. By ignoring it, and the titles and headers, you can isolate the data elements (fields) that must be derived from the database.

By process of elimination, the database consists of the following fields:

```
Course
Description
Day
AM or PM class
Time
Instructor
Credits
```

Identifying Constraints

Any system is bound to be constrained in certain ways. There are two broad categories of constraints: organizational and technical. **Organizational constraints** include budgets, deadlines, and people's capabilities. While we cannot delve into these organizational constraints here, keep in mind that the project's budget and urgency, and the attitudes and skill of users, can play important roles.

Technical constraints are the limitations imposed by the hardware and the software. If there were such a thing as a perfect database program, several steps in the development process could be eliminated. For purposes of explaining technical constraints, we will look at how they influence the process of choosing the record structure of the class-schedule database.

You may want to glance back at Chapter 9, pages 159–163, about creating the record structure. We've already figured out what fields the records should contain. We have also given each field a preliminary name. Now we have to specify their order, and the size and type of each field.

A good way to clarify your thinking about the order of the fields is to look at some course catalogs to see how other people have organized course data. There are some constraints, however. For example, to sort classes in chronological order (morning classes before evening classes), we have to put the AM/PM field before the time field. This is because, when sorting on multiple keys, the TriPac database program sorts from left to right. (The alternative is to use military time, which most people dislike.)

Size specifications impose another technical constraint. You have the option of specifying 2, 4, 8, 12, or 20 characters in a text field; real-world data don't always fit neatly into such categories.

We've now informally specified the requirements for a course-registration application utilizing a class-schedule database. For a database application, specifying requirements means assembling an overall picture of the outputs the application will produce, the inputs it must accept, the searches and/or sorts that must occur to produce the output, and the data that must be present in the database.

Implementing the Database Program

To define the database, use the procedure you learned in Chapter 9, pages 159–163. Point to an untitled database, open it, and name it Class Schedule. Then select the *Define Record Structure...* command in the Layout menu. The record structure for the Class Schedule database should be as follows:

```
Field 1   Name: Course            Type: Text  8
Field 2   Name: Description       Type: Text 20
Field 3   Name: Day               Type: Text  4
Field 4   Name: AP (am or pm)     Type: Text  2
Field 5   Name: Time              Type: Text  8
Field 6   Name: Instructor        Type: Text 12
Field 7   Name: Cr                Type: Text  2
```

When you have finished filling in the record structure, press the Return key. The dialog box will retract, and a reverse-video heading line will appear on the screen directly below the menu bar.

At this point, check your design. It should fit on the screen. Check the spelling of your column headings. If you made any mistakes, go back to the *Define Record Structure...* command and make any necessary changes. If you have to change the record structure after you begin to enter records into the database, you will lose your data.

Now, you can add records to the database. This process is known as **data entry**, and it can be a time-consuming and error-prone task. You're going to enter the sample data in Table 10.1 into your database, using the *N=Add New Record...* command in the Edit menu. Type in the data one record at a time. Then press the Return key to add the record to the database. The program will automatically display it in row-and-column format. If you discover a mistake, move the arrow cursor to the record in question, and use the *E=Edit Current Record...* command to correct the mistake.

Evaluating the Results

Now, let's translate the questions on page 175 into search and sort criteria, to test out the class-schedule database.

Question: "What if I can only go to classes after noon on Monday?"

This question translates into the search & select criteria *Day = M* and *AP = pm*. Select the *Search & Select...* command from the Search menu. Type in the selection criteria for Day and AP, as shown in Figure 10.2, and press the Return key. The records that meet the selection criteria will be highlighted in reverse video. Use the key and the Down and Up arrow keys to scroll through the entire database.

Before you answer the next question, don't forget to clear the selected records with the *Unselect Every Record* command.

TABLE 10.1 *Data for class-schedule database*

Course	Description	Day	AP	Time	Instructor	Cr
EN 101	Intro to Engineering	MWF	am	09:00–10:00	McGinnis	3
CO 201	Public Rel. Writing	TTh	pm	02:00–03:30	Simpson	3
PY 260	Experimental Psych	TTh	pm	05:30–07:00	Kowalski	3
CS 101	Intro to Computers	MWF	am	09:00–10:00	Blissmer	3
LS 220	Human Physiology	MWF	pm	03:00–04:00	Hagen	3
SA 101	Graphic Design I	TTh	am	09:30–11:00	Smith	3
MN 280	Studies in Finance	M	pm	05:00–07:00	McMahon	2
FL 100	Beginning Italian	MWF	am	09:00–10:00	DeCollibus	3
PY 101	Intro to Psychology	TTh	am	09:30–11:00	Jamieson	3
CO 240	Feature Writing	M	pm	06:00–09:00	Ryan	3
HI 121	The Sixties	MW	am	11:00–12:00	Baker	2
CO 260	Broadcast Journalism	TTh	pm	07:30–09:00	Hrynyk	3
LI 100	Freshman Composition	TTh	am	11:30–01:00	Bassis	3
FL 114	Beginning French	MW	pm	07:30–09:00	Vose	3
LI 218	American Short Story	MWF	am	08:00–09:00	Bassis	3
SA 232	Silkscreen Workshop	T	am	09:30–12:00	Nitzberg	2
CS 101	Intro to Computers	M	pm	04:00–07:00	Alden	3
CO 101	Intro to Advertising	TTh	pm	07:30–09:00	Algaze	3
MA 112	Calculus Tutorial	Th	pm	03:00–04:00	Leonardi	1
LS 111	Microbiology	MW	pm	01:00–03:00	Verant	4
CS 220	Pascal Programming	MWF	am	11:00–12:00	Blissmer	3
HI 180	Afro-American Hist	TTh	am	09:30–11:00	Lombard	3
EN 101	Intro to Engineering	TTh	pm	05:30–07:00	McGinnis	3
LI 280	Poetry Workshop	Th	pm	02:00–04:00	Bly	2
CO 101	Intro to Advertising	MWF	am	10:00–11:00	Algaze	3
CS 262	Artificial Intell	TTh	pm	02:00–04:00	Alden	4
CO 220	Copywriting II	W	pm	05:30–07:00	Simpson	3
FL 100	Beginning Italian	MW	pm	05:30–07:00	DeCollibus	3
MN 280	Studies in Finance	TTh	am	09:30–10:30	McMahon	2
LS 221	Human Physiology Lab	T	pm	02:00–05:00	Hagen	2
PY 101	Intro to Psychology	Th	pm	07:00–10:00	Jamieson	3
HI 200	Russian History	MWF	am	10:00–11:00	Neidich	3
CS 220	Pascal Programming	Th	pm	07:00–10:00	Blissmer	3
MN 212	Arts Management	MWF	pm	12:00–01:00	Schiffman	3
CO 201	Advertising Lab	Th	pm	02:00–05:00	Algaze	2
CO 112	Photography Workshop	M	pm	07:00–09:00	Quinn	2
MA 111	Calculus I	MWF	pm	01:00–02:00	Leonardi	3
PY 220	Developmental Psych	W	pm	04:00–07:00	Cook	3
CS 221	Pascal Tutorial	W	pm	12:00–01:00	Blissmer	1
SA 280	Graphic Design II	TTh	am	11:30–01:00	Smith	3
CO 220	Copywriting II	MWF	am	11:00–12:00	Gellert	3
SA 101	Graphic Design I	W	pm	04:00–07:00	Harnicar	3
FL 202	Intermediate Italian	MWF	am	08:00–09:00	DeCollibus	3
CS 101	Intro to Computers	W	pm	06:00–09:00	Blissmer	3
LS 112	Microbiology Lab	Th	am	08:30–11:00	Verant	2
MN 101	Basic Accounting	MWF	pm	02:00–03:00	McMahon	3
LS 220	Basic Nutrition	W	pm	07:30–09:30	Callaghan	2
CO 112	Photography Workshop	T	pm	02:00–04:00	Kestenbaum	2
CO 260	Broadcast Journalism	MWF	am	11:00–12:00	Colburn	3

```
File  Edit  Search  Layout                          Database: Class Schedule

  Course                  any
  Description             any
  Day                     =          M
  AP (am or pm)           =         pm
  Time                    any
  Instructor              any
  Cr                      any

  Press Esc to cancel        Press Return to Search & Select
```

FIGURE 10.2 *Completed Search & Select dialog box.*

> Question: "I've heard that Professor Smith is a great teacher. How do I find out what classes she teaches?"

This question translates into a search criterion of *Instructor = Smith.* Clear the dialog box from the last search; then enter the new search criterion and press the Return key. All the records that meet the search criterion will be highlighted.

> Question: "My work schedule limits me to Monday, Wednesday, and Friday morning classes. What classes can I take?"

To answer this question, you will have to perform several searches. One way to do this is to first search & select with the criterion AP = am. Then perform three search & unselect commands, with the criterion set to Day = T and AP = am, Day = Th and AP = am, and Day = TTh and AP = am. The remaining highlighted records will represent the classes available on Monday, Wednesday, or Friday mornings.

> Question: "I'm only interested in Communication. What classes can I take?"

The course field is a combination of a departmental abbreviation and a class number. If department were a separate field, you could base your search on finding a match for that field. Because it isn't, you must use some other method. For example, if you sort the records in ascending order by course, all the Communication classes will be grouped together.

Generating the Registration Form

Now it is time to test the system's ability to generate a registration form. Use the following search criteria to produce a set of sample data to use:

> Select one English course and two Computer Science courses meeting on Monday, Wednesday, and Friday. Make sure there are no time conflicts in your schedule.

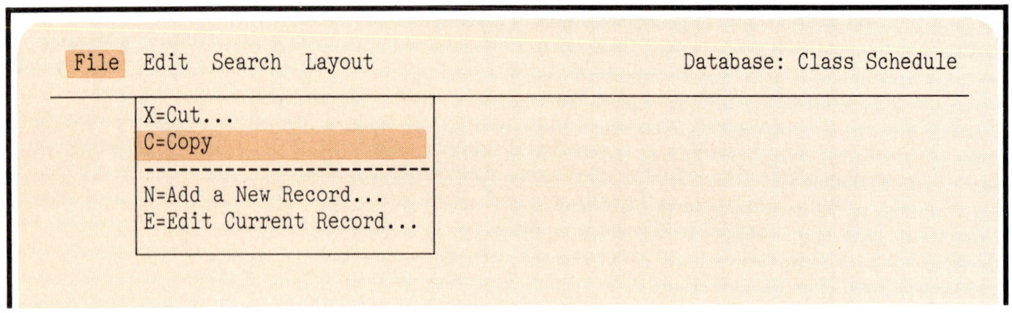

FIGURE 10.3 *The* C = Copy *Command.*

Generating the registration form involves copying records from the database and pasting them into a word-processing document. Begin by using the word processor to create a blank registration form, with the titles and heading line shown in Figure 10.1. Call the document Registration.

After you have selected your three classes, press the Esc key to toggle to the menu bar. Select the *C = Copy* command in the Edit menu, as shown in Figure 10.3.

Quit the database program and open the Registration word-processing document. When it appears, move the cursor to the first position in the line below the dotted line, as shown in Figure 10.4(a), and execute the *P = Paste* command in the Edit menu.

The selected records will be pasted into the document with the fields arranged vertically, one field per line, as shown in Figure 10.4(b). Next, you will need to rearrange the fields horizontally, so that each record can occupy a horizontal row. To rearrange the first record, move the cursor to the paragraph mark following the course number and delete it. The course description will move up one line. Align it under the Description heading by inserting spaces before it. Then move the cursor to the paragraph symbol following the description and delete it. In order to make the database record fit, you will also have to delete the instructor's name.

Continue to delete paragraph symbols and text until the entire first record is horizontally positioned on one line. Then repeat the process with the second and third records. When you have arranged the course information in three rows between the two rows of dotted lines, as shown in Figure 10.4(c), print a copy and hand it in to your instructor.

Advanced Database Features

So far, it may seem easier to select records manually from a database, using your eyes, than to develop search and sort criteria for scanning the database. But a real database can easily contain hundreds or even thousands more rows than you have been working with.

If you had to scan through a database of this size, the advantages of letting the program do the scanning would be much more obvious. The program wouldn't overlook records, and it wouldn't "mind" performing several different searches or sorts to find data.

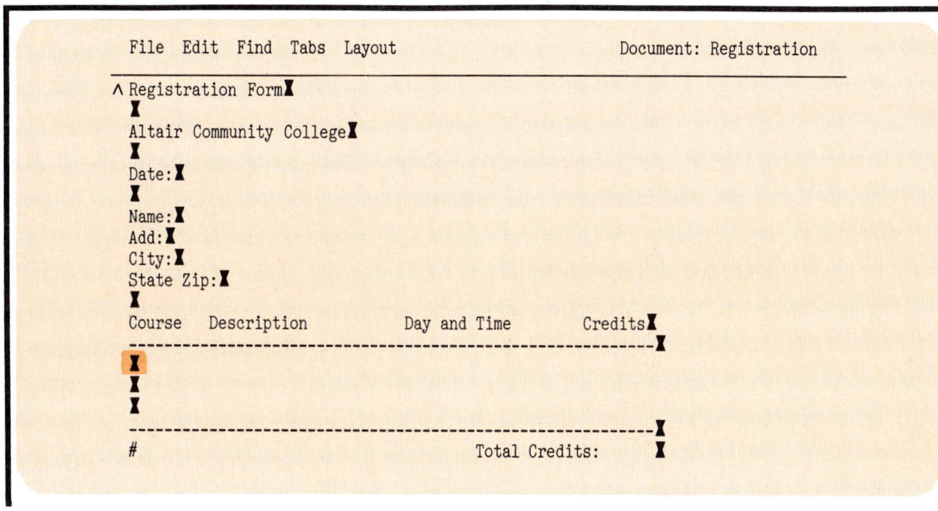

```
File  Edit  Find  Tabs  Layout                         Document: Registration
^Registration Form
Altair Community College
Date:
Name:
Add:
City:
State Zip:
Course   Description           Day and Time         Credits
------------------------------------------------------------


------------------------------------------------------------
#                                    Total Credits:
```

(a) Cursor positioned to paste selected records into documents.

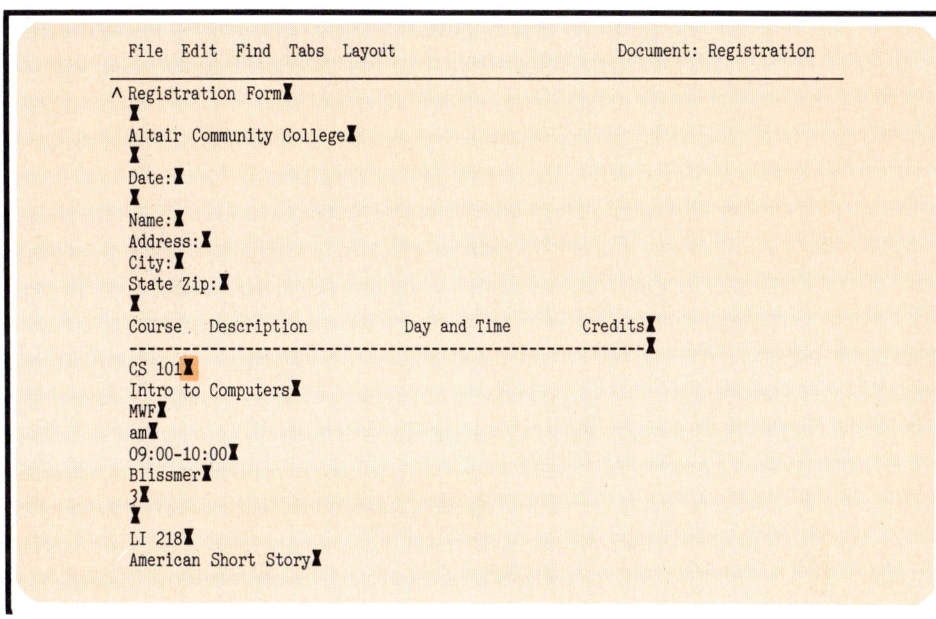

```
File  Edit  Find  Tabs  Layout                         Document: Registration
^Registration Form
Altair Community College
Date:
Name:
Address:
City:
State Zip:
Course   Description           Day and Time         Credits
------------------------------------------------------------
CS 101
Intro to Computers
MWF
am
09:00-10:00
Blissmer
3
LI 218
American Short Story
```

(b) Document scrolled back to first screen after the selected records have been pasted in.

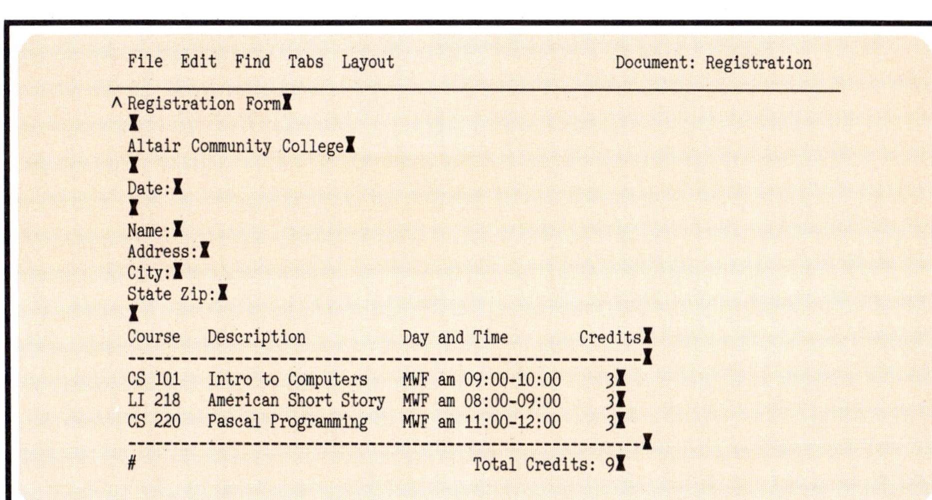

```
File  Edit  Find  Tabs  Layout                         Document: Registration
^Registration Form
Altair Community College
Date:
Name:
Address:
City:
State Zip:
Course   Description           Day and Time         Credits
------------------------------------------------------------
CS 101   Intro to Computers    MWF am 09:00-10:00       3
LI 218   American Short Story  MWF am 08:00-09:00       3
CS 220   Pascal Programming    MWF am 11:00-12:00       3
------------------------------------------------------------
#                                    Total Credits: 9
```

(c) Edited Registration document. Pasted-in records have been formatted to align under headings.

FIGURE 10.4 *Pasting records from database to word processor.*

To understand the benefits of a commercial database program, let's look at the features of advanced database programs.

Relational Databases

A **relational database** organizes files into tabular rows (records) and columns (fields), and enables the user to relate two or more files through a field they have in common, as illustrated in Figure 10.5. Like many database programs, TriPac can only use one file at a time. Multiple interrelated files and relational data-manipulation capabilities are the distinguishing characteristics of a relational database program.

If we were designing a large-scale course-registration database, interrelated files would be a great advantage. There could be a student file containing an ID number, name and address, transcript information, and financial information. Entering the ID number would automatically search the student file

Course	Description	Day	AM/PM	Time	Instructor	Cr.
CO 240	Feature Writing	M	PM	6-9	Ryan	3
.	.	.	.	.	.	.
.	.	.	.	.	.	.
.	.	.	.	.	.	.

Course	Student ID
CO 240	123456
CO 240	731657
CO 240	961121
CO 240	03567

Student ID	Name	Tuition Paid	Bal. Due
03567	Blissmer	500.00	-0-
.	.	.	.
.	.	.	.
.	.	.	.

FIGURE 10.5 *Relationships among files can be created through common fields.*

for the name and address. Linking an accounting database into the system would give access to records of tuition paid and outstanding. Also, the registration process could produce class rosters, linking a database of classes and students into the system.

Database applications can quickly become quite complicated. The more complex the application, the more it pays to approach the problem systematically, and plan ahead.

Database Size

The maximum size of a database is a technical constraint that must be taken into account in the design process. The limits of commercial database packages can vary widely. A large-scale database program might advertise that it supports three open files at once, up to 65,534 records per file, and 127 fields per record (with a maximum of 1024 characters per record).

These numerical limitations can be better understood when they are compared to numbers such as how many students are in a college or how many items are in an inventory. Such figures serve as a starting point for determining the number of records per file. Estimates of characters per record, fields per record, and characters per field then serve as a base for defining the record structure. These types of calculations are important to ensure that the database program can handle the size of a particular application.

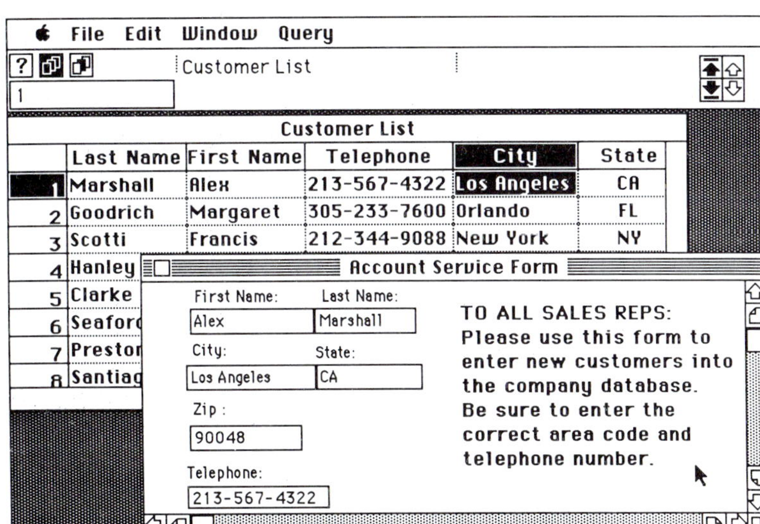

A customer-list database viewed (1) in tabular rows and columns and (2) by individual records when entering data.

Data Manipulation

Advanced data-manipulation capabilities include arithmetic within a record and across records, and wildcard searches.

To understand **arithmetic within a record,** think of the resemblance between a course-registration system and an airline flight-reservation system: both need to keep track of the number of available seats. If it is possible to perform arithmetic within a record, a number-of-seats field could be added to the class-schedule database. Whenever a student enrolled in a particular course, the system would update the field (subtract 1 from it). When the number reached 0, the class could be tagged as unavailable or removed from the class-schedule database.

Arithmetic across records makes it possible to answer "how many"-type questions. For example, to answer the question, "How many classes meet after noon on Monday?," the database program would formulate the search as: Count records where Day = M and AP = pm. The result of such a search would be a count of the number of records that meet the search criteria.

Another use for arithmetic across records is to sum a series of fields in selected records. For example, in the Used Cars database, you could ask a question like, "What is the combined value of all the Mercedes on the lot?" The database program would translate that request into a search as: Sum Price where Make = Mercedes.

A **wildcard search** uses shorthand notation to fill in incomplete search criteria. For example, with wildcard notation, answering the question about what Communication classes are available would be translated into a search criterion like: Course = CO ***. The three asterisks in the field name indicate that any acceptable characters may occupy those positions. Thus all courses with the CO prefix would be selected.

Redefining a Database

Databases tend to grow and change with use. In addition to being constantly revised (new records added, old records deleted), new requirements might mean that the record structure has to be redefined. The capacity to **redefine the record structure** means one can add, delete, rename, resize, and reorganize fields in a record without losing any data.

For example, suppose a new requirement is imposed on your class schedule database: Each record must contain a separate department code, class number, and section number. If you can redefine the record structure, you can make two fields out of the current course field, and insert a section number after the class number, as shown in Figure 10.6. Caution: In TriPac, you can't redefine a database without losing your existing data.

Generating Reports

A **report generator** is a part of a database program that allows you to define and produce printed output. Figure 10.7 shows a report generated by a report generator. Report generators provide a variety of options, including:

- A procedure for defining a report, previewing it on the screen, and saving the format for repeated use.
- Automatic calculation across records (totals, subtotals, counts, and averages).
- Automatic calculation across fields (for example, field 1 minus field 2 equals a new field in the report).
- The ability to select specified records and fields for inclusion in the report, and to produce a report sorted in a particular way.

Course	Description
CO 201	Public Rel. Writing
.	.
.	.
.	.
.	.

Original record structure

Dept.	Class	Section	Description
CO	201	1	Public Rel. Writing
CO	201	2	Public Rel. Writing
CO	201	3	Public Rel. Writing
.		.	.
.	.	.	.

Redefined record structure

FIGURE 10.6 *Original and redefined record structures.*

Enrollment by Department

Dept	Class	Enrollment	
Communications	Intro to Advertising	60	
	Photography Workshop	45	
	Public Rel. Writing	35	
	Advertising Lab	15	
	Copywriting II	25	
	Feature Writing	20	
	Broadcast Journalism	35	
	Subtotal:		235
Computer Science	Intro to Computers	125	
	Pascal Programming	45	
	Pascal Tutorial	25	
	Artificial Intelligence	20	
	Subtotal:		215
	Total:		450

FIGURE 10.7 *A report produced by a report generator. Report generators usually allow you to specify what fields to include in the report and in what order, and to use arithmetic functions that provide subtotals and totals.*

When you use a report generator, the first step is to define the format of the report. Like defining a database, this is usually done through an on-screen dialog, which allows you to specify what to include in the report, and the source of the data. A Print Report command causes the database to be searched, and sorted if necessary, and the results printed in the report.

Data Security

Data security involves protecting the database against unauthorized access. Security is most important in a shared system, which gives many people access to the database. Often users are assigned a **password**, a code that identifies the user to the system. Figure 10.8 shows a typical password dialog. If you have a card that allows you to withdraw money from your bank account via an automated teller machine, you must first enter a password to gain access to the money-dispensing machine.

Passwords can provide variable levels of access. A user can have complete access, access to selected records or fields, or read-only access, depending on the degree of confidentiality to be maintained.

For example, in a three-level password-based course-registration system, students would probably have level-1 (read-only) access to the database. Clerks in the registration office, whose responsibility it is to update and maintain the database, would have level-2 (read/write) access. Only the registrar would have level-3 access: ability to read and write records and to modify the record structure.

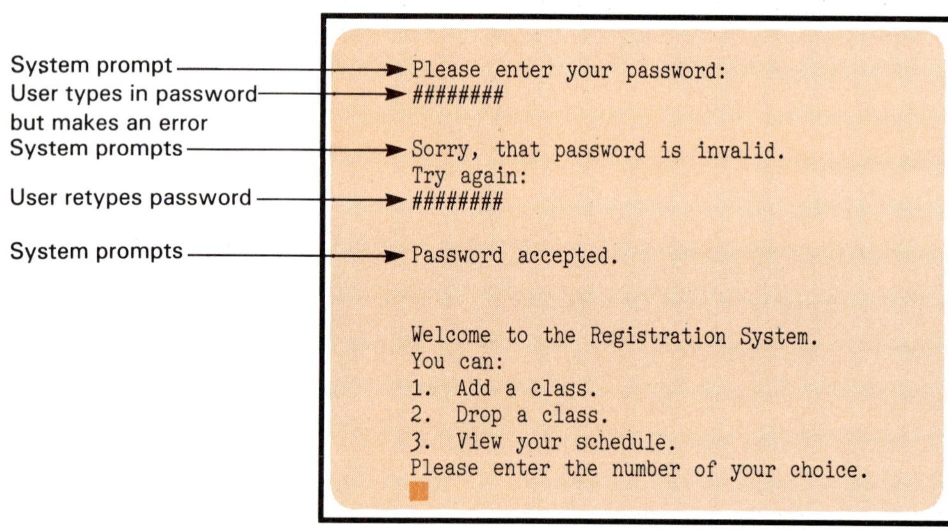

FIGURE 10.8 *Sample password dialog.*

Data Integrity

Data integrity is a matter of the accuracy and validity of the data in the database. In other words, it ensures that the data that is added to the database is correct. There are several ways to handle data integrity. Database programs can perform **edit checks** when data are entered into the database or updated.

The TriPac database program performs a simple edit check on numeric fields. When a field's type is numeric, you cannot enter anything but a number; the keyboard will not respond.

More complex edit checks include range checking, in which upper and lower values are assigned to a field. For example, a field that designates the number of hours worked per week might have a lower limit of 0 and an upper limit of 80. If you attempted to enter a number outside that range, the program would reject the entry.

A commercial database is a significant and valuable resource, and there is always the danger that users could accidentally destroy data, delete the wrong data from a database, or add the wrong data to a database. There is also a danger of losing or damaging the disk itself. For these reasons, provision must be made to back up the database. A **backup file** is a copy made for possible later reconstruction in case the original database is destroyed, lost, or damaged.

Exercises with the Database Program

Translate the following questions into search or sort criteria for the Class Schedule database, print the results, and hand them in to your instructor:

"I am only interested in 2-credit classes. What are my options?"
"Does Professor Alden teach any Monday morning classes?"
"I can only take classes between 3:00 and 7:00 pm. What classes are available?"
"I can only take classes on Monday morning or Wednesday morning. What classes are available?"
"What evening English classes are available on Wednesdays?"

REVIEW AND SELF-TESTING

Key Terms

Application development
Builder-user
Systems analyst
Specifying requirements
Functional specification
Fixed information
Variable information
Organizational constraints
Technical constraints
Data entry
Relational database
Arithmetic within a record
Arithmetic across records
Wildcard search
Redefining the record structure
Report generator
Data security
Password
Data integrity
Edit check
Backup file

Questions for Review and Discussion

1. What makes a database program a particularly useful application-development tool?
2. How is the process of developing a database application similar to the general-purpose problem-solving method?
3. What is a functional specification?
4. Outline the steps involved in specifying requirements for a database application.
5. Name one technical constraint that helps determine the order of fields in a record structure.
6. What command is used to correct mistakes in records?
7. When is it easier to specify search criteria than to scan a database with your eyes?
8. How does a relational database differ from a database used by TriPac?
9. Name two purposes for arithmetic across records.
10. How might you use a wildcard search to search the class database for introductory courses?
11. What is the difference between data security and data integrity?

11

How to Buy a Personal Computer System

PREVIEW

Throughout this book, you have been learning how to use a personal computer. You've also become familiar with several general-purpose applications. In this chapter, we'll give you some ideas for choosing a computer system of your own.

Buying a personal computer system involves decisions that do not lend themselves to clear-cut rules. You will be inundated with other people's preferences and opinions. You will have to use judgment and insight to sort through an immense number of conflicting messages.

Correctly projecting from your own application needs to the capabilities of a specific make and model of personal computer is the most important step for the first-time computer buyer.

In this chapter, you'll discover:

- *How to determine your needs*
- *How to specify your application*
- *Where to find information*
- *How to buy an IBM Personal Computer*
- *How to buy a Macintosh*
- *How to buy a home computer*
- *How to buy a portable computer*
- *How to purchase your computer*

Know Your Applications

Buying a personal computer system, like the problem-solving process we discussed in Chapter 4, starts with getting to know the problem. In thinking about buying a personal computer, the most important consideration is to know your applications, and to buy for those applications. Don't rush off to the computer store before you do your homework.

The problem-solving process applied to buying a personal computer.

- *Get to know the problem: Think about how you will use a personal computer.*
- *Define the problem: Make a general list of the applications you need.*
- *Identify alternative solutions: Research and evaluate a variety of software packages and personal computer systems.*
- *Choose the best alternative: Narrow down the choices and decide which system works best for you.*
- *Implement the solution: Make your purchase.*

Get to Know the Problem

First, examine your expectations about how you will use a personal computer. Some questions to consider include:

- Will you be predominantly interested in one application? Are you a writer (word processing), an accountant (spreadsheets or accounting software), a graphic designer (graphics), or a small-business owner (database or spreadsheet programs)? By eliminating the applications you don't need, you will simplify the decision-making process considerably.
- Will you use the computer in your profession? If your colleagues favor particular hardware and software, you might want to follow suit so you can swap disks and exchange information with them.
- Are you computerizing a small business? A dentist might want a computer to keep track of patient records and billing. A lawyer might use a computer to help prepare legal contracts. The owner of a retail store might need a system for accounting and inventory. The widest variety of software for these specialized needs can be found for the IBM Personal Computer and its equivalents.

- How often do you plan to use your computer? People who use their computers day in and day out want power, performance, and functionality. They are willing to pay more, and they will often put up with complex, hard-to-learn systems to obtain these features. Casual users may prefer a simple, easy-to-learn system.
- Are you planning to write programs or develop software? If so, you may not need any application software. Instead, you will want to find the computer system that best suits the applications you wish to develop, and the system that offers the most development tools.
- Do you travel? Will you want to take your computer with you? Find out whether a portable computer can run the software you need. A reporter, for instance, might want a computer that fits in a briefcase and offers word processing and communications. A manager might just need a computer he or she can take home to finish up the day's tasks.
- Will the computer be primarily for your own use, or for your children's education and entertainment? If business applications are not your primary consideration, a home computer will offer the best value and the widest variety of recreational and educational software.

Of course you may have other ideas in mind. Generate your own questions in light of your needs. No one knows them better than you.

What Do You Want the Computer to Do?

Defining the problem means defining what you want the computer system to do. Start with a general list of applications geared to your needs. Some examples are writing (papers, articles, letters, novels), personal financial planning, inventory control, customer lists, mailing lists, tax preparation, budgeting, payroll, adventure games, simulations, tutorials, music, drawing, computer-aided design, scheduling, forecasting, stock-market quotes, home banking, and conferencing.

Refine the general description into a specific description. Spell out your expectations in more detail. Define what it is you intend to do with your computer. Let's look at some examples:

- A graphic designer wants a computer system to help create charts and graphs, layouts, and illustrations. He wants to draw the graphics, print them, and present them to clients, and also insists on ease of use.
- A journalism student wants to develop a freelance writing and editing business while finishing graduate school. She needs to produce multi-page proposals, articles, reports, and papers. The documents will include typographical elements like boldface, italics, and footnotes.
- The owner of a retail shoe store wants computerized records of customers' names and addresses. She currently files customer records by name and Zip code, and types mailing labels for direct-mail campaigns. The number of customers has grown to 5,000, and the task is becoming unmanageable by hand.

- A contractor wants to prepare estimates and keep track of expenses, materials, and labor hours.
- A stockbroker wants to monitor stock prices, obtain and analyze financial data from on-line databases, and prepare summary reports featuring graphs.
- A homeowner wants to control his solar heating and cooling systems, security, lighting, and home entertainment center.

Even before you've begun collecting information about specific hardware and software, jot down a list or description of all the ways you envision using the computer. These notes will help you define the requirements of the system. By defining and refining your description of applications, you will clarify your alternatives and your priorities.

Evaluate the Alternatives

There are many ways to acquire background information and evaluate your alternatives. Spend some time researching, reading, and talking to people before you make any purchases. This process will help you narrow down your choices.

Computer Users

Talk to people who have similar application interests. Do you have any friends, professional contacts, or teachers who are already using a computer for the types of problems you are going to tackle? Ask people how they use their computers. Ask what problems they have encountered. Ask their opinions on various computer systems and software packages.

Computer Magazines

Computer magazines provide reviews of hardware and software, opinion columns, news, trends, and predictions. There are many personal-computer magazines, targeted to various types of consumers. Magazines are targeted to educators, businesspeople, programmers, kids, users of specific applications, and owners of specific computers.

For trends, news, and reviews, read magazines like the weekly *InfoWorld*, the monthly *Personal Computing* or *Byte*, and the quarterly *Whole Earth Review*. Magazines about specific computers and applications include *PC World*, *PC*, *Macworld*, *A+* (Apple), and *Amiga World*.

Public libraries and school libraries often subscribe to specialized, expensive, or controlled-circulation magazines not available at newsstands or computer stores. These periodicals are a good source of information about particular applications. Names of some of these periodicals are *PC-Week*, *Mini-Micro Systems*, *The Seybold Report on Professional Computing*, *Data Sources*, and *Datapro's Microcomputer Software*.

Books

A relatively small investment in a pertinent, up-to-date book is a valuable way to familiarize yourself with computers and their uses before you buy. Look for user guides in the application areas in which you are interested, and books with hardware or program names in their titles. Before you buy a book, evaluate it as a learning tool and as a reference guide. Check the copyright date to see if the book is current. Read the preface or introduction to find out who the book is written for. Flip through the pages to see whether illustrations and graphics accompany the text. Then flip to the index and glossary at the back of the book, to see if the book is useful as a reference.

Your local or school library will probably have a small- to medium-sized collection of computer books. (For an overview, check number 001.64 under the Dewey Decimal System; in Library of Congress systems, look under QA 76.) If you would rather buy, most book stores and computer stores carry computer books and magazines.

Computer Shows

If you've ever been to an automobile or boat show, you already have an idea of what a computer show is all about. If you want to compare several computer systems and software packages, see demonstrations, or meet people with similar interests and needs, go to a computer show or conference. Check local newspapers for regional shows, and magazines for national shows and/or conventions. Larger cities host many such shows and expositions yearly.

For maximum media and customer exposure, many companies wait for computer shows to announce their latest products. Shows are good places to look at new software and hardware systems, pick up company literature, and often buy products at a discount.

Computer shows and conferences are a good place to see new computer hardware and software and to compare systems.

User Groups

User groups are loosely knit collections of people who meet periodically to listen to lectures, swap problems and solutions, publish newsletters, trade software, and meet other people with similar interests. They are usually organized around a particular brand of computer, such as an Apple II or an IBM Personal Computer. Some are organized around application software, such as a Lotus 1-2-3 user group, and others focus on particular professions (consultants, technical writers, small business systems, and the like). Joining a user group, or attending meetings before you buy a computer, is a good way to get advice and information.

Computer Stores

Computer stores are probably the best sources of information. You can try out various systems, watch demonstrations, and ask questions. Check out several retail stores in your area. Ask about prices and the availability of various systems. Get a sense of the attitude of the salespeople. Are they customer problem solvers? Do they appear knowledgeable about hardware and software? Do they ask you questions about your specific needs? Does the store cater to professionals or hobbyists, and which would you prefer? Ask about after-sale training and support.

Before you begin looking at systems in a store, have some concrete examples of your application in mind. Know specifically what the application must do.

Computer stores are often the best place to see demonstrations and compare different systems.

For example, "I need a database package that will store 10,000 names and addresses, produce a monthly summary report, and print mailing labels sorted by Zip code. I also expect to add 5,000 new names to the file over the next year." Concrete examples help you uncover hardware and software limitations, and eliminate those systems from consideration.

You can also obtain copies of the product literature supplied by software publishers and hardware manufacturers. Of course, descriptive information of this kind is written by the marketing department, and should not be mistaken for an objective evaluation. The product-specification sheets do provide accurate technical information.

Documentation

The manuals that accompany hardware and software products are called **documentation.** You can get an excellent overview of most products by looking at their documentation. Its quality and style also reflect the ability of the manufacturer or publisher to market and support their products.

Evaluate the documentation as a teaching tool. Does it explain how to use the product? Does it proceed logically from the basics to the more advanced functions? Are there plenty of examples? Does it include a tutorial disk? Does it contain illustrations and screen shots?

Then evaluate the documentation as a reference manual. Does it have an index? Does it explain error messages? Is there a quick reference guide? Is there a technical appendix?

Courses

Still in doubt about whether or not to buy? Look around for one-day or weekend seminars on such topics as "Using a Personal Computer" or "Purchasing Your Personal Computer." Also look for application-oriented classes, such as "Word Processing for Personal Computers" or "Using Personal Computers in Small Business." Make sure the course offers hands-on experience.

How to Buy an IBM Personal Computer System

IBM manufactures a family of Personal Computers (PCs). The original IBM PC, introduced in 1981, was followed by the IBM PC XT, which features a built-in hard disk; the transportable PC; the IBM PCjr (discontinued, but still available); and the IBM PC AT (Advanced Technology), which features a more powerful microprocessor.

The IBM PC is an extremely popular personal computer: It has captured over 30 percent of the total personal-computer market. IBM is the world's largest computer and office-equipment manufacturer. This influences many buyers, who feel that the size and prestige of IBM, coupled with the service and backup it can offer, outweigh any other considerations.

Virtually every software company writes programs for the PC. The wide range of software that has been developed for the PC makes it a very versatile computer. The PC has also spawned a large "third-party" industry of software and hardware developers.

The IBM Personal Computer system offers a wide variety of printer, display, disk, and memory options.

The PC was designed as an **open system**, so it is sold as a system of components. This gives the PC tremendous versatility and adaptability, but the trade-off is that there are many decisions to make when buying a PC. You have to decide what memory, disk drives, display, and so forth to buy. The basic IBM PC, the "IBM Personal Computer System Unit with Keyboard," comes with 256K of RAM memory. It is up to the buyer to select the additional hardware components that are needed to make the computer a useful system.

Memory Considerations

You will want to add to the 256K of memory that the computer comes equipped with. But how much memory should you add? You will probably want a minimum of 384K, but the software you plan to use is the major consideration. A good rule of thumb is not to buy more memory than you need, because you can always add more later.

For example, suppose your application involves database management. For small file-management programs, 384K is usually plenty, but sophisticated relational database programs typically require a minimum of 512K, and recommend 640K for optimal operation. Packaged application software always contains a specification of the system it works with, including minimum memory requirements and the number of disk drives required.

Additional memory for the PC comes on memory-expansion boards, which plug into the expansion slots located inside the system unit. You can buy these from IBM, or you can buy third-party memory-expansion boards.

Disk Storage Considerations

Disk drives are not included in the basic IBM PC, but the system unit contains two empty slots for disk drives. You can configure your system to contain either one or two floppy drives, or one floppy and one hard disk. Two disk drives are preferable to one. The combination of floppy and hard disk gives you the most flexibility, versatility, and performance from your system. A hard disk increases the performance of virtually any software: Access time is much faster and storage capacity much greater; the trade-off is a much higher price.

Display Considerations

The two most important points to consider in comparing display devices are graphics and color. Buying an IBM PC requires you to weigh the differences between display devices.

Because of low quality, a television set is not recommended as a display device. Also, the video output of a computer cannot be directly sent to a television. To do so requires an RF modulator. (The exception is the video monitor in a high-priced component television system.)

Display devices range from monochrome (the least expensive), to composite color monitors, to RGB color monitors (the most expensive). Which to choose largely depends on whether you will be using software that takes advantage of color and graphics displays. Word processing, for instance, is normally associated with monochrome displays, but newer word processors like Microsoft Word display text in graphics mode, and WordStar 2000 uses color to highlight various aspects of a document.

The IBM PC requires a video interface or graphics adapter, a board that plugs into one of the expansion slots and connects the PC to the video display device. The Monochrome Display and Printer Adapter is a video interface for a monochrome display. IBM also sells a Color Graphics Adapter, an Enhanced Graphics Adapter, and a very expensive Professional Graphics Controller, all of which can be used with either a monochrome or color display. Third-party graphics-adapter boards are also available.

Printer Considerations

The IBM's versatility means that virtually any type of printer can be connected to it. Figure out what your printing needs will be based on your application; then select the type of printer that suits your needs.

Printers fall into two categories—impact and non-impact. Of the non-impact printers, laser printers (the most expensive) offer the broadest range of desirable features: graphics, high speed, high quality, and quiet operation. Inkjet and thermal-transfer printers cost less, and are the best choice for high-resolution color printing.

Impact printers—dot-matrix and letter-quality—transfer an image by striking the paper. Letter-quality printers produce text that closely resembles the printing of an IBM Selectric typewriter, which is desirable for some business situations; the trade-off is high noise and lack of graphics capability. Dot-matrix printers are the most common and least expensive printers for personal-computer systems. They too are noisy, but they can print graphics and high-quality text, and some can print in color.

Communication Considerations

There are two ways to add communication capability to a PC. The first is to use a modem card, which contains a modem and an interface, and plugs into one of the expansion slots. The alternative is to use a communications interface card. IBM's Asynchronous Communications Adapter, for example, connects the processor to an external modem.

A Note on IBM Compatibility

Should you buy an IBM PC-compatible computer? The term **compatibility** refers to computers on which the same software can be run without alteration. Thus an IBM-compatible personal computer should be able to run programs designed for the IBM PC.

These computers are sometimes differentiated by lower price and additional features (built-in graphics capabilities, or the transportability of the Compaq). IBM PC-compatibles include the ACT Apricot, Canon AS-100, Columbia, Compaq, Corona, ITT XTRA, Leading Edge, Olivetti PC, Sperry PC, Tandy series, TeleVideo, Texas Instruments Professional, and Visual Commuter.

The Compaq Transportable 286 is compatible with the IBM PC AT.

One important question is whether the company that manufactures the compatible will continue to be in the personal-computer business for the next several years. The risk is being stuck with an orphan computer that no one will service or support. If you want to minimize your risk and simplify the buying decision, stick with the IBM PC. If cost is your primary consideration, you can save an average of 10 to 20 percent by buying a compatible.

How to Buy an Apple Macintosh

Apple borrowed graphics concepts and a mouse-driven interface from high-priced engineering workstations and graphics computers, and incorporated them into a lower-priced personal computer. The difference between the Macintosh and the IBM PC is not what each can do, but how they do it. The Macintosh is easy to use, and its built-in graphics and user interface set it apart from other personal computers.

The basic Macintosh is a **closed system** with a built-in floppy disk drive and monochrome display. This makes the decision-making process much easier than it is for the IBM PC. You have fewer options to choose among when buying one. Because of its closed nature, very few third-party hardware devices have been manufactured for the Macintosh.

The basic Macintosh comes equipped with a built-in monochrome display device, one 3 1/2-inch floppy disk drive, and a set of plug receptacles that allow you to connect additional devices. However, there are still some decisions to make when buying a Macintosh.

The Apple Macintosh combines built-in graphics with a mouse-driven interface.

Memory Considerations

The basic Macintosh comes with either 128K or 512K of memory. The newer Macintosh Plus comes equipped with 1 megabyte of memory. Expansion boards can boost that figure to 4MB. Much of the software recently developed for the Macintosh requires 512K.

Disk Storage Considerations

To expand on the built-in floppy, you can add an external floppy drive, an external hard disk drive, or an internal hard disk drive. The external floppy drive is the least expensive alternative. An external hard disk drive offers greater storage, whereas the internal hard disk drive offers greater storage plus higher speed. The trade-off is higher price.

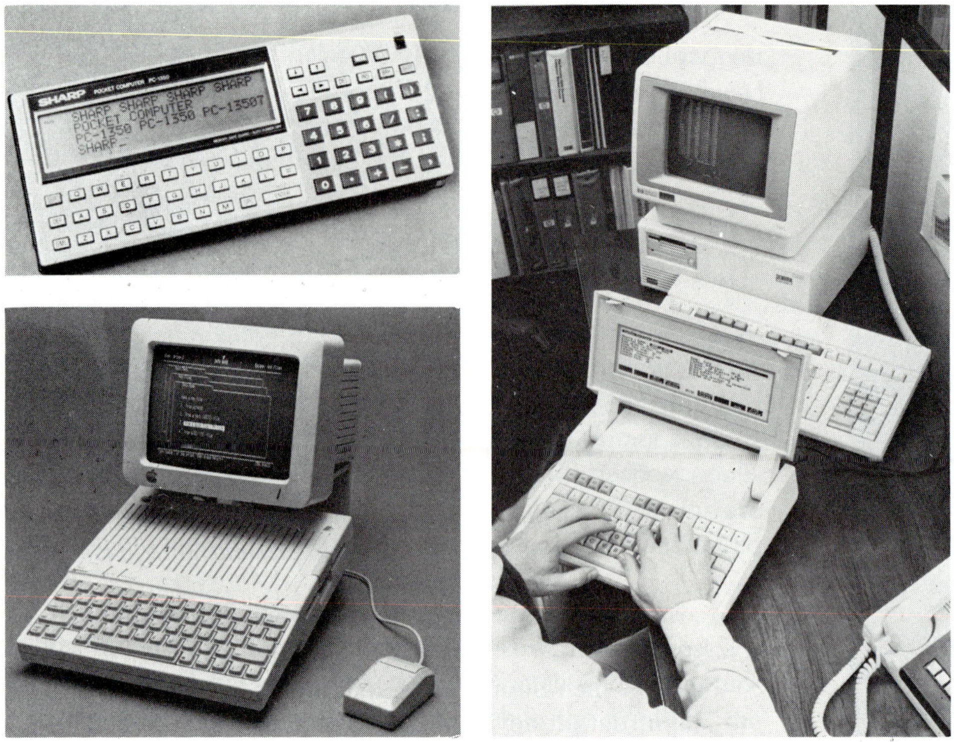

Portable computers come in a wide variety of sizes and prices. Hand-held personal computers, such as the Sharp, are like programmable calculators. Laptop computers, such as the Hewlett Packard Portable, are notebook-sized computers. Transportable computers, such as the Apple IIc, offer functions similar to desk-top personal computers.

and generally weigh 20 to 40 pounds. They usually offer all of the functionality of a desk-top computer, and should be considered if transportability is a requirement.

Choose the Best Alternative

What is the best personal computer system to buy? Each has its own style, features, advantages, and disadvantages to consider. You have to decide which system works best for you. Price usually dictates the overall performance level and functionality of a system.

To find a reasonably priced system that offers everything you want, implemented the way you would like it, you will probably have to make compromises, whether in price, functionality, or simplicity and clarity. Compare hardware prices from several sources using a chart like Table 11.1. Choosing the best alternative will be easier if you follow these guidelines:

- Keep your system simple. It is easy to be intimidated by the technobabble of features, functions, performance, and power. Look for simplicity and clarity in computer systems. Computer design is changing. Keep in mind that simple no longer means less useful or less powerful.

TABLE 11.1 *Comparing hardware costs. When shopping for a computer system, make a list of everything you will need. Then compare prices from several sources.*

Store name	______	______	______	______
Address	______	______	______	______
Phone	______	______	______	______
System unit:				
Base price	______	______	______	______
Extra memory	______	______	______	______
Disk Storage:				
Floppy (KB)	______	______	______	______
Hard (MB)	______	______	______	______
Display:				
Monitor	______	______	______	______
Adapter	______	______	______	______
Printer	______	______	______	______
Printer cable	______	______	______	______
Other:				
Modem	______	______	______	______
10 disks	______	______	______	______
Paper (1 box)	______	______	______	______
Accessories	______	______	______	______
Sales tax	______	______	______	______
Total	______	______	______	______

- Add functions only as you need them. A simple, less-powerful system is often the best choice for the first-time buyer. Your computer system is like a toolbox. A few general-purpose tools can be far more useful than a toolbox crammed with special-purpose tools. You can always add more later.
- Let the system evolve as your learning evolves. Build your computer skills and expertise by accumulating a series of small successes. Only after you experience tangible benefits and results should you move on to more advanced functions.
- Stick to buying popular middle-of-the-road hardware and software. When you buy hardware and software, you are buying a company as well. The computer industry is full of well-publicized failures, whose customers wind up with an orphan computer and no software. Good software is available for any major system.

How to Make Your Purchase

First-time buyers should buy from a computer store that offers service and support. Insist that the dealer show you how to set up the hardware, how to connect the cables, and how to install the software. Establish a clear understanding of what support and training the dealer will provide. Find out if support and training are separately priced. Ask what happens, and whom to call, if your computer breaks. Find out the policies of the hardware manufacturer and software publisher on damaged or faulty equipment, faulty disks, updates, copy protection, and telephone "hotline" services.

Other costs will crop up in your initial purchase. Don't forget that you may also need blank disks, disk storage boxes, ribbons or cartridges and paper for your printer, and cables to connect various devices.

REVIEW AND SELF-TESTING

Key Terms

User group	Home computer
Documentation	Hand-held personal computer
Open system	Laptop computer
Compatibility	Transportable computer
Closed system	

Exercises for Review and Discussion

1. Pick an application, such as word processing, spreadsheets, or database management. Search out magazine reviews of packaged software for that application. Make a comparison list of prices and features.
2. Check your daily newspaper for computer sales. (The business and sports sections contain most computer ads.) Compare prices for various systems, noting what is included in the sale price.
3. Make an exploratory visit to a local computer store to inquire about hardware, software, and prices. Caution: Be honest with the salespeople. Tell them that you are working on a class assignment.
4. Survey your school's library to familiarize yourself with books, reference volumes, and periodicals that will help you find information quickly.
5. Develop a requirements list for a personal computer system. Shop and compare prices by phone.

12

The Future of Personal Computers

PREVIEW

It is easy to forget that the personal computer was born in 1973 and is still in its adolescence. As the personal computer matures over the next decade, today's most sophisticated applications will seem like child's play.

Tomorrow's powerful personal computers will enable us to do things we have yet to imagine, at no greater cost than today's computers. And they will be even easier to use. This chapter speculates on what personal computers might be like in the next decade.

In this chapter, you'll discover:

- *Trends in personal-computer hardware*
- *Trends in communication technology*
- *The anatomy of a super personal computer*
- *Applications for the future*
- *Artificial intelligence*
- *Robots*
- *The pitfalls of software development*

The Personal Computer Revolution

Since the middle of the 1970s, the "personal computer revolution" has been advertised as a panacea. Revolution sells. Intrigued by the prospect of owning one, people bought personal computers in record numbers. Since the early personal computers were offered in build-it-yourself kit form, the number of personal computers in use has grown to approximately 80 million today.

At first, people bought them not so much to make practical use of them as to explore what a personal computer could do. They played games, wrote programs, and experimented with application software. Schools used them at first for drill and practice, then for teaching programming, and now to teach application skills. Businesspeople bought personal computers for accounting, word processing, recordkeeping, and inventory control.

Then people began to discover the limitations of personal computers. Though computers kept on selling, some of the computer revolution's promises remained unfulfilled: They were ornery machines, unnecessarily complicated and hard to use. Using them meant learning a new language of technical jargon. Sometimes they didn't perform as advertised, and software was frustratingly weak. But the pace of improvements was rapid. The personal computer has since proven to be one of the most powerful agents of change in our society, and its as-yet-unrealized benefits are still enormous.

We can anticipate dramatic advances in hardware technology, and application programs with the power to handle virtually all of our information-related needs. In the next decade, everyone will be capable of using personal computers for access to information, to organizations, and to other people. What changes will bring this transformation about?

The Technical Outlook

All the personal computers in existence today will eventually be replaced by more cost-effective and powerful computers. This is because the technological base on which computers are built is constantly advancing. Furthermore, no new discoveries need to take place for this change to occur.

What will happen instead is a vast increase in the cost/performance and power of the various components. The advances in component technology that will make personal computers more powerful will be (1) larger memory capacity, (2) more powerful microprocessors, (3) higher-capacity mass storage devices, (4) improved high-resolution display devices, and (5) high-speed communication networks.

Memory and Processors

We know from experience that miniaturization contributes to the development of more powerful and cheaper components. Over a relatively short span, as Figure 12.1 shows, memory-chip capacity has increased from 8K to 64K to 256K bits. We can expect this trend to continue. Several chip producers are distributing sample 1-megabit RAM chips, and 4-megabit RAM chips are being built in laboratories. Microprocessors are experiencing the same evolution. Experts

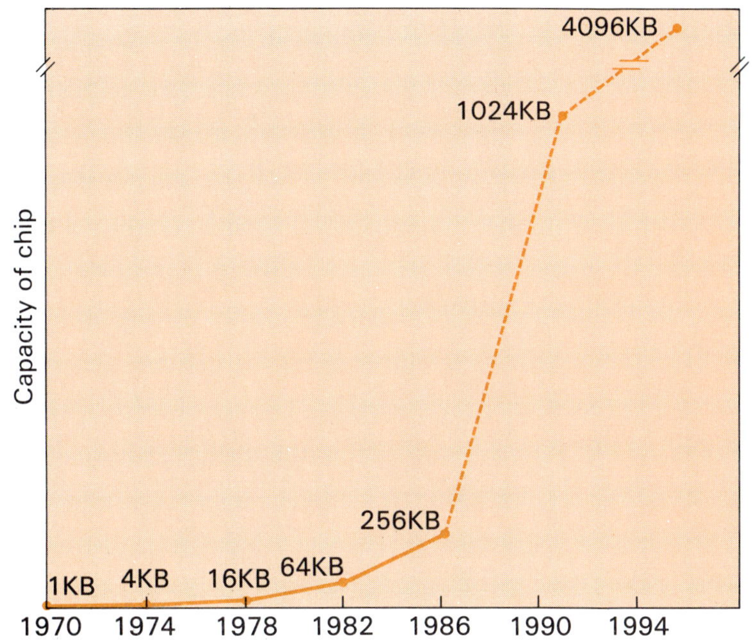

FIGURE 12.1 *Evolution of memory technology. Since 1970, memory densities have quadrupled every four years.*

predict that within five years, one microprocessor chip will do the work of today's mainframes.

Component technologies have also undergone an extraordinary anti-inflationary trend. Components have simultaneously become smaller, faster, and cheaper, giving us more computer power per dollar. When we speak of **cost/performance,** we mean that the dollar that today buys 64K of memory will buy 256K of memory in five years and 1MB of memory in ten years. We can expect similar improvements in the microprocessor in tomorrow's personal computers.

Mass Storage

New technologies are also reducing the costs of disk storage. Magnetic disks will continue to dominate personal computers, but the introduction of new recording techniques will provide improved performance at lower cost. In ten years, floppy disks with capacities of several megabytes and hard disks with capacities of hundreds of megabytes will be available at the same price as today's lower-capacity disks.

Laser disks, now used by consumers for video and audio recording, will soon play an important role in mass storage. A version of the 4 3/4-inch audio compact disk (CD) is now available for computers. Called the Compact Disk Read-Only Memory (CD ROM), the disk will store 540 megabytes, more than 1500 times the capacity of today's 360K floppy disks.

Laser disks that can be recorded on but are not erasable are already beginning to replace microfilm storage-and-retrieval systems. They are unprecedentedly versatile: They can store data, sound, and images. Documents, pictures, drawings, and music can be recorded and stored on write-once laser disks.

Digital's compact disk read-only memory (CD ROM) disks store 540 megabytes of information, or 200,000 single-spaced pages, on a 4¾-inch plastic disk. A commercially available database is recorded on the disk shown here.

Erasable laser disks merge the high storage capacities of the nonerasable laser disk with the reusability of conventional magnetic disks. A personal computer connected to laser disks could integrate data, text, audio, and video in a single storage medium and would provide users with tremendous versatility. Documents annotated with drawings and spoken words will become common in business. On a broader front, computer users will have access to music, animated graphics, and pictures to form the basis for totally new computer applications.

Display Technology

Computer graphics, the capacity to draw pictures and display images on computer screens, will benefit from new low-cost high-resolution display technology. By way of analogy, imagine a display screen as a spreadsheet with a very large number of rows and columns visible. Instead of a cell, the intersection of row and column is a picture element, shortened to **pixel.** The more rows and columns there are, the higher the resolution. A television screen displays 525 rows by 484 columns. The Macintosh displays 512 by 342 pixels, and the IBM PC with Enhanced Graphics Adapter 640 by 350 pixels.

The trend in display technology is toward higher resolution in color. For very high-quality images, future CRTs will provide resolutions of 4096 by 2048 pixels per screen. Thin **flat-panel displays** will provide similar resolution in portable devices. As display capabilities grow, it will be possible to display photograph-quality still and animated pictures from laser disk files with accompanying sound, text, graphics, still images, and slow-motion and regular-motion videos.

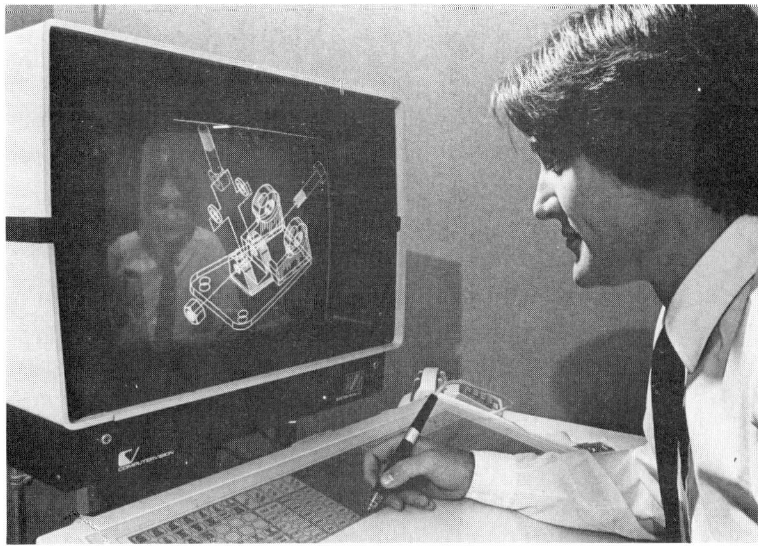

High-resolution graphics capabilities, as displayed by this engineering workstation, will soon be incorporated into low-cost personal computers.

Communication Technology

Communications, from an engineering standpoint, is simply the movement of electronic traffic from one point to another. It makes no difference whether the signals represent a written memo, a conversation, or a television picture. Today's primary communication channel, the telephone network, moves elec-

Low-cost satellite dishes may soon enable personal computers to connect to a wide variety of services.

tronic mail at speeds of up to 9600 bits per second over ordinary telephone wires. This is acceptable for simple messages or conversations, but it is too slow to carry pictures and moving images effectively.

Tomorrow's communication channels will utilize fiber-optic cables and satellite links for high-speed two-way communication between any two points on the globe. The telephone network will go far beyond simply transmitting the human voice. It will be a highly distributed information system consisting of a wide variety of communication and information-processing services. This means that personal computers will be able to connect to dozens of new services, as well as to one another. On a personal computer equipped with communication devices, a user will be able to compose a document, annotate it with voice and graphics, and quickly transmit it anywhere across the network.

The Anatomy of a Super Personal Computer

How might these advances in component technologies be combined into one personal computer? Personal computers combining several new component technologies are the subject of research at Carnegie Mellon University (Project Andrew) and Massachusetts Institute of Technology (Project Athena). Researchers are working on software for graphics-based engineering workstations—hardware based on 32-bit microprocessors, 1 megabyte of memory, and high-resolution color displays. These projects are being sponsored by IBM and Digital, in the hope that new products will emerge.

In the longer term, we can anticipate the emergence of a "super personal computer." A super personal computer would be self-contained and portable, about the size of a briefcase, with optional battery power. A color flat-panel display with a resolution of at least 1024 by 1024 pixels would unfold from the case. A mouse and keyboard would also fit in the case.

Inside the case, the system components would include an advanced microprocessor, 1 to 8 megabytes of memory, 100 megabytes to 1 gigabyte of magnetic or laser disk storage, and interfaces to connect to telephone lines, local-area networks, and printers. Such a personal computer could handle applications that today are only practical on large-scale computers.

The Software Outlook

While hardware follows a fairly predictable course of progress, software displays a tendency to progress in spurts. Software is the dominant challenge in designing tomorrow's personal computer systems. Hardware will be viewed as a mechanism for running software. It will take unprecedented efforts on the part of software developers to continue to create imaginative and novel uses of computer systems to meet the needs of users.

What will we do with the next generation of personal computers when they arrive? Clearly, the first order of business is to put them to work on general-purpose applications that are now being stretched to their limits. Word processing is one kind of general-purpose software that will evolve considerably in the next decade.

The Future of Word Processing

Word processors trace their current design largely to their secretarial-typing heritage, which has emphasized the mechanical aspects of composing, revising, formatting, and printing text. In addition to mechanical typing functions, word processors now offer spelling and grammar checkers and style checkers. The Writers Workbench, developed by AT&T's Bell Laboratories, pioneered such features as finding and correcting duplicated words, such as "the the," correcting punctuation, and finding and correcting excessive wordiness, such as "at this point in time."

As we saw in Chapter 4, the process of composition consists of three broad steps: prewriting, writing, and revising. Today's word processors are most useful in the later stages of writing. Tomorrow's word processors might prove useful in the prewriting stages as well.

One indicator of this trend is the outline generator, an example of which is shown in Figure 12.2. Today's typical word processor does not support outlining, which is very useful in prewriting. A word processor integrated with an outline generator would allow you to more easily manipulate and rearrange blocks of text and ideas.

Another limitation is that word processors are dependent on the keyboard. What about a word processor that accepts the spoken word, bypassing the keyboard and the mouse? With a voice-activated word processor, you could create a document by dictating to the computer, reading the resulting text on the display screen, and then revising with the keyboard or mouse.

Today, **speech recognition** systems for personal computers are speaker-dependent word recognizers. They must be trained by the user, and their

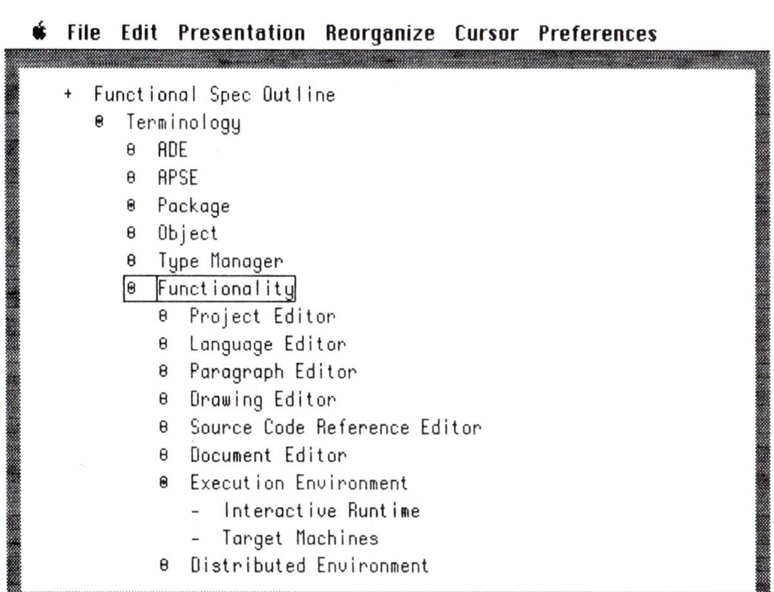

FIGURE 12.2 *Outline generators allow users to easily manipulate and rearrange blocks of text. For example, each heading shown in the display can be expanded to full-screen size so that text can be added, and then the heading can be contracted back into a single line.*

vocabularies are limited to about 100 words. Figure 12.3 shows how a computer recognizes spoken words. Very high-priced experimental systems offer larger vocabularies, higher accuracy, and the ability to cope with background noise.

IBM and other companies are developing devices called talkwriters, which can understand approximately 5000 words. In Japan, Toshiba has developed an experimental voice-activated word processor that is speaker-independent and can handle a very large vocabulary. But it is not practical for use with English, because spoken English uses far more syllables than spoken Japanese.

What is needed is a device that can decipher the speech of different speakers, without setting limits on vocabulary or requiring lengthy training to recognize words. One promising technique is voice spectrograms, which are electronically produced voiceprints. Dr. Victor Zue of MIT taught himself to read spectrograms, which had previously been thought impossible, and computers are being programmed to reproduce his skill. This technique paves the way for a computer to analyze and interpret voiceprints and convert them into text—and thus for truly speaker-independent voice recognition.

Word processors perform the mechanics of manipulating language, but they do not understand language. To do so would require interpreting the meanings of words. So far, the only programs in practical use that respond to the meanings of words are the natural-language interfaces to database programs. With one of these interfaces, the user can request information from the database in written English. The program then responds with English statements or displays of data.

In the future, we can expect language-understanding programs that will aid users in generating messages and keeping track of what needs to be done.

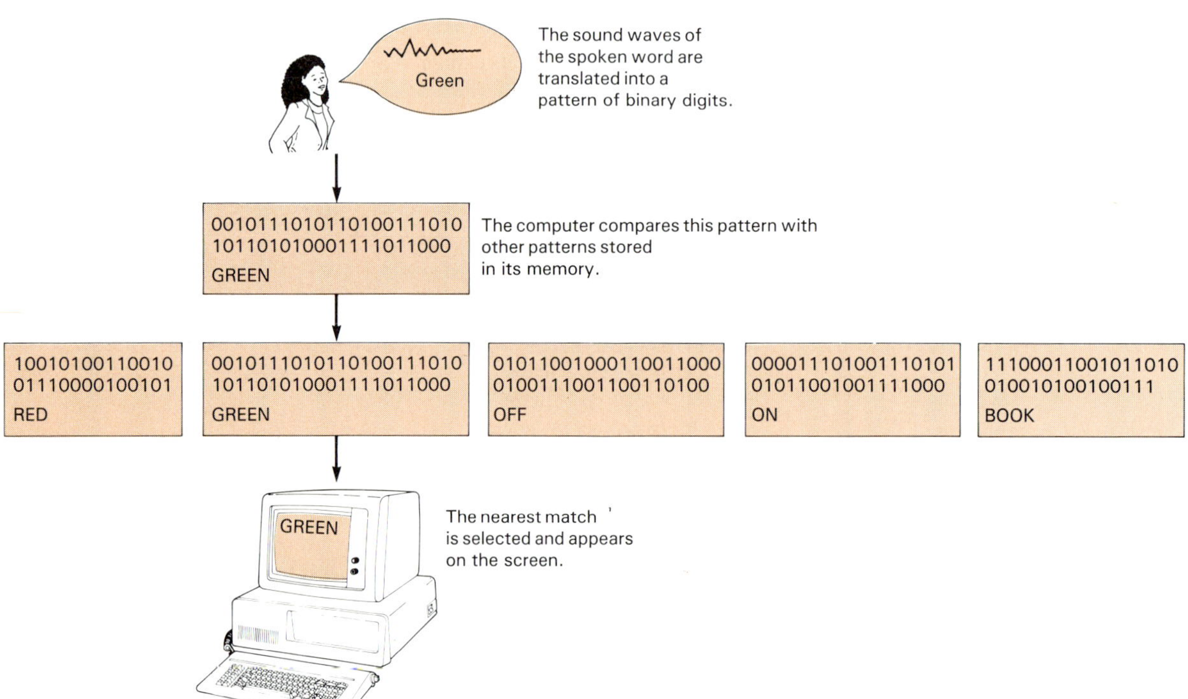

FIGURE 12.3 *How a computer recognizes speech.*

For example, if an electronic-mail user writes "I'll get you a copy of that report" in response to a request, the program could interpret the message, remind the user to send a copy of the report via electronic mail, and monitor its completion.

Software that mimics the human understanding of language is not a foreseeable development. Natural-language interfaces and speech-recognition systems deal with meaning in an acceptable way because they operate in a narrowly defined range of possible meanings. The software does not understand the full range of human language. To do so would require knowledge of the unarticulated background expectations of the speaker and hearer.[1]

The Friendly Frontier

How can computers be made easier to use? The user interface is an often-studied problem in research laboratories. The long-term goal of such research is to make the human-to-computer interface as fluid and fluent as the human-to-human interface. In addition to language-understanding programs, several interesting experiments may pave the way for improved user interfaces.

Personal computers now allow users to point at items on the display screen, either by moving a mouse or by touching a finger to a touch-sensitive screen. Could a computer system respond to hand movements? In experiments at MIT, users wore a wrist-watch-sized band that detected arm movements; this enabled the user to move objects on a large display screen by pointing to them. Meanwhile, a speech recognizer interpreted the user's oral commands to display particular objects, and to change their shapes and colors. By combining pointing with talking, the researchers minimized some of the problems associated with speech recognition.

By the same token, could a computer respond to the direction in which you are looking? In an experimental eye-tracking system, researchers outfitted users with special eye-tracking glasses and asked them to watch simultaneous video programs projected on a single screen. If the glasses detected that the user was watching one particular program, the system would fill the screen with that program. By monitoring which part of the display screen the user is looking at, software could detect what the user is interested in, and respond accordingly. The system might also be able to determine when to move on, or gauge the effectiveness of its displays, by monitoring a user's gaze. If a user ignored a particular part of the display, for example, the system could reorganize its display.[2]

The goal of these and other experiments is to make computers as easy to talk to as a person. Communicating with people, we use gestures, speech, eye movement, and body language, and we adapt our method of communicating with specific people based on previous interactions. Will software ever be able to respond to the same things? As with language-understanding programs, such software is years away, but experimentation is giving researchers clues to developing software that resolves ambiguities and more closely resembles a human-to-human interface.

[1]Winograd, Terry. "Computer Software for Working with Language," *Scientific American*, September 1984, pp. 142–144.

[2]Bolt, Richard. "Conversing with Computers," *Technology Review*, February/March 1985, pp. 38–40.

The gaze-orchestrated dynamic windows experiment at MIT helps researchers study how people focus their visual attention when confronted with complex displays.

Meanwhile, the output of computer systems will be enriched by the addition of color graphics, advancing the techniques that are currently available on expensive graphics-based engineering workstations and on the Macintosh personal computer. In addition to enhancing the interfaces of general-purpose application programs, graphics will open up new means of communicating with personal computers. Graphics programs with stored libraries of images will function as an electronic canvas for artists, designers, and architects. Strikingly realistic depictions and animation will be commonplace.

Artificial Intelligence

Clearly, the personal computer will become a much more capable assistant. Could it also become a more intelligent assistant?

Artificial intelligence (AI) is the branch of computer science that attempts to understand the nature of human intelligence and to produce intelligent computers by programming them to perform tasks that require humanlike qualities such as reasoning and perception.

Examples include systems that play games like checkers and chess, robots that work in factories, and systems that use the same knowledge and rules of thumb that experts use to solve problems.

AI research uses highly specialized forms of programming, such as the languages LISP and PROLOG. Its long-term goal is to understand human intelligence well enough to develop software that exhibits intelligent behavior. This is an emotionally charged issue. But anyone who looks closely at AI cannot fail to see that a great gap remains between human self-awareness and intelligence

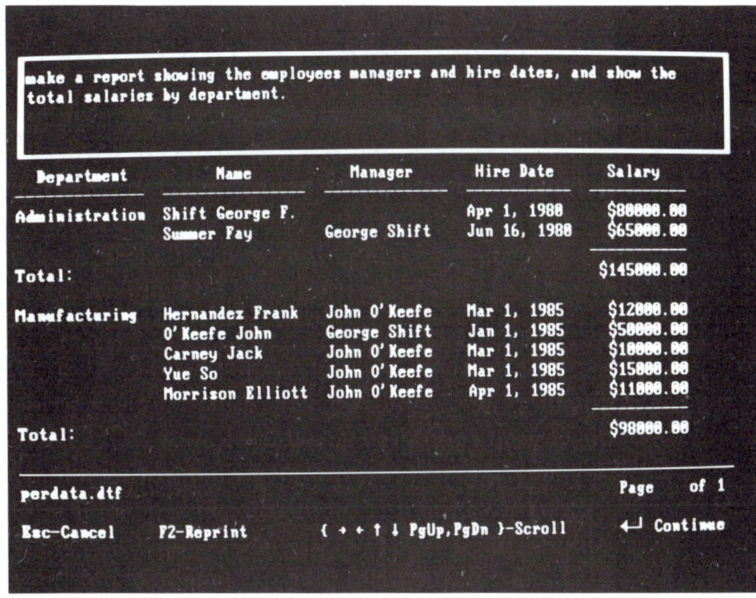
make a report showing the employees managers and hire dates, and show the total salaries by department.

Department	Name	Manager	Hire Date	Salary
Administration	Shift George F.		Apr 1, 1988	$80000.00
	Summer Fay	George Shift	Jun 16, 1988	$65000.00
Total:				$145000.00
Manufacturing	Hernandez Frank	John O'Keefe	Mar 1, 1985	$12000.00
	O'Keefe John	George Shift	Jan 1, 1985	$50000.00
	Carney Jack	John O'Keefe	Mar 1, 1985	$10000.00
	Yue So	John O'Keefe	Mar 1, 1985	$15000.00
	Morrison Elliott	John O'Keefe	Apr 1, 1985	$11000.00
Total:				$98000.00

perdata.dtf Page of 1

Esc-Cancel F2-Reprint { ← → ↑ ↓ PgUp,PgDn }-Scroll ↵ Continue

Natural-language interfaces to database programs allow a user to type requests in English. Shown above is Symantec's Q&A's product which allows users to type in requests in their own words.

and AI programs. The problem is that nobody really knows how people think. One of the byproducts of AI research is to help psychologists understand how people think. But instead of experimenting with humans, AI researchers experiment with computer programs.

AI researchers have not been very successful in getting computers to do simple things that virtually every child can do, like learn from experience, understand language, or exhibit common sense. But they have had some success in getting computers to solve highly structured, highly specialized problems. **Expert systems** are computer programs that solve specialized problems at the level of a human expert; they represent applied artificial intelligence. Expert systems are used in medical diagnostics, chemistry, geology, and business. Their major shortcoming is their inability to handle novel or unique situations. They only work in narrowly defined circumstances, and only after they have been fed information by human experts.

Personal Computers as Agents

A computer with the mentality of a human being is not something that we can anticipate in the near future. However, by coupling artificial intelligence techniques with a friendly interface and communication capabilities, we can create systems that appear to act intelligently.

Artificial intelligence researchers John McCarthy and Oliver G. Selfridge at MIT coined the term **agent** for a system that, given a goal, could carry out the appropriate computer operations and ask for and act on advice when necessary. To put it another way, an agent would be a software version of a robot, doing its work within the computer.[3]

[3]Kay, Alan. "Computer Software," *Scientific American*, September 1984, p. 58.

Industrial robot arms can be programmed to perform a wide variety of material handling and assembly tasks.

What might an agent do? One aim of current research is to design an agent that could act as an intelligent personal electronic newspaper. Having stored a profile of the user's preferences, interests, and needs, it would then search through library databases and wire services for articles the user would be interested in. Then it would present them to the user to read or save for future reference.

It is also conceivable that an agent could act as a personal secretary. It would handle appointments and scheduling; like an electronic newspaper, it would scan databases and wire services and inform the user of events of interest; and it could even take over some routine chores, producing scheduled reports, periodically backing up files, and scanning sources for data to input to the user's programs.

Eventually, the kind of robots we read about in science fiction and see in the movies may appear. We already have some of the pieces. Industrial robot arms weld cars and assemble parts. Robot eyes guide parts-carrying vehicles through factories. Robot fingers pick parts from bins. But creating a useful, intelligent general-purpose robot is a larger intellectual task by far than any that has been undertaken.

The Tar Pit

In *The Mythical Man-Month*, Frederick P. Brooks uses the analogy of the primeval tar pit to describe large-scale software development efforts: "No scene from prehistory is quite so vivid as that of the mortal struggles of great beasts in the tar pits. In the mind's eye one sees dinosaurs, mammoths, and sabertoothed tigers struggling against the grip of the tar. The fiercer the struggle, the more entangling the tar, and no beast is so strong or so skillful but that he ultimately sinks."[4] Software development has been such a tar pit; it is one of the most

[4]Brooks, Frederick P. *The Mythical Man-Month: Essays on Software Engineering*, Reading, MA: Addison-Wesley Publishing Company, 1975, p. 4.

complex tasks ever undertaken. The ability to manage this complexity and turn ideas into software products often remains slightly beyond the grasp of software developers.

It has become commonplace to read about the imminent release of a product so revolutionary that it will forever alter the course of personal computing. The software industry has coined the term **vaporware** to describe software whose glories reside solely in its press releases. Nevertheless, software is the key to any progress we will make with computers in the future. The computers themselves are immaterial; it is the software that is the limiting factor.

The future will contain tar pits in which many an unwary developer and user will flounder. But it will also be filled with exciting and unforeseeable developments that will extend our capabilities far beyond anything we can envision now.

REVIEW AND SELF-TESTING

Key Terms

Cost/performance
Laser disk
Computer graphics
Pixel
Flat-panel display
Communications
Speech recognition
Artificial intelligence
Expert system
Agent
Vaporware

Questions for Review and Discussion

1. What advances in component technology will make personal computers more powerful?
2. What is the dominant challenge in designing tomorrow's personal computer systems?
3. Describe how a future word processor might handle the prewriting stage of the composition process.
4. How might gesture recognition improve today's user interfaces?
5. How might eye-tracking systems improve today's user interfaces?
6. What is the long-term goal of user interface design?
7. Why have artificial intelligence systems only been successful in highly specialized areas?

Appendix A

Using TriPac and DOS Utilities

Managing Your Disk

TriPac Version 1.00 is designed as a two-disk application. Because of its limited capacity, your data disk may fill up with files before the end of the semester. If so, and you want to create additional TriPac files, you have two options:

1. Selectively delete unneeded data files in the TriPac directory, using commands in the File menu.
2. If you don't want to lose any of your data files, copy the entire TriPac disk, and erase selected data files from the new copied disk.

TriPac File-Management Commands

The File menu of the TriPac Applications Manager contains several commands that manage the files used by the application programs. In addition to opening and closing files, you can use TriPac commands to copy, delete, and rename files.

Copy

You can make a duplicate of any TriPac file as long as (1) there is enough room left on the disk, and (2) the column headed DOCUMENTS, SPREADSHEETS, or DATABASES has at least one untitled entry remaining. To copy a file, use the *Open a Copy...* command in the Application Manager's File menu.

1. Highlight the name of the file you wish to duplicate. Press the Esc key to toggle to the Menu bar.

2. With the pointer on the File menu, press the Down arrow key to highlight the *Open a Copy...* command. Press the Return key.
3. A dialog box will appear. The name of the file you want to duplicate will be highlighted. You can edit the name or leave it unchanged. (TriPac permits duplicate file names.)
4. Press the Return key. You will be transferred to the file you want to duplicate, and its contents will be copied into the new file. You can then quit the application program. The new file name will appear in the Application Manager directory.

Delete

You can delete any file in the TriPac directory. Move the pointer to the file you wish to delete.

1. Toggle to the menu bar. With the pointer on the File menu, highlight the *Delete...* command and press the Return key.
2. A dialog box will appear, verifying the name of the file you wish to delete. Once you delete a file, it cannot be recovered. Use the Esc key to cancel the delete command if you change your mind.
3. After you press the Return key, the name of the deleted file will disappear from the workspace.

Rename

You can rename any file in the TriPac directory. Move the pointer to the file you wish to rename.

1. Toggle to the menu bar. With the pointer on the File menu, highlight the *Rename...* command and press the Return key.
2. A dialog box will appear. The name of the existing file will be highlighted. Edit the name, or type in a new name, and press the Return key. The only unacceptable file name is all blanks (spaces).
3. After you press the Return key, the new file name will replace the old file name in the workspace.

Disk Operating System Commands

The Disk Operating System (DOS) is a collection of programs that manages the resources of a computer system. There are two Disk Operating Systems for the Apple IIe, ProDOS and DOS 3.3. Because your TriPac disks are not DOS disks, it is not possible to use either ProDOS or DOS 3.3 except to make a copy of your program and data disks.

The following is meant as a set of guidelines for copying an entire disk. For more specific information about your operating system, consult the *Apple IIe Owner's Manual* or the *Apple IIc Owner's Manual.*

The following discussion assumes that you have Quit TriPac and are about to use DOS. Before you begin, be sure you have the following components:

- A program disk containing the TriPac software, or a data disk containing the TriPac data files.
- A disk labeled *ProDOS User's Disk* or *DOS 3.3 System Master.*
- One or more blank disks.

OPERATING INSTRUCTIONS

Recall that starting up the computer is often called booting. There are two ways to boot an Apple® computer. The computer you are using has two floppy disk drives. The left disk drive is called drive 1; the right disk drive is called drive 2.

Booting the Computer with the Power Off

1. Insert any program disk into drive 1, handling it by the label. Never touch the exposed magnetic surface of the disk.
2. The Apple computer has an on/off switch on the back of the computer. The display device also has an on/off switch. First turn on the display device; then turn on the computer.

Booting the Computer with the Power On

1. Insert a program disk into drive 1, handling it by the label.
2. Hold down the and Control keys while you press the Reset key.

COPYING DISKS

The procedure for copying a disk varies depending on whether your computer uses the ProDOS or the DOS 3.3 operating system. Use one of the following procedures to copy a disk. If your operating system is called DOS 3.3, skip this section and go on to the next section, "Copying Disks with DOS 3.3."

Copying Disks with ProDOS

The ProDOS User's Disk contains a program for copying disks.

1. Insert the ProDOS User's Disk in drive 1 and boot the computer, using one of the procedures described in the previous section.
2. A menu will appear listing your options. Press F to activate the ProDOS filer.
3. Another menu will appear. Press V to activate the Volume commands.
4. A list of volume commands will appear. Press C to copy a volume. (Volume is just another name for disk.)

Apple is a registered trademark of Apple Computer, Inc.

5. The copy program presents you with a number of default (that is, preset) responses. For example, the first default response is

```
--COPY--
  THE VOLUME IN SLOT: (6)
```

Press the Return key four times to use the default responses. Check with your instructor to determine whether the default responses need to be changed.

6. At the bottom of the screen the message

```
--INSERT DISKS AND PRESS <RET>--
```

will appear.

7. Remove the ProDOS User's Disk from drive 1 and replace it with the disk you wish to copy.

8. Place a blank disk in drive 2. Press the Return key. You'll hear a whirring and clacking noise. The words FORMATTING, READING, and WRITING will alternate on the screen while the program disk is being copied, and the disk drives' lights will flash on and off. When the program is finished, you'll see:

```
COPY COMPLETE
--PRESS <RET> TO ACCEPT: <ESC> TO EXIT--
```

Remove your new disk from drive 2 and label it.

If you wish to make another copy, remove the disk from disk drive 1 and insert the disk you wish to copy. Then insert a blank disk into drive 2. Press the Return key. The copy program will be repeated. When the program is finished, you'll see:

```
COPY COMPLETE
--PRESS <RET> TO ACCEPT: <ESC> TO EXIT--
```

Remove your disk from drive 2 and label it. Then press the Esc key.

Copying Disks with DOS 3.3

The DOS 3.3 System Master disk contains a program for copying disks.

1. Insert the DOS 3.3 System Master disk in drive 1 and boot the computer, using one of the procedures described earlier.

2. A series of messages will appear on the screen. Make sure the Caps Lock key is pressed, type *RUN COPYA*, and press the Return key.

3. The Apple Disk Duplication program will appear. The copy program presents you with a default (that is, preset) response. Press the Return key four times to activate the default responses. Check with your instructor to determine whether the default responses need to be changed.

4. At the bottom of the screen the message

```
--PRESS 'RETURN' KEY TO BEGIN COPY--
```

will appear.

5. Remove the DOS 3.3 System Master disk from drive 1 and replace it with the disk you wish to copy.

6. Place a blank disk in drive 2. Press the Return key. You'll hear a whirring and clacking noise. The words READING, INITIALIZING, and WRITING will appear on the screen while the program disk is being copied. When the program is finished, you'll see:

   ```
   DO YOU WISH TO MAKE ANOTHER COPY?
   ```

   If you wish to make another copy, press the Y key for yes, then press the Return key. The message

   ```
   --PRESS 'RETURN' KEY TO BEGIN COPY--
   ```

   will appear.

   Remove your new disk from drive 2 and label it.

   Remove the disk from drive 1 and insert the disk you wish to copy. Then insert a blank disk into drive 2 and press the Return key. When the program is finished, you'll see:

   ```
   DO YOU WISH TO MAKE ANOTHER COPY?
   ```

   Press the N key for no, then press the Return key.

Appendix B

TriPac Commands and Messages

General Information

Commands preceded by a letter and an equal sign (=) can be performed by holding down the Control key while pressing the specified letter key.

Commands followed by an ellipsis (. . .) cause a dialog box to appear. The dialog box contains additional instructions. Some contain data-entry fields to complete the command. Dialog boxes always allow you to cancel the command by pressing the Esc key.

When a command cannot be performed, you cannot select it. For example, if the workspace pointer is on an untitled file, the *Open a Copy. . .*, *Delete. . .*, and *Rename. . .* commands in the File menu cannot be selected and will be bypassed.

Application-Manager Commands

File Commands

Commands in the **File menu** perform operations on the selected (highlighted) file. The appropriate file name should be highlighted in the directory before executing a command in the File menu.

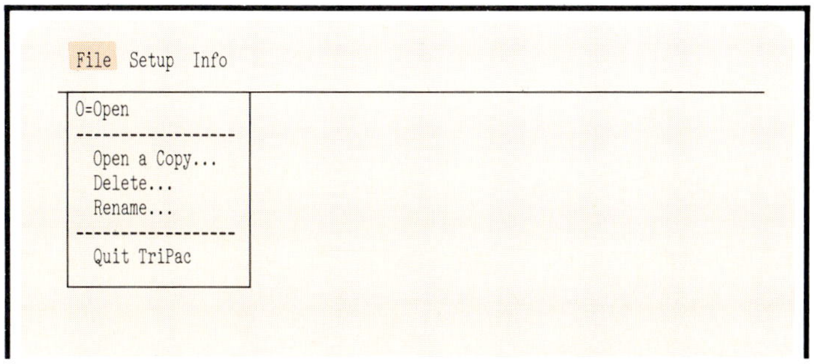

The *O=Open* command (1) opens the selected file for processing and (2) loads the corresponding application program (word processor, spreadsheet, or database).

If the file to be opened is untitled, the command appears as *O=Open*. . . and a dialog box asks you to name the new file. The only unacceptable file name is all blanks (spaces).

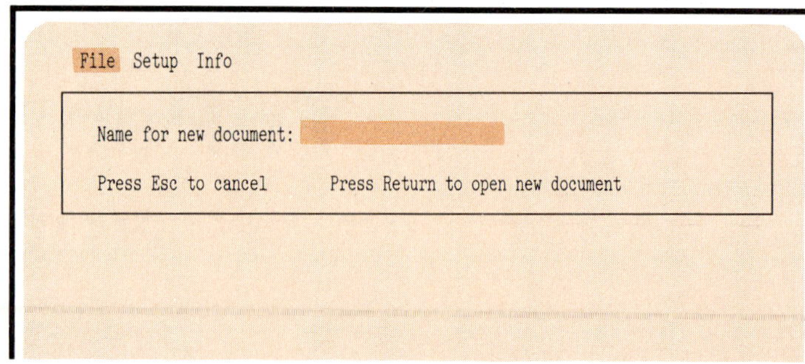

The *Open a Copy*. . . command makes a duplicate of an existing file. A dialog box asks you to name the new file. The existing file name remains in the dialog box data-entry field. You can edit the name or leave it unchanged. (TriPac permits duplicate names in the directory.)

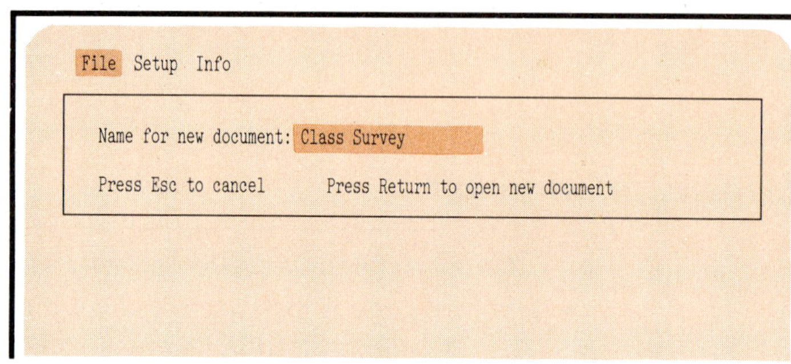

The *Delete*. . . command erases an existing file from the directory. A dialog box confirms the name of the file to be deleted. Be careful. Deleted files cannot be recovered.

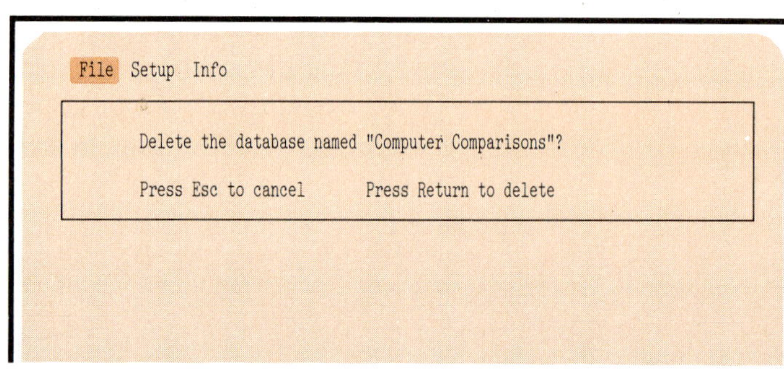

The *Rename*. . . command gives an existing file a new name. A dialog box allows you to edit the old name of the file.

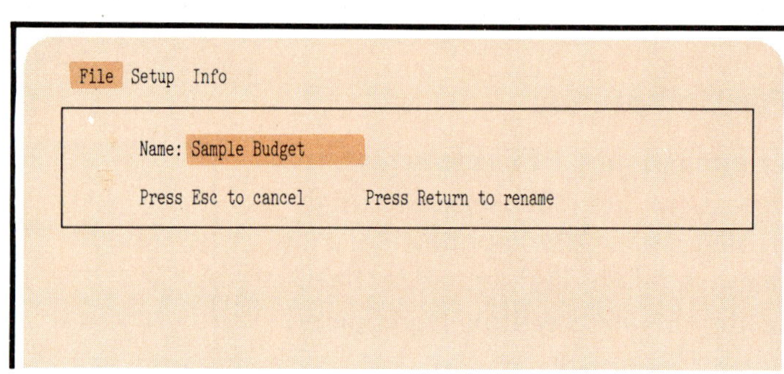

The *Quit TriPac* command returns you to the operating system.

Setup Commands

Commands in the **Setup menu** enable you to change the interface between the computer and the printer.

The *Printer*. . . command enables you to change the slot in which the printer interface board is plugged. A dialog box initially shows the default value Slot 1. Pressing any key causes the highlighted printer-connection field to toggle between Slot 1 through Slot 7.

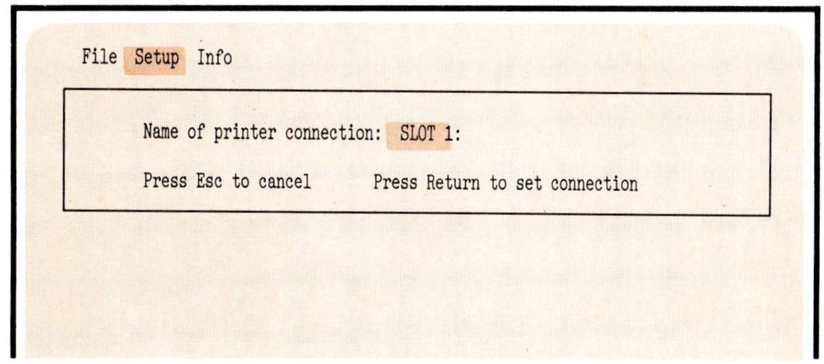

The Info Command

The *About TriPac*. . . command in the Info menu displays the version number of the program you are using.

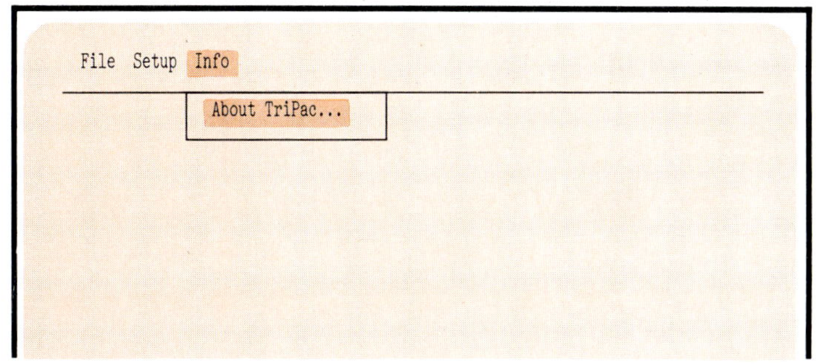

It also gives general directions for using specified keys.

```
File  Setup  Info

  TriPac Software Version 1.0 designed by R. Alden, M. Esserlieu and
  R. Blissmer. Programmed by ibidinc.
  Copyright (c) 1986 by Houghton Mifflin Company.
  All rights reserved. Written license agreement required for any use
  other than with Houghton Mifflin Company publications.

  Key Term          Description
  Cursor            Reverse video block, now highlighting Info on menu bar.
  Menu bar          Top line of the screen.
  Workspace         Area of the screen below the menu bar.
  Escape key        To toggle control between menu bar and workspace.
  All arrow keys    To move cursor within workspace or menu bar.
  Up/Down arrows    Down arrow to drop pull-down menu from menu bar.
                    Up or Down arrow to move cursor within a menu.
                    One or more Up arrows to close up a pull-down menu.
  Return key        To activate a menu command.
  Dialog box        To provide additional information for selected commands.
  Tab key           To move from field to field in a dialog box.

  Press Return to return to workspace.
```

Word-Processor Commands

File Commands

Commands in the **File menu** perform operations on a selected document.

The *Save Document* command writes the contents of the document onto disk.

```
File  Edit  Find  Tabs  Layout                    Document: Appendix B

  Save Document
  Print Document...
  ------------------------------
  Revert to Last Version...
  ------------------------------
  Quit Word Processor
```

The *Print Document...* command prints a copy of the document. A dialog box informs you whether the document is single-spaced or double-spaced. The command prints one page at a time. If the document is longer than one page, the dialog box asks you to press Enter to print each page. The dialog box also informs you if the printer is not ready. Check first to see that the printer is connected to the computer and turned on.

```
File  Edit  Find  Tabs  Layout                    Document: Appendix B

      Note: Document is single-spaced

      Press Return to print page:  1

      Press Esc to cancel
```

The *Revert to Last Version...* command enables you to restore the last saved version of the document after you have made changes. A dialog box informs you that all changes made since the last save will be lost.

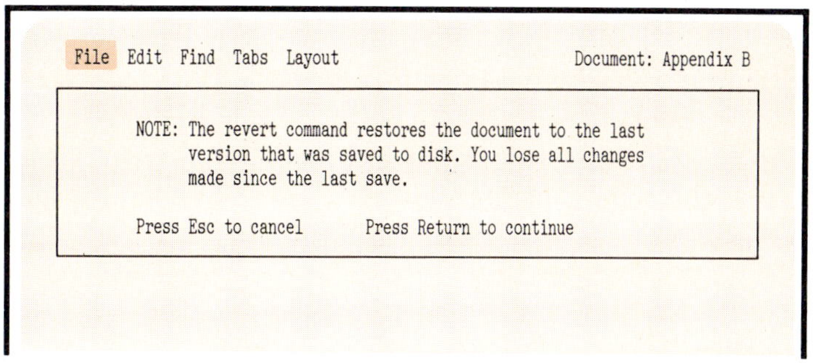

The *Quit Word Processor* command (1) saves the contents of the document and (2) returns you to the Application Manager.

Edit Commands

Commands in the **Edit menu** enable you to select text and then manipulate it.

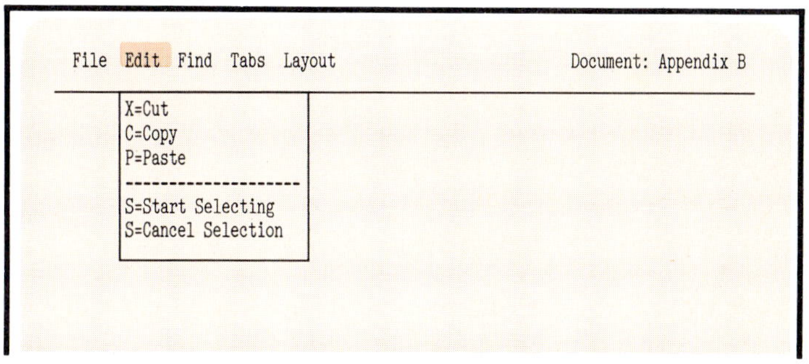

The *X=Cut* command enables you to remove a selected block of text from the document into a clipboard. The remaining text closes up to fill the gap. The text in the clipboard can then be (1) inserted elsewhere in the document, (2) inserted in another document, or (3) discarded.

The *C=Copy* command enables you to duplicate a selected block of text into a clipboard without removing it from the document. The text in the clipboard can then be (1) inserted elsewhere in the document or (2) inserted in another document.

The *P=Paste* command enables you to insert the clipboard text into a document. Text may (1) be inserted beginning at the location of the blinking cursor or (2) replace any selected text.

The *S=Start Selecting* command enables you to highlight text for cutting, copying, or deleting.

The *S=Cancel Selection* command enables you to change highlighted text back to normal video.

Find Commands

Commands in the **Find menu** enable you to search a document for selected words or phrases, and replace them with other words or phrases.

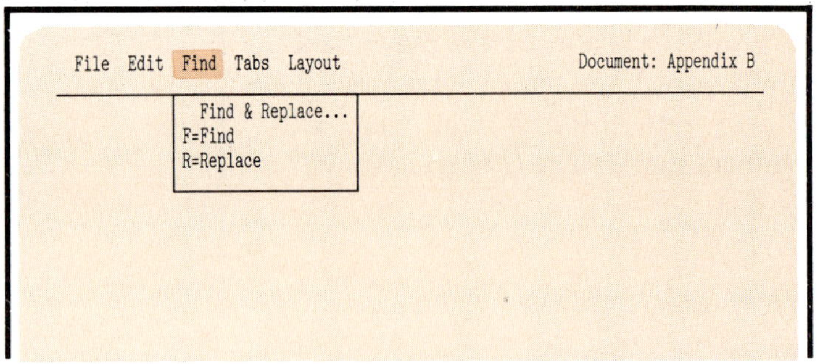

The *Find & Replace...* command enables you to specify the text to be found and the text that will replace it. A dialog box asks you to enter both texts. The Tab key moves forward between the find and replace fields.

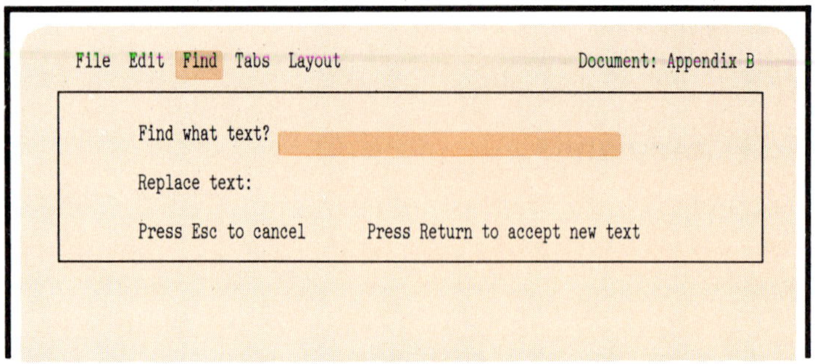

The *F=Find* command enables you to search the document for the specified text. The command must be repeated for each search. The Find command searches the entire document, beginning and ending at the location of the cursor.

The *R=Replace* command enables you to replace highlighted text with the contents of the replace-text field.

Tabs Commands

Commands in the **Tabs menu** enable you to set and clear tab stops.

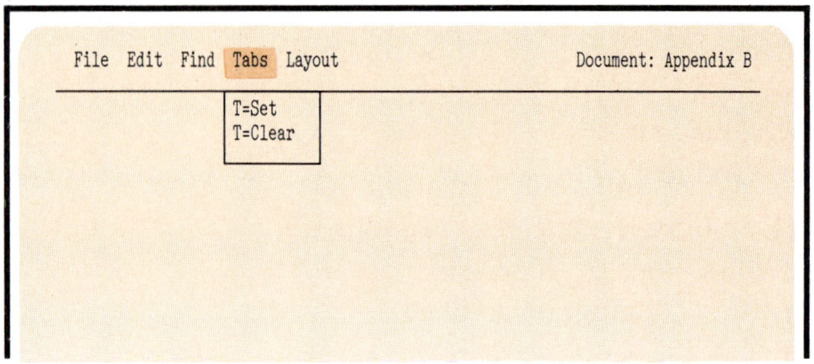

The *T=Set* command places a tab stop along the horizontal line underneath the menu bar, at the current position of the cursor.

The *T=Clear* command erases an existing tab stop. The cursor must be positioned on the tab stop to be cleared. Text in the document that has already been tabbed will not be affected.

Layout Commands

Commands in the **Layout menu** enable you to change the appearance of the printed document.

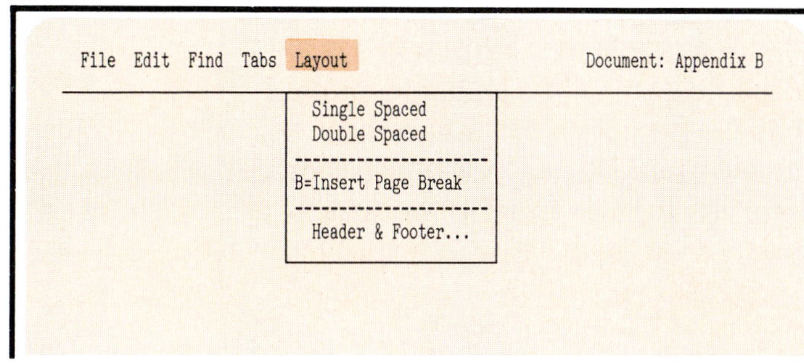

The *Single Spaced* command enables you to print your document single spaced. Single Spaced is the default spacing. The *Double Spaced* command enables you to select double spacing for your document. The current spacing of the document is indicated by an *X*.

The *B=Insert Page Break* command enables you to begin a new page anywhere in the document. The page break is inserted at the position of the cursor, and appears on the screen as a horizontal row of hyphens.

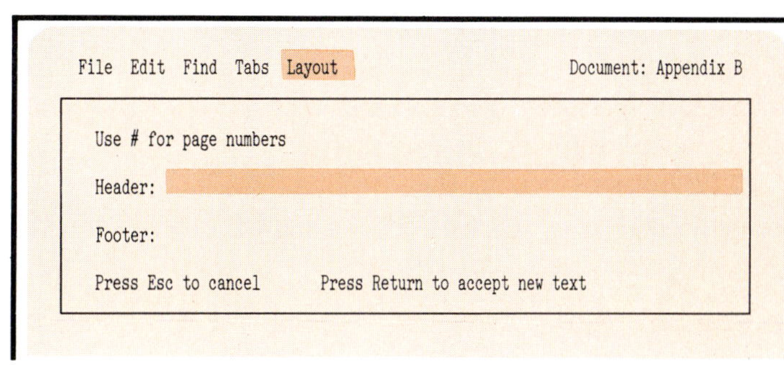

The *Header & Footer...* command enables you to specify one user-defined header to appear at the top of each printed page and/or one user-defined footer to appear at the bottom of each printed page. A dialog box asks you to enter the header and footer text in a 65-character data-entry field. The Tab key moves forward between the header and footer fields. Wherever a # character is placed, a page number will appear. TriPac does not check for duplicate page numbers. Page numbering always starts with 1.

Spreadsheet Commands

File Commands

Commands in the **File menu** perform operations on the selected spreadsheet.

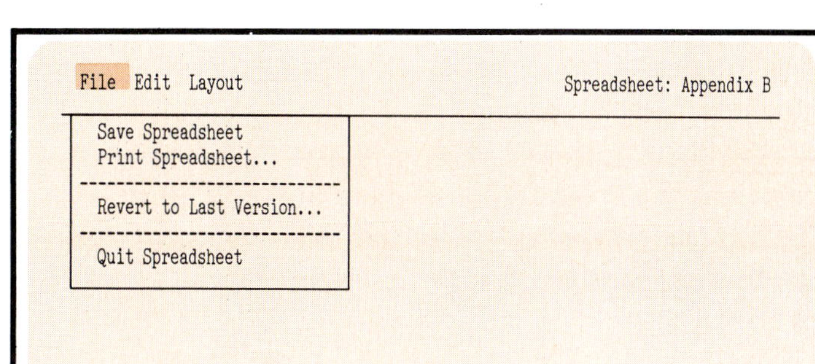

The *Save Spreadsheet* command writes the contents of the spreadsheet onto disk.

The *Print Spreadsheet*. . . command prints a copy of the spreadsheet. A dialog box asks you to press Enter to print page 1. The command prints one page at a time. If the document is longer than one page, the dialog box asks you to press Enter to print each page. The dialog box also informs you if the printer is not ready. Check first to see that the printer is connected to the computer and turned on.

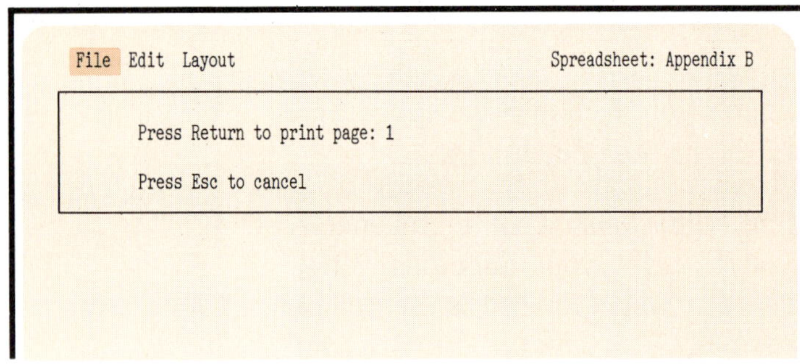

The *Revert to Last Version*. . . command enables you to restore the last saved version of the spreadsheet after you have made changes. A dialog box informs you that all changes made since the last save will be lost.

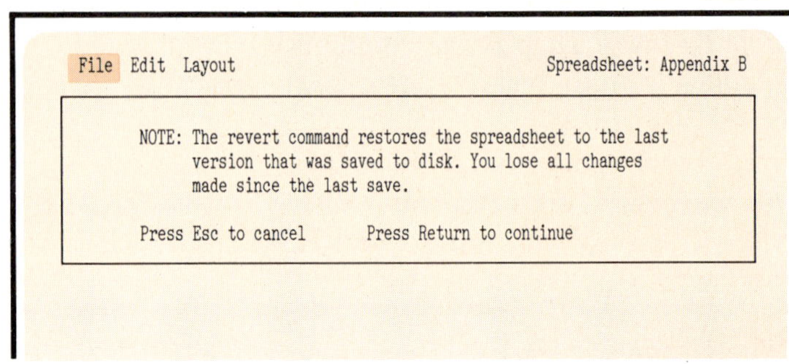

The *Quit Spreadsheet* command (1) saves the contents of the spreadsheet and (2) returns you to the Application Manager.

Edit Commands

Commands in the **Edit menu** enable you to select cells and then manipulate them.

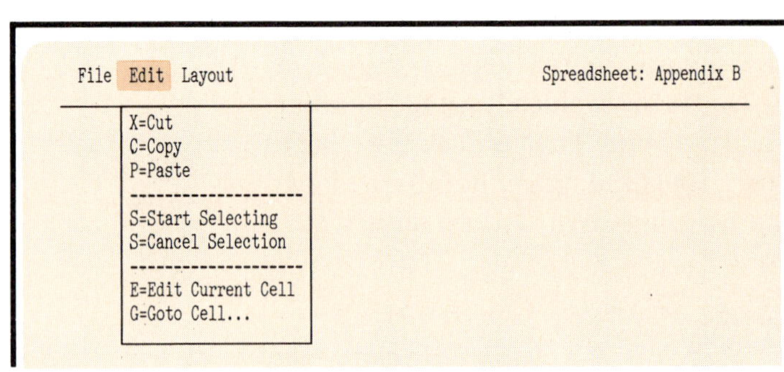

The *X=Cut* command clears selected cells in the spreadsheet and places them in a clipboard. They can then be (1) inserted elsewhere in the spreadsheet, (2) inserted in another spreadsheet, (3) inserted in a word-processing document, or (4) discarded.

The *C=Copy* command duplicates selected cells into a clipboard. They can then be (1) inserted elsewhere in the spreadsheet, (2) inserted in another spreadsheet, or (3) inserted in a document.

The *P=Paste* command enables you to move a block of cells from the clipboard into a spreadsheet. Cells are pasted beginning at the location of the cursor. When cells containing formulas are inserted at new locations, they retain their original cell coordinates.

The *S=Start Selecting* command enables you to highlight cells to cut or copy, or to perform layout commands.

The *S=Cancel Selection* command enables you to change highlighted cells back to normal video.

The *E=Edit Current Cell* command enables you to change the contents of a cell that already contains numbers, text, or a formula.

The *G=Goto Cell* command enables you to jump to any cell in the worksheet.

Layout Commands

Commands in the **Layout menu** enable you to change the appearance of selected cells in the spreadsheet. The changes appear on the display screen and in the printed spreadsheet.

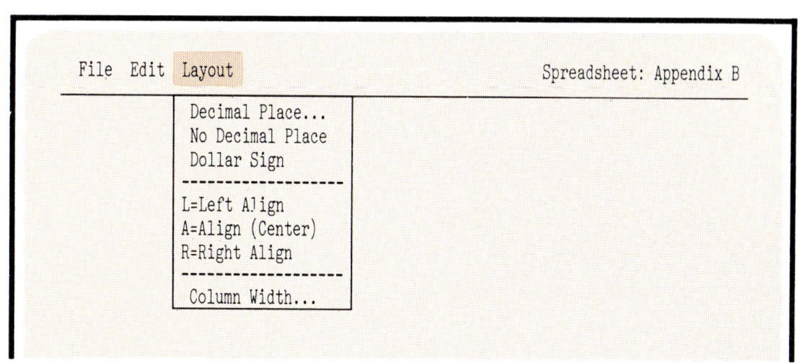

The *Decimal Place...* command enables you to specify the number of decimal places in selected cells. Only cells containing numbers are affected. A dialog box informs you of the current number of decimal places. Typing in a new number causes all selected cells containing numbers to change. The default for numeric cells is two decimal places. The valid range of decimal places is 0 to 10. TriPac has a precision of 11 digits.

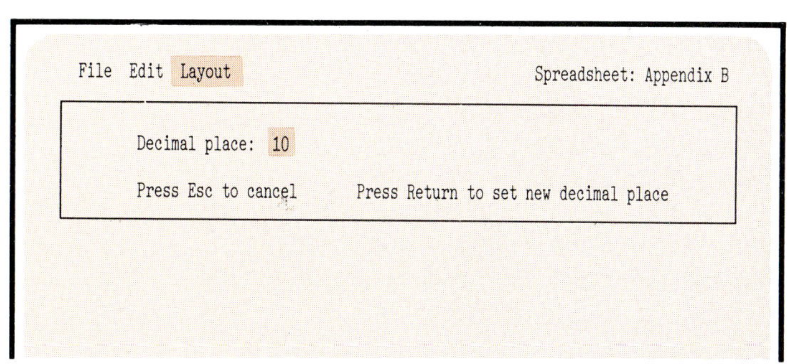

The *No Decimal Place* command performs the same function as specifying zero decimal places in the *Decimal Place...* command. Only cells containing numbers are affected.

The *Dollar Sign* command places a dollar sign ($) to the left of the contents of selected cells. Only cells containing numbers are affected. The command is a toggle: Performing the command on cells that already contain dollar signs removes the dollar sign.

The **Align** commands affect both text and numbers. They override the default of aligning text to the left and numbers to the right, as follows:

The *L=Left Align* command aligns the contents of selected cells to the left.

The *A=Align* (center) command centers the contents of selected cells.

The *R=Right Align* command aligns the contents of selected cells to the right.

The *Column Width...* command enables you to change the widths of selected columns. A dialog box informs you of the current width of selected columns. Typing in a new number causes the selected columns to change to new widths. The default column width is 12. The valid range of column widths is 0 to 74.

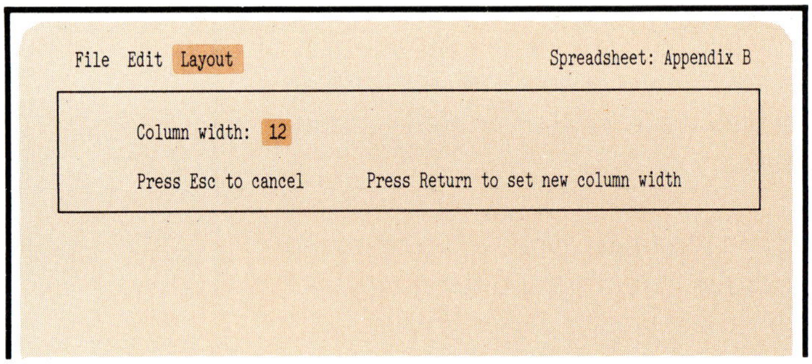

Database Commands

File Commands

Commands in the **File menu** perform operations on the selected database.

The *Save Database* command writes the contents of the database onto disk.

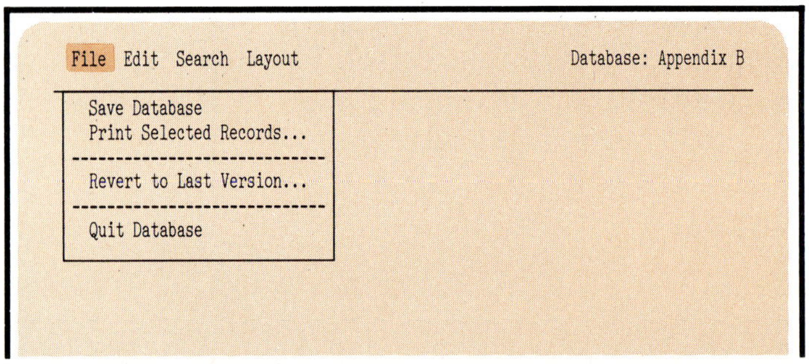

The *Print Selected Records*. . . command prints all selected records in the database. A dialog box asks you to press Enter to print page 1. The command prints one page at a time. If the document is longer than one page, the dialog box asks you to press Enter to print each page. The dialog box also informs you if the printer is not ready. Check first to see that the printer is connected to the computer and turned on.

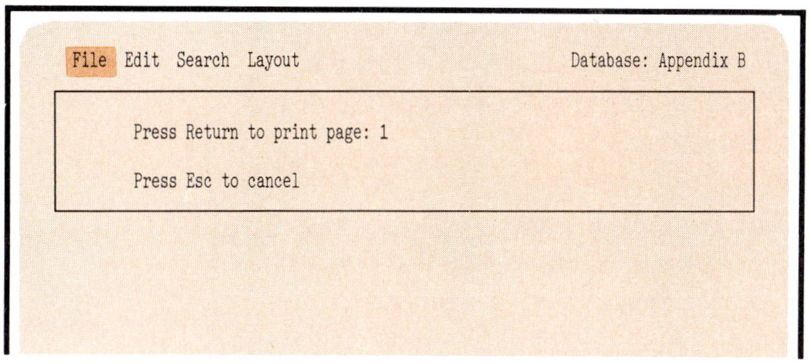

The *Revert to Last Version*. . . command enables you to restore the last saved version of the database after you have made changes. A dialog box informs you that all changes made since the last save will be lost.

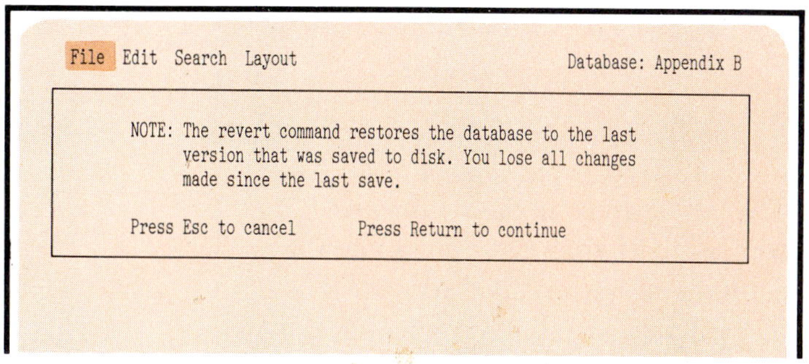

The *Quit Database* command (1) saves the contents of the database and (2) returns you to the Application Manager.

Edit Commands

Commands in the **Edit menu** enable you to manipulate selected records, add new records, and edit the current record in the database.

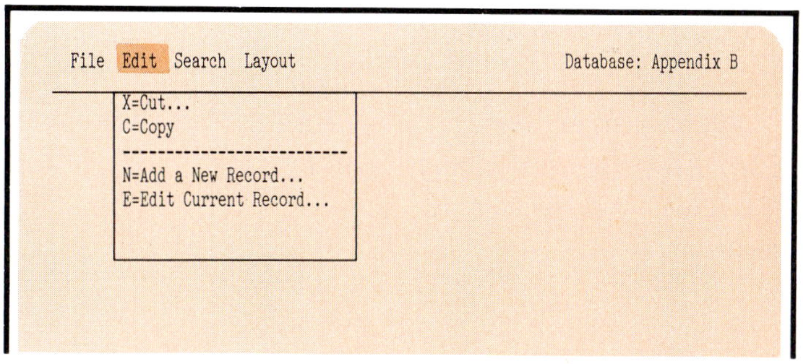

The *X=Cut*. . . command removes selected records from the database. A dialog box informs you that, since no paste command exists, cut records cannot be replaced in the database. Be careful. Cut records cannot be recovered.

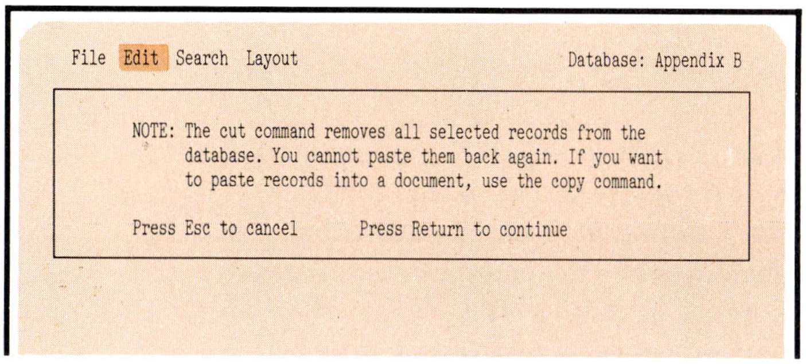

The *C=Copy* command copies selected records into a clipboard. The copied records can be pasted into a document.

The *N=Add a New Record...* command enables you to add a record to the database. New records are always appended to the end of the database. A dialog box asks you to type in the contents of each of the fields. The Tab key moves forward through the fields in the dialog box.

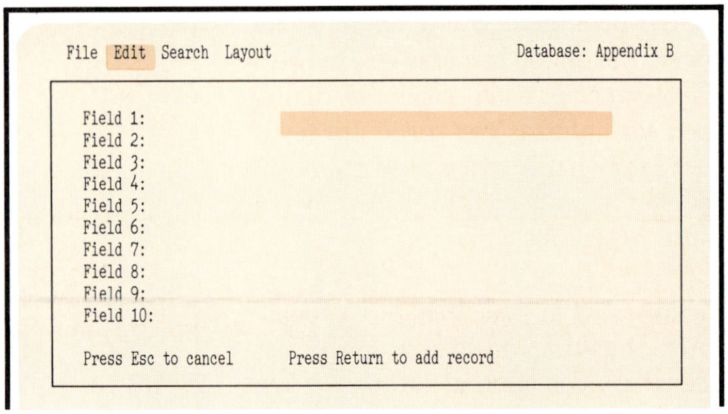

The *E=Edit Current Record...* command enables you to change the contents of an existing record. The current-record pointer indicates the record that will be edited. A dialog box enables you to edit individual fields. The Tab key moves forward through the fields in the dialog box.

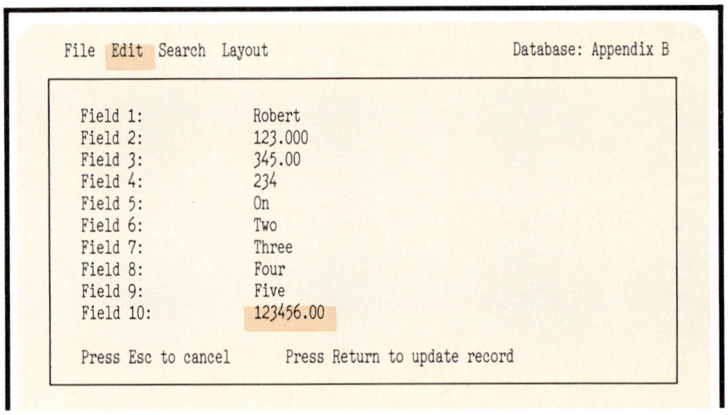

Search Commands

Commands in the **Search menu** enable you to (1) search for records that meet specified search criteria, (2) select records, or (3) unselect records.

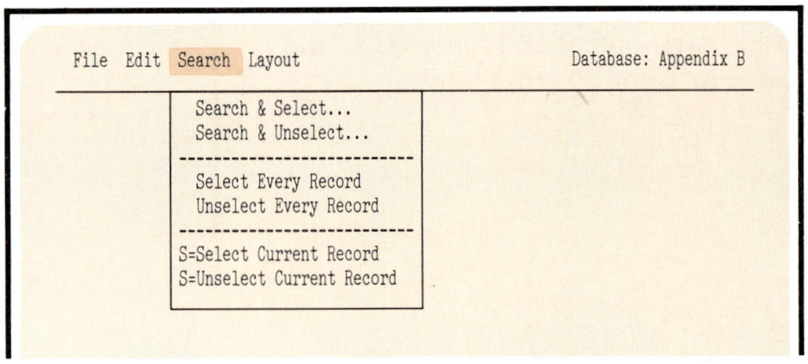

The *Search & Select...* command enables you to specify search criteria for selecting records. A dialog box enables you to enter the search criteria. Pressing the space bar toggles between search criteria for each field. Valid search criteria are: >=, <=, =, NOT=, >, and <. The Tab key moves forward through the fields.

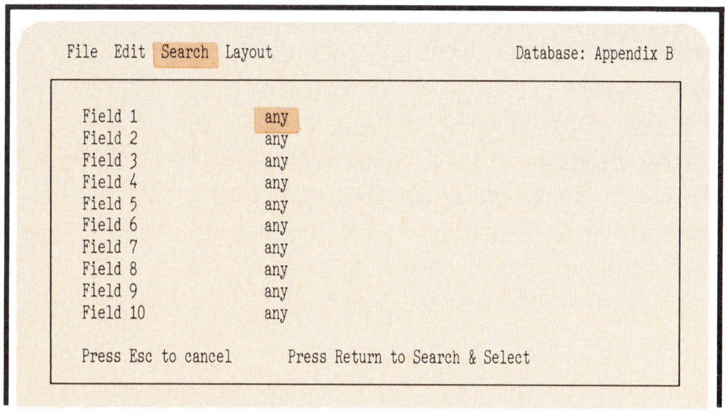

The *Search & Unselect...* command enables you to specify search criteria for unselecting records. The format of the dialog box is identical to that of the Search & Select dialog box.

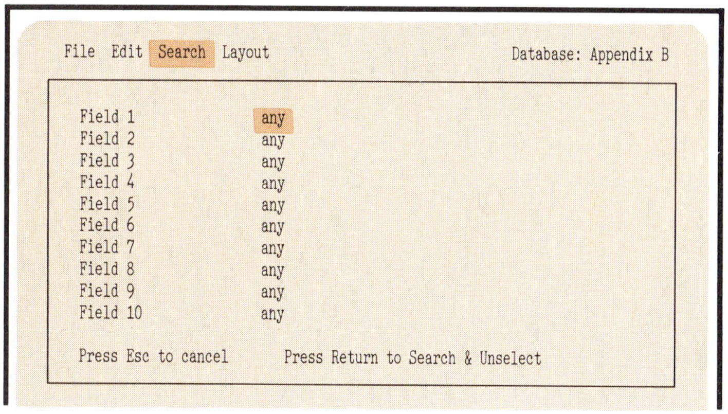

The *Select Every Record* command selects all records in the database.

The *Unselect Every Record* command unselects all records in the database.

The *S=Select Current Record* command selects the record that the current record pointer is indicating.

The *S=Unselect Current Record* command unselects the record that the current record pointer is indicating.

Layout Commands

Commands in the **Layout menu** enable you to sort records, and to view and alter the format of the records.

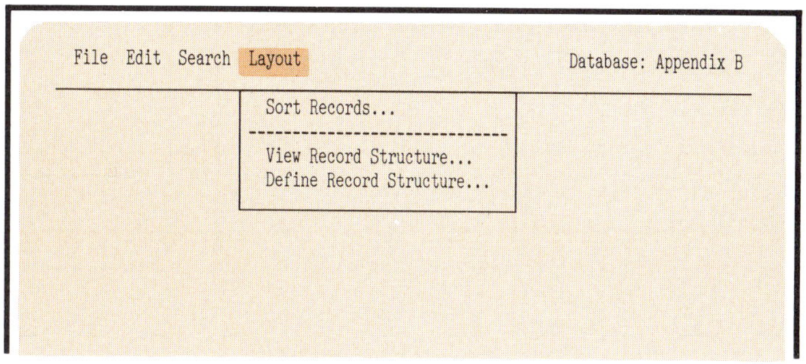

The *Sort Records*. . . command sorts all records in the database. A dialog box enables you to specify the sort criteria. Sorting proceeds from left to right. Pressing the space bar toggles between sort criteria. Valid sort criteria are ascending order and descending order. The Tab key moves forward through the fields in the dialog box.

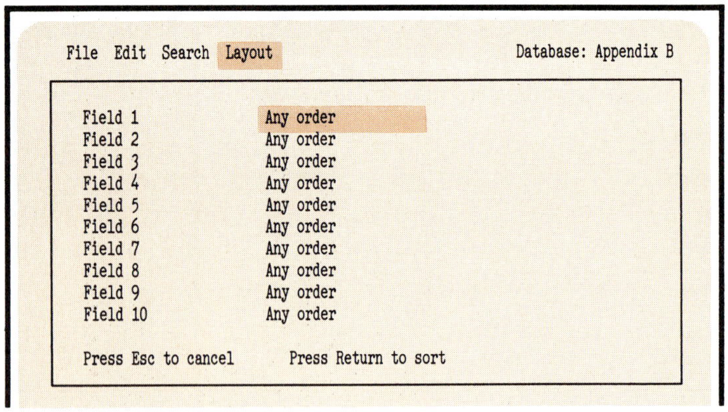

The *View Record Structure*. . . command enables you to look at the record structure of an existing database. A dialog box shows you the record structure.

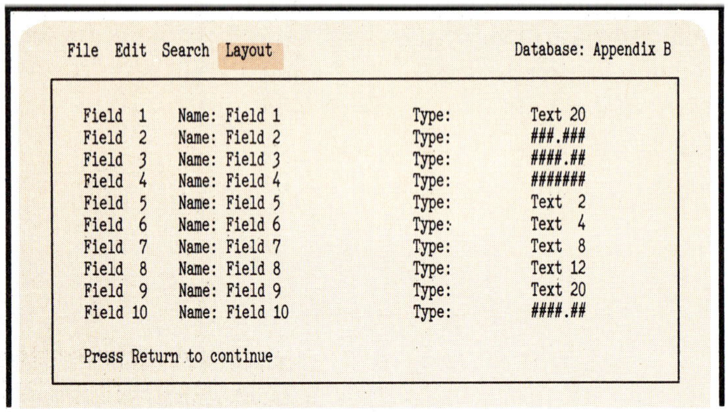

The *Define Record Structure*. . . command enables you to create the record structure of a new database. A dialog box enables you to name the fields and to specify a type for each field. Valid text fields can be 2, 4, 8, 12, or 20 characters in length. Valid numeric fields are 11 characters in length, and can contain zero, two, or three decimal places.

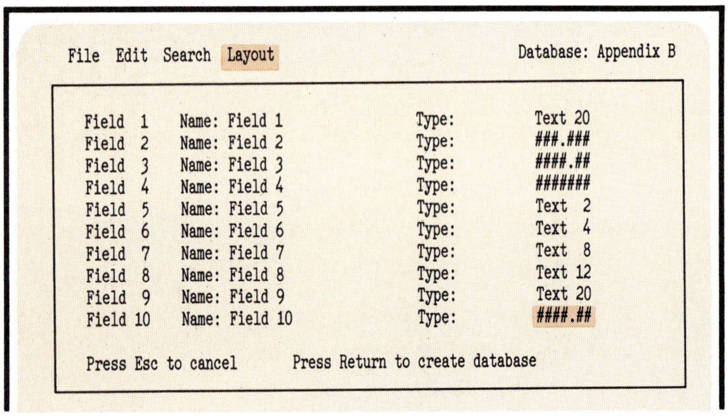

If the database structure is already defined, and current records exist, the *Define Record Structure*. . . command will delete existing records.

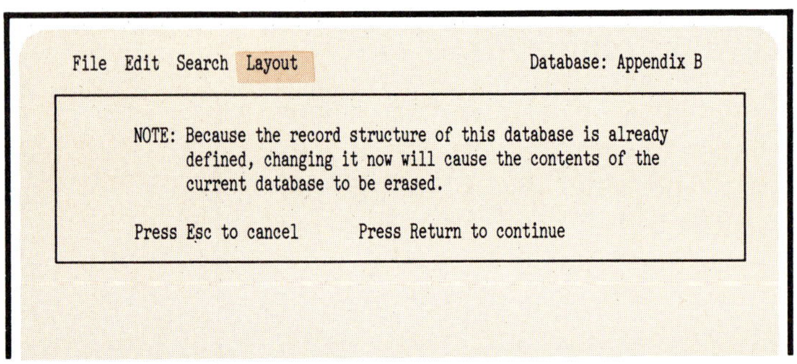

Messages

All TriPac messages appear in dialog boxes.

Explanation: You tried to open a file but there is not enough room on the disk to store the file. Delete one or more files to make room for the new file. Alternatively, you tried to open a copy when not enough room exists in the directory; delete one or more files to make room for the copy.

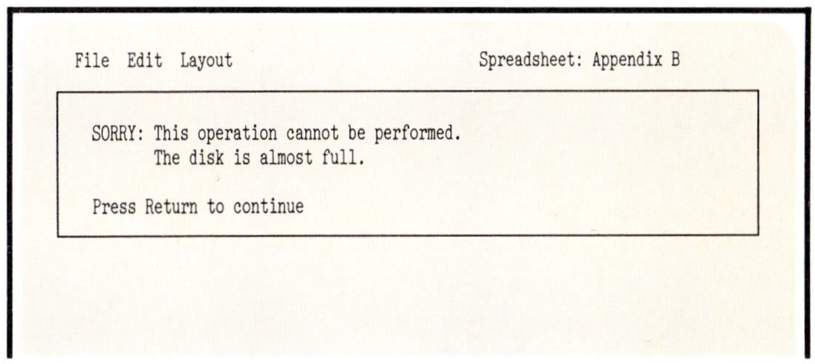

Explanation: You attempted to copy, cut, or type into a document text that is larger than the remaining space in the document.

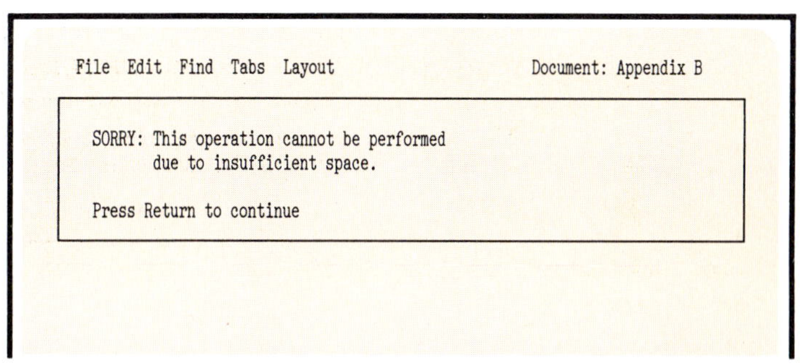

Explanation: You attempted to add too many records to a database.

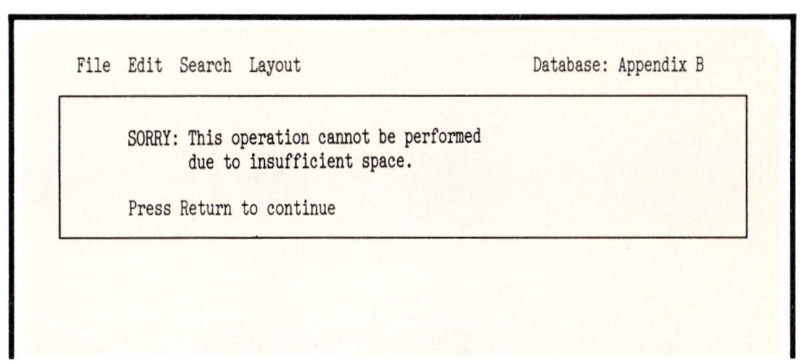

Explanation: You entered an unacceptable expression in the spreadsheet edit line. Check for unbalanced parentheses, an invalid cell reference, or unacceptable characters in the formula.

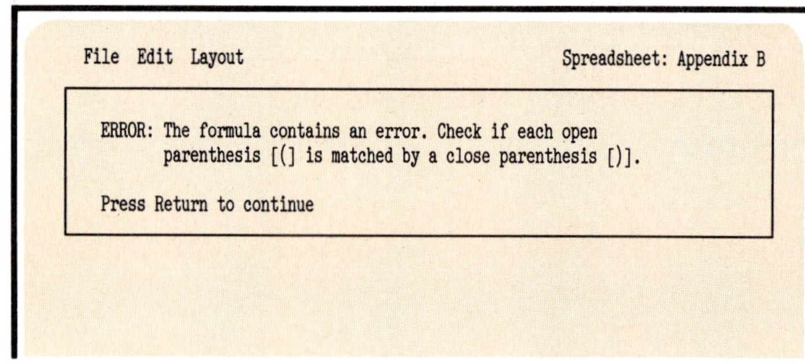

Explanation: Your TriPac disk is almost full. You must delete some files to make room on your disk.

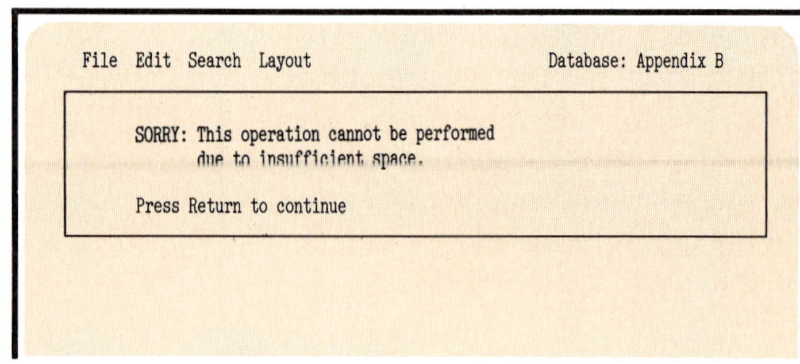

Appendix C

Glossary

Absolute cell reference. A cell reference that does not change.

Acronym. A word formed from the first letters or sounds in a phrase. For example, DOS is an acronym for *disk operating system*.

Active cell. The cell at which the cursor is pointing. (See Cell.)

Agent. A system that, given a goal, could carry out the appropriate operations and ask for and act on advice when necessary.

Application. The use to which a computer system is put.

Application development. A problem-solving process that begins with the needs of the user and ends with a system that does what the user wants it to do.

Application manager. A computer program that manages application programs.

Application program. A computer program that enables a user to perform a particular kind of task.

Artificial intelligence. The branch of computer science that attempts to understand human intelligence and to program computers to perform tasks that require qualities such as reasoning and perception.

Ascending order. Sequential arrangement from lowest to highest; for example, a telephone directory lists names in ascending order. (See Descending order.)

ASCII. An acronym for *American Standard Code for Information Interchange*. A code that specifies and standardizes the binary digits used internally by microcomputers to represent letters, numbers, and special characters.

Backup file. A copy of a file made for safekeeping in case the original is lost or damaged.

BASIC. An acronym for *Beginners All-purpose Symbolic Instruction Code*. A programming language commonly used for personal computers.

Bit. Short for **bi**nary digi**t**. The smallest unit of information in a computer system, represented by an electronic circuit that can be either on or off.

Bit map. A special segment of RAM where bits represent pixels on a display screen. (See Pixel.)

Block. In word processing, text that is consecutive and can therefore be manipulated as an entity, such as by moving, copying, or deleting it.

Boldface. Text that appears thicker or darker on the screen or printout for purposes of emphasis.

For example, the terms listed in this glossary are in **boldface** type; the explanations are in ordinary type.

Booting. Starting up a computer, accomplished by a set of instructions called the bootstrap program.

Brainstorming. Unrestrained thought or discussion, without prejudging or rejecting any ideas.

Buffer. A temporary memory-storage area.

Bug. An error. A software bug is a programming error; a hardware bug is a malfunction or design error.

Builder-user. A person who designs and develops an application for his or her own use.

Byte. A unit of storage that can hold one character of information. Equivalent to eight consecutive bits.

Cell. In a spreadsheet, the space representing the intersection of a row and a column.

Cell reference. In spreadsheet formulas, the use of a cell's name instead of an absolute number.

Centering. Aligning a block of text at an equal distance from the left and right margins.

Central processing unit (CPU). The part of a computer system that interprets and executes instructions, performs arithmetic and logic operations, and directs storage and input and output operations. (See Microprocessor.)

Channel. A pathway for the transmission of data to and from a computer system.

Character. Any letter, number, punctuation mark, or other symbol that a computer can read, process, store, and write.

Clipboard. A temporary storage area used to store the contents of a Cut or Copy command until a Paste command is given. The clipboard holds one piece of information at a time. When you issue a new Cut or Copy command, the previous contents are erased. (See Cut, Cut-and-Paste, Paste.)

Closed system. A system which does not permit additional components to be added without some difficulty. (See Open system.)

Command. An instruction that tells a program to perform an operation.

Command processor. A program that interprets and responds to the commands you type in on the keyboard.

Communication. (1) The process of exchanging information using a commonly agreed-upon set of symbols. (2) From an engineering standpoint, the movement of electronic traffic from one point to another.

Communication software. Programs that enable hardware devices to communicate with one another.

Compatibility. Refers to computers on which the same software can be run without alteration.

Computer graphics. The capability to draw pictures and display images on computer display screens.

Computer system. A system consisting of a computer, the programs that control it, the problem-solving procedures for accomplishing tasks, and the people who use it.

Control (CTRL) key. A keyboard key that activates a particular function when pressed in combination with other keys.

Copy. To replicate information, leaving the original intact.

Copy-and-paste. To replicate information from one location in another location in a word-processing document, spreadsheet, or database.

Copy protect. A technique used to make a disk difficult or impossible to copy.

Current record pointer. An arrow-shaped cursor that points to the record that can be selected or edited (the current record).

Cursor. A visual aid on the display screen, denoting the position that will be affected. For example, in word processing, a rectangular blinking box indicates where the next character you type will appear on the display screen.

Cursor-movement keys. Keys that move the cursor in a particular direction when pressed.

Cut. To remove text, cells, or records from their original location for pasting into a different location. (See Cut-and-Paste, Paste.)

Cut-and-Paste. To remove information from one location and place it in another location in a word-processing document, spreadsheet, or database.

Data. (1) The raw facts that are used to create information. (2) A general term for all the information that can be produced or processed by a computer system. (See Information.)

Database. A collection of various categories of data, organized according to a logical structure.

Database management system. The hardware and software that organize and provide access to databases.

Database program. A computerized record-keeping program that stores, organizes, manipulates, retrieves, and summarizes data.

Data integrity. The accuracy and validity of the data in a database.

Data manipulation. Processing data or requesting information from a database such as searching for and sorting records.

Data processing. Collectively, all the logical, arithmetic, and input and output operations that can be performed by a computer.

Data security. Techniques for protecting a database against unauthorized access.

Data type. The specification of the characteristics, features, or properties of data such as text or numbers, or size.

Decimal tab. The capability to line up columns of numbers on their decimal points.

Decision making. A problem-solving approach for situations in which only partial information is available about a problem.

Dedicated system. A computer dedicated to a single task; for example, a computer dedicated to the task of word processing.

Default. An action or value that the computer automatically assumes unless a different action or value is specified.

Delete. To remove information from the screen or a disk.

Descending order. Arrangement of information in sequence from highest to lowest. (See Ascending order.)

Dialog box. An on-screen box in which the user responds to the system's request for more information.

Directory. A listing of all the files on a disk.

Disk. A circular platter coated with a magnetic or optical material, which can store information.

Disk drive. The device that can read information from a disk and write new information on it. A disk drive mounts the disk on a spindle, which spins it around like a record player while reading and/or writing.

Display screen. An output device for displaying information from a computer system. Commonly a cathode-ray tube (CRT), sometimes a liquid-crystal display (LCD), light-emitting diode (LED), electroluminescent screen, or plasma screen.

Distributed processing. Information processing distributed among physically separate computer systems.

Document. Any text or collection of characters (letters, numbers, spaces, punctuation marks, and other symbols).

Documentation. The books or manuals that accompany a software package, hardware component, or computer system.

DOS. An acronym for *disk operating system*. (See Operating system.)

Dot-matrix printer. An impact printer that prints characters and images composed of patterns of dots.

Dynamic values. In a spreadsheet, values that change automatically if the values that they depend on change. (See Static values.)

Edit checking. A process for determining the accuracy or validity of data entered into a system. For example, if a field's type is numeric, you should not be able to enter anything but a number.

Editing. The process of composing text, revising (inserting, deleting, correcting, and formatting) it, and periodically saving the document onto disk.

Edit line. In spreadsheet programs, a reserved space for entering and editing text, numbers, and formulas.

Electronic library. Files stored in a mainframe or minicomputer disk storage system, which can be accessed by terminals or personal computers.

Electronic mail. A technology for sending and receiving electronic messages.

Electronic worksheet. The part of a spreadsheet program displayed on the screen as rows and columns.

End-user computing. In organizations, a configuration in which computers are controlled by users rather than by the data-processing department.

Escape (Esc) key. A keyboard key used to toggle from one mode of operation to another. For example, if you are in a word-processing edit mode and you want to transfer to a print mode, you will press the Esc key.

Execute. To carry out a specified command.

Expert system. A computer program that solves specialized problems at the level of a human expert.

Field. The smallest unit of meaningful information in a record. (See Record.)

File. A collection of logically related information.

Find. A word processing command that searches a document for a particular word or phrase. Also called search.

Find-and-Replace. The capability of a word processor to search a document for a particular word or phrase, and to replace it wherever it occurs with another word or phrase.

Floppy disk. A flexible platter, coated with magnetic oxide and encased in a protective jacket, capable of storing information. (See Disk.)

Footer. A line of text that appears at the bottom of each printed page. Footers are entered only once; the software takes care of inserting them on each page during printing. (See Header.)

Form. (1) In a database program, a list of fields illustrating the structure of a record and the correspondence between field names and sizes. (2) In word processing, a standard document for sending to a number of recipients.

Format. The way information is physically organized on a display screen, printed page, or disk.

Front-end processor. A processor that collects information from local sources, performs a limited amount of processing on it, and forwards it to another computer system.

Function. A predefined routine or formula.

Functional specification. A problem definition that specifies the functions a system must perform.

Function keys. Keyboard keys used to initiate commands or operations that would otherwise require several keystrokes.

General-purpose application software. Software designed to handle a wide variety of tasks that employ the same general capabilities; for example, word processing, spreadsheet, database management, graphics, and communications.

Gigabyte (GB). A unit of measure equal to 230 or 1,073,741,824 bytes.

Global search. In word processing, an instruction to search through an entire document to find a particular word or phrase.

Graphics. The methods and techniques used to draw pictures or images.

Hard disk. A disk made with a rigid base such as aluminum, then coated with a magnetic or reflective recording surface, capable of storing information.

Hardware. (1) The electronic and mechanical components of a computer or other system. (2) The tangible part of a system. (See Software.)

Header. A line of text that appears at the top of each printed page. Headers are entered only once; the software takes care of inserting them on each page during printing. (See Footer.)

Highlighting. Emphasizing information on a display screen, often in reverse video, for the purpose of selecting or manipulating it.

Horizontal scrolling. The ability to shift the contents of the screen to the left or the right in order to view information that is wider than the screen display.

Icon. A picture on a display screen of an object such as a file, a wastebasket, an in-basket, or a memo representing a particular function.

Index. A list of the contents of a file or document, with references for locating each item.

Information. Data used in decision making. (See Data.)

Information processing. Performing systematic operations on information, such as typing, adding, sorting, and thinking.

Information system. A set of interconnected parts whose purpose is to gather, manipulate, store, transmit, and communicate information.

Input. (1) The process of transferring data into a computer system. (2) Devices that convert data into a form that a computer's processor and memory can use.

Instruction. A basic unit of a program that specifies what action is to be performed on what data.

Integrated software. Software that combines two or more functions with the ability to share data among the functions. For example, TriPac integrates word processing, spreadsheets, and databases.

Interface. (See User interface.)

Justify. In word processing, to align text at both the left and right margins.

Key. In a database program, a unit of information (usually a field) associated with a record and used to identify it for purposes of sorting or retrieval.

Keyboard. A device containing keys that convert finger pressure into electronic codes the computer can recognize.

Kilobyte (KB). A unit of measure equal to 210 or 1024 bytes.

Large-scale information system. A system associated with large centralized computer installations of one or more mainframes and/or minicomputers.

Laser disk. A disk that uses a laser to retrieve and/or record data instead of magnetic methods.

Laser printer. A printer that uses a laser to transfer an image to a drum, and then to record the impression on paper.

Layout commands. Commands that enable the user to change the appearance of a document, spreadsheet, or database.

Letter-quality printer. An impact printer that closely simulates the printing of an IBM Selectric typewriter.

Linking spreadsheets. A technique for consolidating information from two or more spreadsheets. When data are changed in the source spreadsheet, the target spreadsheet is automatically updated.

Local-area network (LAN). A geographically limited communication channel linking personal computers for the purpose of (1) communicating with one another and (2) sharing such resources as a mass storage device or a printer.

Macro. A single command or instruction that invokes a sequence of options.

Macro language. A programming-like facility found in spreadsheets and database programs, used to create macros.

Mainframe. A room-sized high-performance computer, capable of running complex programs that would be impractical or impossible on smaller computers.

Manual recalculation. In a spreadsheet program, an option in which formulas are evaluated and recalculated only when the user issues a command to do so.

Margin. The left or right boundary of a document.

Mass storage. Devices that store information before and after processing, such as disks and tapes.

Megabyte (MB). A unit of measure equal to 220 or 1,048,576 bytes.

Memory. The functional component of a computer system that stores information used by the processor.

Menu. A list of commands available for a computer user to choose from.

Menu bar. A one-line horizontal on-screen display of a list of menus.

Microcomputer. A computer system whose central processing unit is a microprocessor. Also called a personal computer.

Microprocessor. (1) The part of a computer that controls its operation. (2) A silicon chip that contains all the circuitry necessary to carry out the instructions it receives.

Microsecond. A unit of time equal to one millionth of a second.

Minicomputer. A medium-sized medium-capacity computer system whose performance rivals that of a small mainframe.

MIPS. An acronym for million instructions per second. A unit of measure for comparing the processing speeds of different computers.

Model. A simulation of a real-world event or phenomenon.

Modem. A hardware device that enables two computers to exchange data over standard telephone lines.

Monitor. (See Display screen.)

Mouse. A device used to move the cursor on the display screen and to select commands or functions. Typically used as an alternative to the equivalent keyboard keys.

Multiprocessing. Two or more processors sharing the same memory and input-output devices.

Multiuser system. A computer system that allows multiple users to share the processor, memory, disk storage, and software simultaneously.

Nanosecond. A unit of time equal to one billionth of a second.

Natural-language interface. A user interface that accepts commands or requests typed in ordinary English, and then translates them into equivalent commands or actions.

Network. A group of interrelated computers capable of exchanging information.

Numeric model. A simulation or model of a number-based problem.

Office automation. The application of computer and communication technologies to enhance office functions and procedures.

On-line system. A system in which input is transmitted directly from the point of origin to a central location for processing.

Open system. A system which permits a variety of components to be added. (See Closed system).

Operating system. A set of programs that controls the operation and manages the resources of a computer system; for example, MS-DOS, C/PM, UNIX, ProDOS, and Apple DOS 3.3.

Orphan. In word processing, the first line of a paragraph when it appears at the bottom of a page, separated from the rest of the paragraph.

Output. (1) The results of information processing. (2) Devices that convert the results of processing into information that people can use; for example, display terminals, printers, and plotters.

Page break. The point in a document where one page ends and another begins.

Paragraph symbol. The character (¶) that word processors use to designate the end of a paragraph.

Password. A code that identifies a particular user to a computer system.

Paste. To place information in a spreadsheet or word-processing document.

Peripheral. A device that operates in conjunction with a computer, but is not part of the computer; for example, a printer or disk drive.

Personal computer. A computer small enough to fit on a desktop, affordable enough to be owned by a single person, yet powerful enough to perform many different tasks. Also called a microcomputer.

Pixel. Short for *picture element*. A light or dark point on the surface of a display screen.

Pointer. Reverse-video highlighting that functions as a selection cursor. (See Selection.)

Printer. A device that produces printed output by transferring characters and images onto paper.

Printout. A document or listing, printed on paper.

Problem. Any question or matter characterized by doubt, uncertainty, or difficulty.

Procedure. A sequence of steps that specifies one or more actions and the order in which they must be taken.

Process. A systematic series of actions aimed at a specific goal.

Processor. The part of a computer that controls its operation and does the actual processing. Also called the central processing unit (CPU).

Program. A sequence of instructions that makes the computer carry out a given set of tasks.

Programmer. A person who creates computer programs.

Programming language. A set of precise rules for formulating statements so that a computer can understand them; for example, BASIC, Pascal, C, Ada, COBOL, RPG.

Prompt. A request from the system for input from the user.

Protocol. A formal set of rules for specifying the format and relationships of information transmitted between two or more communicating devices.

Pull-down menu. A menu that is hidden from view until needed.

Query. A question or request for information.

Query language. A language for questioning or requesting information from a database.

RAM. An acronym for *random-access memory*. A processor's temporary working area, which stores data and programs while the computer is on. (See Memory.)

Range. In spreadsheet programs, a series of cells. Examples include an entire or partial column, or an entire or partial row.

Range search. In database programs, a search for records that fall between two criteria; for example, a search for all names between L and N.

Record. A collection of information consisting of one or more related items or fields. (See Field.)

Relational database. A database that organizes files into tabular rows and columns, and enables the user to relate two or more files through a field they share.

Relative copy. In spreadsheets, the ability to adjust a formula's cell reference in accordance with its new location.

Replace. The substitution of one piece of information for another, in combination with Find, Cut, or Copy.

Report generator. The part of a database program that allows a user to define and produce printed output.

Return key. A keyboard key used to enter commands, respond to prompts, and begin new paragraphs. (Also called the Enter key.)

Reverse video. Highlighting of selected data on a display screen by reversing the normal light-dark contrast between the characters and the background area.

ROM. An acronym for *read-only memory*. A permanent memory, containing data and instructions loaded into it at the time of manufacture.

Save. To store information in a file.

Scroll. To move the contents of a display screen up, down, left, or right to bring hidden parts of the document, spreadsheet, or database into view.

Search-and-Replace. (See Find-and-Replace.)

Searching. A technique for locating a particular record in a database.

Sector. The smallest unit of data that can be written to or read from a disk. (See Track.)

Selection. The choosing (highlighting) of data for the purpose of manipulating it. In word processing, for example, a block of text can be selected for deletion; in a database, particular records can be highlighted in response to your questions.

Sequential. A method of organizing information in a series based on one or more key fields.

Shared-logic system. A computer system that connects several terminals to a single microcomputer or minicomputer's processor.

Simulation. A computerized representation of a process or a set of activities or events.

Software. The programs that control the operation of a computer.

Software package. One or more floppy disks on which a program resides. The package should also include documentation.

Solution. An answer or explanation to a problem.

Sort. To arrange a set of items in a predetermined sequence. For example, the telephone book is sorted alphabetically by customer name.

Special-purpose application software. Software designed for the special needs of particular kinds of businesses, education, or professions; for example, medical billing, patient tracking, or contract writing.

Specifying requirements. To define a problem in a sufficiently well-organized way to guide the development of an appropriate system.

Speech recognition. (See Voice interface.)

Spelling checker. A program that checks documents for spelling errors.

Spreadsheet program. A program that helps solve problems that can be expressed in numbers and formulas. It organizes information into rows and columns; stores numbers, formulas, and text; performs automatic calculations; and saves the results for future reference.

Static values. In spreadsheets, values that do not change unless a new number or text is entered manually. (See Dynamic values.)

Structure. In database programs, the manner in which the fields of a record are organized or interrelated. Also called record structure.

Style checker. An electronic proofreader that hyphenates words, checks for punctuation errors, and flags awkward or redundant usage and excessive wordiness.

System. A set of parts, each with a specific purpose, that work together to accomplish a desired goal.

System restart. A procedure used to restore the operation of a computer system to its original start-up mode without turning the computer off.

Systems analyst. A person who interprets needs, analyzes requirements, and develops functional specifications for a system.

Tab. A stopping point along the horizontal dimension of a document.

Tab key. A keyboard key used to move the cursor to a prespecified location to the left or right, or above or below its current location.

Template. A partially completed worksheet, containing text and formulas but not data.

Terminal. An input/output device used to enter and receive information.

Title command. The capability to freeze titles, so that they remain in view when scrolling through a worksheet.

Toggle. To alternate between functions by means of successive presses of a particular key.

Top-down design. A problem-solving method in which the solution is first specified in general terms, and then broken down into finer and finer detail.

Touch screen. A plastic membrane or set of infrared sensors placed over a display screen to enable the user to select commands and actions by touching the screen.

Track. One of many concentric circles on which data are stored on a disk.

Transaction. An event about which data are recorded and processed; for example, a request for a seat on an airline flight.

Transaction-oriented system. A multiuser system in which transactions activate processing; for example, an airline reservation system and a credit-approval system.

Tutorial. An interactive teaching tool, often a program, designed to help you learn to use a software package.

Typing cursor. An underline or reverse-video box that indicates the location on the screen of the next character you type. (See Cursor.)

Undo. A feature that enables a user to recover data deleted by the preceding command.

Update. To modify information by replacing it with more timely information.

User-defined function. A single command or instruction that invokes a macro. Used primarily to customize a spreadsheet application.

User-defined page break. A word processing command that inserts a page break into a document, thus beginning a new page.

User interface. Software that acts as an intermediary between an application program and the person using it.

Utilities. Programs that perform functions required by many of the application programs using the system; for example, utilities can copy, rename, and delete files.

Voice interface. (1) An input technology that enables the computer to recognize spoken words or phrases. (2) An output technology that simulates the human voice.

Volatile. In memory, the characteristic of losing contents when electrical power is shut off.

What-if analysis. Use of a spreadsheet to compare alternatives.

Wide-area network. A geographically dispersed communication network linking computers for the purpose of communicating with one another; for example, a nationwide network of airline reservation terminals connected to a central computer.

Widow. In word processing, the last line of a paragraph when it appears at the top of a page, separated from the rest of the paragraph.

Wildcard search. A search that uses a shorthand notation to fill in an incomplete search criterion.

Winchester disk. A hard disk sealed in a container to prevent contaminants from touching the disk's surface (from the code name of the project that developed it).

Windows. A technique for dividing the display screen into variable-sized rectangles in order to view different sets of information simultaneously.

Word processing. Software that aids in the composition, revision, storage, and printing of text.

Word wrap. In word processing, the automatic carryover of text to the next line, along with the cursor.

Worksheet. The row and column portion of a spreadsheet program.

WYSIWYG. An acronym for *what-you-see-is-what-you-get*. The display of information in a form that resembles very closely what will eventually be printed.

List of Art Credits

Page 3 Courtesy of Apple Computer, Inc.
Page 8 Courtesy of International Business Machines Corporation
Page 12 (c) Lotus Development Corporation 1985. Used with permission.
Page 35 (Top) Courtesy of Hewlett-Packard Company
Page 35 (Bottom) Alan Oddie/99 Graphics
Page 36 (Top) Courtesy of Hewlett-Packard Company
Page 36 (Bottom) Courtesy of Texas Instruments, Inc.
Page 47 (Top) Courtesy of Honeywell, Inc.
Page 47 (Center) Courtesy of Data General Corporation
Page 47 (Bottom) Courtesy of Apple Computer, Inc.
Page 50 Courtesy of Microsoft, Inc.
Page 53 Courtesy of Hewlett-Packard Company
Page 55 Photo courtesy of NCR Corporation
Page 86 (Left) Courtesy of Xerox Corporation
Page 86 (Right) Courtesy of Apple Computer, Inc.
Page 118 SSI Software "Word Perfect"
Page 120 Courtesy of Apple Computer, Inc.
Page 121 (Top) Used with permission of Digital Research Incorporated
Page 121 (Bottom) Courtesy of Microsoft Corporation
Page 126 (c) Lotus Development Corporation 1985. Used with permission.
Page 150 Alan Oddie/99 Graphics
Page 151 Courtesy of Microsoft, Inc.
Page 153 Courtesy of Microsoft, Inc.
Page 158 Courtesy of Infocom
Page 183 (c) Lotus Development Corporation 1985. Used with permission.
Page 196 Courtesy of International Business Machines Corporation
Page 198 Courtesy of COMPAQ® Computer Corporation
Page 199 Courtesy of Apple Computer, Inc.
Page 200 Courtesy of Apple Computer, Inc.
Page 201 Courtesy of Apple Computer, Inc.
Page 202 (Top) Courtesy of Sharp Electronics Corporation, 10 Sharp Plaza, Paramus, New Jersey
Page 202 (Bottom) Courtesy of Hewlett-Packard Company
Page 202 (Right) Courtesy of Apple Computer, Inc.
Page 208 Courtesy of Sony Corporation of America
Page 209 (Bottom) Courtesy of Satellite Broadcast Network
Page 211 Courtesy of Apple Computer, Inc.
Page 214 Courtesy of MIT Media Laboratory

Index